CITY SYMPHONIES

CITY SYMPHONIES

SOUND AND THE COMPOSITION OF URBAN MODERNITY, 1913–1931

DANIEL P. SCHWARTZ

McGill-Queen's University Press

Montreal & Kingston • London • Chicago

© McGill-Queen's University Press 2024

ISBN 978-0-2280-2139-1 (cloth)
ISBN 978-0-2280-2140-7 (paper)
ISBN 978-0-2280-2142-1 (ePDF)
ISBN 978-0-2280-2143-8 (ePUB)

Legal deposit second quarter 2024
Bibliothèque nationale du Québec

Printed in Canada on acid-free paper that is 100% ancient forest free
(100% post-consumer recycled), processed chlorine free

This book has been published with the help of a grant from the Canadian Federation for the Humanities and Social Sciences, through the Awards to Scholarly Publications Program, using funds provided by the Social Sciences and Humanities Research Council of Canada.

We acknowledge the support of the Canada Council for the Arts.
Nous remercions le Conseil des arts du Canada de son soutien.

McGill-Queen's University Press in Montreal is on land which long served as a site of meeting and exchange amongst Indigenous Peoples, including the Haudenosaunee and Anishinabeg nations. In Kingston it is situated on the territory of the Haudenosaunee and Anishinaabek. We acknowledge and thank the diverse Indigenous Peoples whose footsteps have marked these territories on which peoples of the world now gather.

LIBRARY AND ARCHIVES CANADA CATALOGUING IN PUBLICATION

Title: City symphonies : sound and the composition of urban modernity, 1913–1931 / Daniel P. Schwartz.
Names: Schwartz, Daniel P. (Professor), author.
Description: Includes bibliographical references and index.
Identifiers: Canadiana (print) 20230583962 | Canadiana (ebook) 20230584101 | ISBN 9780228021407 (softcover) | ISBN 9780228021391 (hardcover) | ISBN 9780228021421 (PDF) | ISBN 9780228021438 (EPUB)
Subjects: LCSH: City symphonies (Motion pictures) | LCSH: City symphonies (Motion pictures)—History and criticism. | LCSH: Sound in motion pictures. | LCSH: Sound motion pictures. | LCSH: City sounds. | LCSH: Cities and towns in motion pictures. | LCSH: City and town life in motion pictures.
Classification: LCC PN1995.7 .S39 2024 | DDC 791.4302—dc23

CONTENTS

Figures vii
Acknowledgments ix

Introduction: City Symphonies: Sound and the Composition of Urban Modernity, 1913–1931 3

1 **In the Concert Hall:** Luigi Russolo's *The Art of Noises* and *The Awakening of a City* 26

2 **On the Street:** The Sound and Silence of Arseny Avraamov's *Symphony of Sirens* in Baku (1922) and Moscow (1923) 59

3 **On the Screen:** Sounding the Inaudible in the City Symphonies of Walter Ruttmann and Dziga Vertov 96

4 **On the Air:** German Experimental Radio and the Radio City Symphony 131

5 **Around the World:** Sight and Sound in the Global Symphonies of Vertov and Ruttmann 162

Coda: Listening to City Symphonies 187

Notes 191
Index 217

Figures

0.1 László Moholy-Nagy's "Dynamic of the Metropolis." In László Moholy-Nagy, *Painting, Photography, Film*, trans. Jillian DeMair and Katrin Schamun (Zurich: Lars Müller, 2019), 127. 4

1.1 "Nel Laboratorio degli Intonarumori a Milano," in Luigi Russolo, *L'Arte dei rumori* (Milan: Edizioni Futuristi di "Poesia," 1916). 31

1.2 "Risveglio di una città," in Luigi Russolo, *L'Arte dei rumori* (Milan: Edizioni Futuristi di "Poesia," 1916). 31

1.3 Umberto Boccioni, *Città che sale* (1910–11), New York, Museum of Modern Art. 43

1.4 Luigi Russolo, *La Rivolta* (1911), The Hague, Netherlands, Kunstmuseum Den Haag. 44

1.5 Luigi Russolo, *Linee-froza della folgore* (1912), Portogruaro, Collezione del Comune di Portogruaro. 45

2.1 An idealized sketch of the steam-whistle machine (*magistral'*). Arseny Avraamov, "Simfoniya Gudkov," *Gorn* 9 (November 1923): 110. 60

2.2 Examples of drawn sound from Arseny Avraamov's article "Synthetic Music." Arseny Avraamov, "Sinteticheskaia muzyka," *Sovetskaia muzyka* 8 (1939): 313–33. 67

2.3 Text-notes to the "Internationale." Arseny Avraamov, "Simfoniya Gudkov," *Gorn* 9 (November 1923): 114. 76

2.4 The steam-whistle machine (*magistral'*) at the 1923 Moscow *Symphony of Sirens*. Arseny Avraamov, "Simfoniya Gudkov," *Khudozhnik i zritel'* 1 (January 1924): 50. 83

2.5 Artist's rendering of the *Symphony of Sirens* in Baku. Arseny Avraamov, "Simfoniya Gudkov," *Gorn* 9 (November 1923): 113. 91

3.1 The visual sound of typewriters (*Berlin, Symphony of a Great City*, dir. Walter Ruttmann, 1927). 103
3.2 Financial rollercoaster (*Berlin, Symphony of a Great City*, dir. Walter Ruttmann, 1927). 105
3.3 A radio-ear (*Man with a Movie Camera*, dir. Dziga Vertov, 1929). 108
3.4 Ornamental soundtracks drawn by Arseny Avraamov. *Left* image (1930); *right* image (1931). Andrei Smirnov, *Sound in Z: Experiments in Sound and Electronic Music in Early 20th Century Russia* (London: Koenig Books, 2013), 179. 115
3.5 Elementary shapes emerging from water (*Berlin, Symphony of a Great City*, dir. Walter Ruttmann, 1927). 117
3.6 Examples of original strips used in Oskar Fischinger's *Ornament Sound* experiments. Oskar Fischinger, c. 1932. Courtesy of Center for Visual Music, Los Angeles. (c) Center for Visual Music. 118
4.1 Sasha Stone, book jacket design for Alfred Döblin, *Alfred Döblin: Im Buch, zu Haus, auf der Strasse* (Berlin: S. Fischer Verlag, 1928). 133
5.1 HAPAG sailor purchasing bananas (*Melody of the World*, dir. Walter Ruttmann, 1930). 170
5.2 The *Komsomolka* (*Enthusiasm: Symphony of the Donbass*, dir. Walter Ruttmann, 1931). 179
5.3 A coal worker speaking with the voice of a telegraph (*Enthusiasm: Symphony of the Donbass*, dir. Walter Ruttmann, 1931). 181
5.4 Shock worker pledging to overfill her quota and the machine's approving response (*Enthusiasm: Symphony of the Donbass*, dir. Walter Ruttmann, 1931). 182

Acknowledgments

Despite the solitary nature of writing, no book is written alone. Countless people have touched this book, whether through discussion, commentary, or even imagined conversation. One, however, stands out. I am very grateful to Anne Eakin Moss for all her support. She has been with this project from its inception to its completion, and through countless drafts, revisions, changes of course, setbacks, and successes. There isn't a question or idea in this book that I haven't run by Anne at least once, though it should go without saying that responsibility for all its shortcomings lies with me.

I would also like to express my gratitude to past and present faculty and graduate students at Johns Hopkins University, particularly the once-upon-a-time Humanities Center: Meredith Ward, whose class on sound was a major inspiration; Leonardo Lisi, who gave numerous early drafts closer readings than they perhaps merited; and Andrea Krauss, who was more than patient as my German caught up with the subject matter of her courses on topics ranging from Goethe to the avant-garde. Benjamin Stein, Samantha Carmel, Ben Gillespie, David Sugarman, Willy Blomme, Grégoire Hervouet-Zeiber, and Luce de Lire were all ideal interlocutors on ideas that made it into this book as well as many more that did not.

This book would not have been possible were it not for a semester spent at Stanford University taking a class with Gabriella Safran on Russian realism. She will hopefully hear echoes of this class in the chapter on Arseny Avraamov.

At McGill University, where I currently teach, past and current members of the Junior Faculty Working Group – Anna Berman, Daniel Pratt, Stephanie Posthumus, Tove Holmes, Cecily Raynor, and Vanessa Ceia – have been a tremendous source of support and inspiration. I am also very grateful for the advice and insights of Jonathan Sterne, Ara Osterweil, Alanna Thain, and Will Straw, whether through casual conversation, co-taught courses, or comments on drafts.

Portions of this book were worked and reworked as conference presentations; others, as articles for journals. I would like to thank *Slavic Review* for permission to republish and expand upon my 2020 article "Between Sound and Silence: The Failure of the 'Symphony of Sirens' in Baku (1922) and Moscow (1923)." I would also like to thank *Music, Sound, and the Moving Image* for permission to republish "Sounding the Inaudible: Rethinking the Musical Analogy in the City Symphonies of Walter Ruttmann and Dziga Vertov." Finally, I would like to thank all those conference participants and anonymous reviewers who offered comments and encouragement that helped me improve this book.

Finally, I would like to thank my parents and grandparents – Emilia, David, Ida, Pinchas, Rosa, and Leonid – for their love and support, and for being the reason I began studying so much of this material in the first place. And, Laura, for her patience and love.

CITY SYMPHONIES

INTRODUCTION

CITY SYMPHONIES

Sound and the Composition of Urban Modernity, 1913–1931

Tem Po-O-PO-o-O

László Moholy-Nagy's "Dynamic of the Metropolis" is perhaps the most important city symphony never to be filmed. First published in 1924 in the Hungarian avant-garde journal *MA* (Today), then later republished in 1925 in his iconic *Painting, Photography, Film*, the city symphony was billed as a "sketch of a manuscript for a film."[1] This sketch, on which the artist had begun working as early as 1921, was no ordinary film treatment.[2] For one, it did not proceed in a linear fashion; indeed, it resisted any attempt to be read linearly. What is more, descriptions of particular scenes and instructions for camera operators were but one feature of the text, which consisted of photographs, photograms, arrows, shapes, and individual words in a range of font sizes. Intersecting vertical and horizontal lines of varying thickness reminiscent of the compositions of Piet Mondrian segmented the text into montage-like fragments (figure 0.1). Such graphic elements caused the viewer's eye to jump from one image to the next in no particular order while still maintaining a sense of temporal flow. In a word, the text sought to re-create the movement of the metropolis on the page through the logic of film.

A close reading of "Dynamic of the Metropolis" suggests the three main points of this book: first, that the city symphony is not simply a silent film genre but an avant-garde multimedia experiment; second, that it expresses

City Symphonies

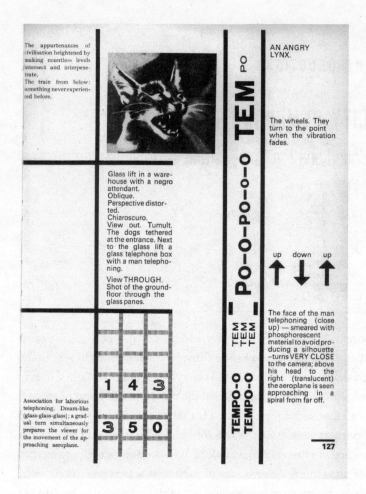

Figure 0.1 / László Moholy-Nagy's "Dynamic of the Metropolis."

not only visual relationships characteristic of urban environments but also audial ones that encompass both cities and new technologies of sonic reproduction; and third, that by engaging audible phenomena the city symphony does not merely represent the metropolis but treats it as a medium for sound as well as sight.

"Dynamic of the Metropolis" was a manifestation of Moholy-Nagy's idea of the "typophoto," a "new visual literature" born of the combination of typography and photography. The typophoto – or "phototext," as

Moholy-Nagy also called it – promised to be "the most visually exact rendering of communication."[3] Instead of progressing linearly and intellectually in the form of typography, the phototext communicated in terms of "optical and associative relationships."[4] These relationships aimed at a visual-conceptual synthesis "so objective as to permit no individual interpretation" – a "hygiene of the optical"[5] that sought to do away with ambiguity through the objectivity of a technical apparatus. As a phototext, "Dynamic of the Metropolis" may not be as closed to interpretation as Moholy-Nagy might have wished. Its mode of communication, however, is nothing if not direct. The city symphony palpably renders the experience of city life through juxtapositions of text, photographic images, and graphic patterns – elements that Moholy-Nagy would later use to compose city symphony films such as *Impressions of the Old Marseille Port* (1929–32) and *Berlin Still Life* (1931–32). In "Dynamic of the Metropolis," images, texts, and shapes do not merely resemble the city; they reproduce the flux and oscillations of urban experience. The dynamics of the city symphony re-create the shifting perspectives and unstable environment of the city itself.[6] As such, the text does not so much represent the city, nor treat it as a character, as reproduce its medium of perception.

Despite Moholy-Nagy's insistence that the effect of "Dynamic of the Metropolis" is "meant to be visual, **only** visual,"[7] sound nevertheless plays an important role in his city symphony. Sound is given visual expression through alternating font sizes and syllabic breakdowns of words such as "tempo," "fortissimo," and "pianissimo"; it also manifests itself through the audible pronunciation of these words, which, were they to be read aloud – "Tem Po-O-PO-o-O" – would no doubt remind the listener of Dada poems such as those of Moholy-Nagy's friend Kurt Schwitters, particularly his "Ursonata." Moholy-Nagy's sketch is likewise littered with references to such audible phenomena as jazz bands, military marches, and wild felines – one of which, "an angry lynx," is photographed mid-roar. Last, the city symphony's visual principles are articulated in musical terms that would guide the composition not just of city symphonies but also avant-garde visual arts, narrative films, and literature throughout the 1920s and '30s.

One senses that, though vision is a key mode of perception for Moholy-Nagy's city symphony, the audible is not far off – that its role is more than that of a metaphorical support. This is also the case in Moholy-Nagy's theoretical discussions of cinema. His understanding of cinema as a tool uniquely positioned to render the dynamic simultaneity of urban life is predicated on a theory that echoes the ideas of the sociologist Georg Simmel. Unlike Simmel, however, Moholy-Nagy did not believe that the daily shocks and kaleidoscopic impressions experienced by the city-dweller led to an irrevocably blasé attitude.[8] Rather, they prepared the ground for a new kind of creative production by augmenting the viewer's capacity to make ever-finer distinctions. As Edward Dimendberg points out, whereas Simmel perceived the "flat and gray tone" of urban experience, Moholy-Nagy saw "organized grey-relationships, the living relationships of chiaroscuro."[9] These relationships were not necessarily visual. Indeed, in a passage that closely resembles Simmel's ideas on the metropolis, Moholy-Nagy transitions from the mode of sight to sound. "The immense development of technology and the big cities," Moholy-Nagy writes, "have increased the capacity of our perceptual organs for simultaneous acoustical and optical activity." Berliners crossing Potsdammer Platz "hear simultaneously ... the horns of the motor-cars, the bells of the trams, the tooting of the omnibuses, the greetings of the coachman, the roar of the underground railway, the shouts of newspaper sellers, the sounds of loudspeakers, etc." Paying attention to how the city symphony renders such sounds is one of the main aims of this book. Berliners, Moholy-Nagy points out, "can keep these different acoustical impressions separate from one another," while "a provincial man" would be "greatly confused by the number of impressions" and incapable of reacting accordingly."[10] Distinction among urban phenomena is thus not a matter for sight alone. Insofar as it is rooted in this ability to distinguish, the city symphony addresses audial as well as visual relationships. In so doing, it is concerned with how light and sound are produced by – and make their way through – urban infrastructure.

Optical and acoustic phenomena are brought even closer together in one of the most important aspects of Moholy-Nagy's aesthetic theory – the transformation of technologies of reproduction (the photograph and phonograph) into technologies of production. Indeed, it is here that Moholy-Nagy, typically considered a visual artist, makes some of the greatest advances in sound art.

> The task of the gramophone to date has been to reproduce existing acoustical phenomena. The sound vibrations to be reproduced are scratched with a needle onto a wax plate and later transferred, using a cast of this plate, back into sound with the aid of a membrane.
>
> An expansion of the apparatus for productive purposes could occur if a person were to make freehand scratches into the wax plate without external mechanical intervention ... ; these would, when reproduced, produce sounds, which, without new instruments and without an orchestra, enable a **fundamental renewal** of sound creation (new, previously nonexistent sounds and sound relationships) and thus help to bring about a modification in the presentation of music and in compositional possibilities.[11]

Moholy-Nagy's comment, which comes by way of a footnote, sums up the ideas of several articles he published in *De Stijl* (1922), *Sturm* (1923), and *Broom* (1923).[12] As Thomas Y. Levin notes, with respect to the gramophone, Moholy-Nagy's ideas were never realized; yet, by 1930, another technology had emerged to make them possible.[13] Optical-sound film – the technology that allowed filmmakers to synchronize images and sounds – also made it possible to "draw" sounds onto a film strip – that is, to draw sound patterns in the form of lines, bars, and curves, photograph them, and play them through a projector. The dream of sound synthesis – of graphically producing (writing) sounds – had been realized.

What Moholy-Nagy called the "groove-script" of the phonograph thus became the "sound-script" of optical-film technology. As Levin notes, Moholy-Nagy hailed this invention with the self-congratulation of a visionary artist whose ideas had been vindicated by history:

> Sound-script makes possible acoustic phenomena which conjure up out of nothing audible music without the previous play of any musical instrument. We are in a position today to be able to play written sounds, music written by hand, without involving an orchestra, by the use of the apparatus of sound film. It is a great pleasure for me to be able to report on this acoustical phenomenon; inasmuch as I had already explained it in articles and lectures ten years ago, although I

was not fortunate enough to be able to experiment with it then, I am very happy today to witness the successful realization of those of my suggestions previously labelled absurd.[14]

Indeed, Moholy-Nagy's ideas were successfully realized by the Swiss composer Rudolf Pfenninger (whom Moholy-Nagy credited with the first animated sound experiments) and German composer Oskar Fischinger (whose "sound ornaments" are perhaps the most well-known examples of animated sound), as well as by lesser-known Soviet composers and sound engineers such as Arseny Avraamov and Evgeny Sholpo (see chapter 2). While these composers each had their own ideas about the relationship between the graphic trace and the sonic phenomenon itself, they all shared an investment in the notion that the production of sound through the film strip was a direct expression of the composer's idea. Orchestras, musicians, and conductors were, in principle, superfluous. For the first time, a composer could set his ideas down on paper (or, rather, on celluloid) and have them sound exactly as intended, thus forming an unbroken chain from the composer's idea to the audience's ear.

In the sound-script, the exactness of the optical extends to the ambience of the audial through the principles of the typophoto. Graphic patterns – lines, squares, curves, triangles, and bars – not only systematize sonic phenomena; they create novel sounds of their own. The relationship of these patterns to sound is similar to that of a phototextual language. It is the combination of a limited series of graphic forms that give rise to infinite possibilities of sound and meaning. Exploring how this principle of graphic composition manifests itself in city symphonies – be they composed on the page, on celluloid, or on actual streets and squares – is a further aim of this book. Graphic patterns may be used to render the sounds of the city, but they may also be used as principles for composing real cities such as Baku and Moscow into symphonies, as was the case with Arseny Avraamov's *Symphony of Sirens* (chapter 2). The desire to make sound-reproduction technologies productive combines with the creative impulse to compose the metropolis as a sonic medium – to turn the city into an orchestra. As an avant-garde multimedia experiment, the city symphony is about more than representing kaleidoscopic visual relationships in musical terms; it engages material manifestations of urban sounds (car horns, bells, whistles, and loudspeakers), as well as novel technologies of sound reproduction and production. Such is the overarching argument of this book.

The Musical Analogy

The "symphony" in *city symphony* is more than a metaphor for musical form. Typically, the label *city symphony* is reserved for a loose grouping of avant-garde silent films that are said to organize the visual elements of urban experience according to musical principles such as rhythm, harmony, dissonance, and counterpoint. Grouped according to family resemblances such as non-narrative approaches and day-in-the-life structures, the films comprising this genre include Paul Strand and Charles Sheeler's 1920 *Manhatta*, Alberto Cavalcanti's 1926 *Nothing but Time*, Walter Ruttmann's 1927 *Berlin, Symphony of a Great City*, and Dziga Vertov's 1929 *Man with a Movie Camera*. They also include many lesser-known gems such as Robert Florey's 1929 *Skyscraper Symphony*, Rudolf Rex Lustig's 1930 *Sao Paulo, A Metropolitan Symphony*, and Liu Na'ou's 1933 Vertov-spinoff, *The Man Who Has a Camera*.[15] That said, to truly grasp the significance of these films, along with experiments such as Moholy-Nagy's film sketch, it is important to look further afield to sonic city symphonies such as Luigi Russolo's 1913 *Awakening of the City* (chapter 1), Arseny Avraamov's 1922 *Symphony of Sirens* (chapter 2), and Walter Ruttmann's 1930 *Weekend* (chapter 4). Read alongside silent city symphony films such as Ruttmann's *Berlin, Symphony of a Great City* and Vertov's *Man with the Movie Camera* (chapter 3), as well as sound symphony films such as Ruttmann's 1930 *Melody of the World* and Vertov's 1931 *Enthusiasm: Symphony of the Donbass* (chapter 5), these sonic, avant-garde city symphonies provide insight into the relationship between sonic phenomena, sound technologies, and urban environments in the early twentieth century. They deserve to be considered city symphonies in their own right and in terms of their insight into the sonic dynamics of urban environments and sound-reproduction technologies.

In this book, I ask how city symphonies across media register, capture, or represent urban sounds: What are the aesthetic and political implications of how they tune into (or ignore) different sounds? What role do they ascribe to sonic phenomena such as noise, vibration, and rhythm? In what listening practices are they embedded? How do they respond to technological shifts in recording and transmission? And how do they render such reproductive technologies productive? I also ask how city symphonies engage the material networks of cities. How do they mediate the sounds of the city, and how do they treat the city itself as a sonic medium? In posing such questions, this book aims to place equal emphasis on the terms *city* and *symphony*. City symphonies engage sonic phenomena and are themselves expressions of sound; they encompass a greater variety of artistic and distinctly sonic practices than their cinematic definition allows. For this reason, I will use the general term *city symphony* to refer to a range of sonic practices that engage the city, while using more specific terms such as *city symphony film*, *city symphony novel*, and *radio city symphony* to describe specific media manifestations of this phenomenon.

Through a comparative analysis of these manifestations, I aim to understand the role of sound in the city symphony as an intermedial phenomenon – one that manifests itself across media practices (music, mass spectacle, radio, and cinema), translates media products from one qualified medium into another (e.g., music into film, film into radio, and so on), or mixes media in novel ways. Instead of viewing city symphonies as quintessential expressions of visual urban modernity, I *listen* to them as attempts to tune into urban and modern sounds. The city symphony, I argue, records, processes, and composes the sounds of the city with specific purposes in mind. These include communicating with the spiritual world (Russolo; chapter 1), fostering an inter-ethnic, proletarian community (Avraamov; chapter 2), and rethinking the relationship between humans and machines (Vertov; chapters 3 and 5). In doing so, the city symphony actively negotiates between the sonic registers of different media (film, radio, text) and the cities in which they are embedded. Just as it brings the sounds of the city into music, radio, and film, it also transforms the city into its own auditorium and orchestra.

In making these arguments, this book takes issue with the musical analogy as the dominant mode of understanding the "symphony" in *city symphony*. According to David Bordwell, in the cinema of the 1920s and '30s, this analogy played a primarily heuristic role that allowed filmmakers to experiment with film's non-representational qualities. It functioned to "break a tendency to think of cinema as an art of the real"[16] while simultaneously ennobling film's status in accordance with a romantic conception of music as, in the words of Friedrich Schlegel, "the highest of all arts."[17] Directors and theorists of city symphonies regularly invoked the musical analogy to articulate their films' theoretical basis, even coming to disagreements over who was the first to apply symphonic form to documentary content. In an article written to a German newspaper, for instance, Dziga Vertov accused Walter Ruttmann of stealing the symphony film idea from his own Kino-Eye group. Since 1919, he argued, "the majority of Kino-Eye films were constructed as a symphony of labor, as a symphony of the whole Soviet country, or as a symphony of a single city." For this reason, Vertov continued, "Ruttmann's recent experiment, along with those of other avant-garde filmmakers, should be viewed as the result of years of pressure from Kino-Eye films and exhibitions on workers in abstract film (and not the other way around, which is absurd both chronologically and conceptually)."[18]

Vertov's accusations clue us into the fact that what we today refer to as city symphony films were never discussed in isolation.[19] There were symphonies of labour and symphonies of the Soviet Union; there were also abstract animated symphonies (Hans Richter's *Rhythmus 21*, Viking Eggeling's *Symphonie Diagonale*) and symphonies of horror (F. W. Murnau's *Nosferatu*). The notion of a symphonic approach to filmmaking entered into numerous discussions pioneered by notable critics and filmmakers such as Rudolf Arnheim, Béla Balázs, Jon Grierson, Siegfried Kracauer, Abel Gance, Germaine Dulac, Walter Ruttmann, Dziga Vertov, and Sergei Eisenstein. These figures discussed symphonic form and other musical analogies with regard to a diverse set of narrative, documentary, and non-narrative or "absolute" films. City and symphony were no more akin to each other than symphony and horror; rather, the notion of the symphonic provided a licence to experiment with forms of visual organization and representation across cinematic genres and practices. In this respect, film was not unique. As Werner Wolf points out, in literature, the musical analogy performed a similar function to its role in cinema.[20] Authors turned to the notion of music in a moment of crisis when the fragmentation of modern, urban experience seemed to burst the boundaries of traditional mimetic storytelling. Not only that, but in works such as Alfred Döblin's *Berlin, Alexanderplatz* the notion of music combined with a cinematic analogy that rendered this fragmentation all the more palpable. Indeed, Döblin's novel (see chapter 4) is considered closer in style and spirit to Ruttmann's *Berlin, Symphony of a Great City* than to its own screen adaptation.[21]

As a generic grouping of films, as Floris Paalman notes, the term *city symphony* is part of a "retroactive teleology," one that emerges in the 1980s and '90s from a discourse on the cinematic city.[22] This discourse tends to view city symphonies as demonstrating a special affinity between cinema, cities, and modernity.[23] Inspired by the urban and critical theories of figures such as Simmel, Siegfried Kracauer, and Walter Benjamin, theorists in this discourse subscribe to what Bordwell calls the "modernity thesis," the notion that, in the words of Ben Singer, "key formal and spectatorial similarities between cinema – as a medium of strong impressions, spatiotemporal fragmentation, abruptness, mobility – and the nature of metropolitan experience" speak to a complete overhaul of the human perceptual apparatus in modernity.[24] The musical analogy is an essential component of this thesis insofar as it relates to the visual dynamics of city symphony films. However, restricting the city symphony film – not to mention the city symphony in general – to this analogy creates an artificial dichotomy between form and content. Music becomes a metaphor for film form, while the city itself – or, rather, its image – becomes the content. The city symphony film's musical structure thus functions as a container that allows it to capture, represent, and imitate the dynamics of the city.[25] However, as one scholar warns, we should be wary of taking this "container" metaphor too far.[26]

By contrast, I suggest that the metaphor has not been taken far enough; or rather, that it eclipses the manner in which city symphonies, cinematic or otherwise, handle sound, not to mention their deeper connection to the sonic avant-garde. Music in the city symphony is more than a metaphor for form; it is the site of sonic experiments that challenge not only what counts as "musical" sound but also the borders between seeing and hearing. Paying closer attention to this dynamic reveals that the cinema, in the words of Thomas Elsaesser, is "not primarily referenced to visuality, and thus hint[s] at processes that wear visual modernity as a sort of mask, a foil or skin that could be shed, or thrown off like a disguise."[27] Pulling off this mask underscores the fact that "sound in modernism," as Sam Halliday suggests, "is irreducible to sound alone. Sound, instead, is best conceived as a configuration, with 'real' sound at its centre, to be sure, but other sense phenomena, such as touch and vision, rarely at more than one or two removes on its periphery."[28] Such a fluid exchange between the senses, I argue, is at the heart of the city symphony's musical conception.

Such an idea gives a fuller sense to the influence and development of Schlegel's conception of music as the "highest of all arts." Schlegel's notion was more than just a way for different "non-musical" arts to ennoble themselves; rather, via the influence of figures such as Arthur Schopenhauer, Richard Wagner, and Friedrich Nietzsche, it made its way into modernist and avant-garde theories and artworks as a desire to aesthetically transform life. The desire to break with the mimetic tradition in art, to break with the "art of the real," to transform sight into sound (synesthesia), and to search for the spiritual in the material, is intimately tied to the modernist avant-garde's striving for *mythopoesis*, the founding of a new communitarian basis for art in which art does not so much imitate life as rules over it. In this regard, music is not merely a formal mould for an artwork, be it a novel, painting, mass spectacle, or film; rather, it is deeply entangled with a new approach to their material basis whether it's breaking words down into their syllabic units or putting one's ear to the pavement and hearing a symphony (Russolo). How such avant-garde artworks engage sound provides insight into this new entanglement. The city symphony as an intermedial art form, I argue, emerges not simply from an interest in making cinema more "artistic," but rather as part this aesthetic movement that sought to break through the banal and everyday by releasing the spiritual energies of the material world.

The City as Medium

And what about the city? In focusing so much on the city's representation, scholars often forget that the city itself is a medium, one that can be manipulated for aesthetic and communicative purposes. In "The City Is a Medium," Friedrich Kittler argues that the city should be understood as a system of material networks for recording, transmitting, and processing information. "In a city," he writes, "networks overlap upon other networks. Every traffic light, every subway transfer, and every post office, as well as all the bars and bordellos, speak for this fact."[29] Bridges, highways, automobiles, oil refineries, gates, and ports all constitute a dense series of interconnections designed to address, command, transfer, and control. If this is the case, then why not play the city as an instrument, tuning and plucking the connections of each network like strings? This, I suggest, is what the city symphony attempts to do – it seeks to rewire and reconnect the networks that constitute a polis by treating them as instruments in an orchestra. As Kittler points out, "Plato, as a lawmaker for an ideal city, proposed that its size be limited to the range of a voice, which would broadcast laws or commands."[30] The city symphony inverts this idea. Instead of reducing the size of the city, it amplifies the sound of the voice, using the city's material infrastructure as a megaphone. In this regard, the city is not so much the "representational content" of the city symphony, nor its "main character," as the material medium through which it sounds.

This is quite literally the case for one of the city symphonies in this book, Avraamov's *Symphony of Sirens*, which sought to re-sound the October Revolution through the material networks and assemblages of Baku. But even city symphonies that did not directly attempt to play music through the industrial spaces of specific cities still relied on, engaged with, or otherwise sought to compose their material networks. In *Enthusiasm: Symphony of the Donbass*, for instance, Dziga Vertov attempted to broadcast the sounds of coal and electricity production through the networks of film and radio, thus integrating the two material networks on the basis of a power-station metaphor (chapter 5). In *Weekend*, Ruttmann sought to tune the network of the city to that of the radio (chapter 4), thus laying the groundwork for his global city symphony *Melody of the World* (chapter 5). In *The Awakening of the City*, Russolo attempted to articulate an alternative sonic city whose vibrations would tap into the network of the dead (chapter 1). In thus composing the material infrastructure of cities, the city symphony exploits the city's capacity as a sonic medium – as a configuration of networks that convey and produce sound.

The rise of "smart cities" has led many scholars to question how cities can manifest intelligence without being reduced to rational-computational metaphors and models designed to streamline capitalist production. In this regard, many studies of media cities such as Scott McQuire's fascinating *The Media City: Media, Architecture and Urban Space* tend to focus on visual phenomena such as glass houses, which were instrumental in the articulation of modern conceptions of transparency.[31] By contrast, sound-studies scholars such as Shannon Mattern have sought to unearth how cities amplify and transmit sound as well as adapt to new sonic conditions (e.g., industrial noise) and technologies. In "Ear to the Wire: Listening to Historic Urban Infrastructures," Shannon Mattern asks how one might excavate the "sonic city" – a city composed of radio waves, public address systems, and everyday conversations. How might one *"dig into"* such forms "of mediation that seemingly *have* no physical form?"[32] And how "might the city itself function as a sounding board, resonance chamber, or transmission medium" for music, public address, interpersonal communication, or any other form of sonic expression.[33] Mattern characterizes her strategy as taking the media-archaeology metaphor literally, "productively 'confusing' media archaeology and archaeology proper."[34] While media archaeologist of the "Kittlerian variety" – notably Jussi Parikka and Erkki Huhtamo – focus on "media artifacts and their representations," Mattern seeks to dig into the material infrastructures where technical media and cities connect – the wires, cables, pneumatic tubes, and deep-sea channels that make media function.

City symphonies, I suggest, are excellent sites for such media-archaeological digs. By listening to them, we can excavate the sounds of specific cities and technologies, not to mention the ideas and power structures behind them. One can, for instance, dig up the hand organs, telephones, and radios of Ruttmann's *Berlin, Symphony of a Great City* and listen to their visual representations (chapter 3); one can unearth the vibratory technologies behind Russolo's *Awakening of a City* and hear their occult resonances (chapter 1); one can trace the lines of a film such as Henri Storck's *Images d'Ostende* (1929) back to the earliest experiments in sound reproduction; one can listen to industrial changes that transformed Baku into a proletarian capital (chapter 2); one can even hear the world become a global village through a media-supported play of call-and-response (chapter 5). All these phenomena provide insight into how the city symphony approaches the city as a medium for sound.

Yet city symphonies are more than just sites for media-archaeological digs, sonic or otherwise; oftentimes, they are doing the digging themselves. For instance, as Devin Fore points out, Vertov's camera shows a predilection for unearthing ancient artifacts such as Scythian skeletons at the sites of future electric dams (*The Eleventh Year*).[35] In this regard, Vertov reveals one of the ways in which cities function as historical media; they are, in the words of Lewis Mumford, "the molds in which men's lifetime have cooled and congealed."[36] In the city, this cooling and congealing finds audible expression. Mumford writes:

> By the diversity of its time-structures, the city in part escapes the tyranny of a single present, and the monotony of a future that consists in repeating only a single beat heard in the past. Through its complex orchestration of time and space, no less than through the social division of labor, life in the city takes on the character of a symphony: specialized human aptitudes, specialized instruments, give rise to sonorous results which, neither in volume nor in quality, could be achieved by a single piece.[37]

City symphonies such as Vertov's dig up the material resonances of heterogeneous temporalities. They do not simply compose cities into symphonies; rather, they re-mediate the city as an already-existing medium of sonic expression in both a metaphorical and literal sense. Mumford writes that "the city, as it develops, becomes the center of a network of communications: the gossip of the well or the town pump, the talk at the pub or the washboard, the proclamations of messengers and heralds, the confidences of friends, the rumors of the exchange and the market."[38] Such "sonorous results" are the materials of city symphony compositions, whether cinematic, sonic, or anywhere in between. City symphonies are not only repositories for information about how such urban networks may have sounded; they are also audible expressions of those networks, especially as their velocity and reach expanded with modern media technologies.

Messengers and heralds, gossips and newspaper boys, telephone operators and radio engineers make up the rotating cast of city symphonies. Their equipment generates the sound that city symphonies sought to connect and compose across time and space.

As such, a further argument of this book is that city symphonies seek to re-mediate the sonic city. For Jay David Bolter and Richard Grusin, the term *re-mediation* describes "the representation of one medium in another," specifically as a characteristic of digital media – for example, the representation of a painting on a computer. Re-mediation may be self-effacing – i.e., it may attempt to sustain an illusion of *immediacy* – or it may seek to draw attention to itself – what Bolter and Grusin call *hypermediacy*. Similarly, I suggest that the city symphony does not so much represent the city as re-mediate it – that is, repurpose the ways in which the city already functions as a medium. Such re-mediations may strive for immediacy – a city symphony such as Ruttmann's, for instance, may appear to provide unmediated access to the city – or they may draw attention to themselves through self-reflexive devices in the manner of Vertov's *Man with a Movie Camera*. They may even attempt to re-mediate the city by rearranging its sounds and spaces as in Avraamov's *Symphony of Sirens*. In all these cases, the city symphony composes the already symphony-like quality of cities. It gives audible expression to the time of buildings, monuments, and streets and composes the material networks of cities as already audible phenomena.

Sound

In making the above arguments, I turn to the insights and methods of sounds studies to investigate the city symphony. The challenge of sound studies, writes Jonathan Sterne, "is to think across sounds, to consider sonic phenomena in relationship to one another – *as types of sonic phenomena rather than as things-in-themselves* – whether they be music, voices, listening, media, buildings, performances, or another other path into sonic life."[39] I take up this challenge with respect to the city symphony as a practice that is not specific to any single medium or mode of expression, but rather one that seeks to express both the sonic manifestations of the city and explore the sonic potential of the city as a medium. My aim is not only to account for the bearing sonic phenomena have on city symphonies, but also to examine the social, political, philosophical, and even spiritual aims of their engagement with sound. City symphonies, I argue, re-mediate the sounds of the city for various ends including communicating with the dead, forging proletarian communities, colonizing territory, bringing art into politics, and renewing art's spiritual foundations. In all these, sonic phenomena such as noise, vibration, and rhythm, as lived realities and concepts, have played an overlooked role.

City symphonies also offer insight into the soundscapes of urban and industrial environments, be they the concrete spaces of Berlin, the oil fields of Baku, the coal mines of the Donbass, or the virtual spaces of cities on radio and film. This book aims not only to better understand the sounds of these spaces but also to highlight discrepancies between particular city symphonies and the spaces they sought to compose. It pays attention, in other words, to the sounds *and* silences of city symphonies. Consider, for example, Avraamov's *Symphony of Sirens*. The mass spectacle is often described as an earth-shattering, cacophonous event, one that, in the words of Hillel Schwartz, "flexed its mightiest muscles in Baku in November 1922, where numerous conductors on special towers used coloured flags and pistols to coordinate multiple choirs, the foghorns of the Soviet flotilla on the Caspian, two batteries of cannon, a machine-gun division, the rifles of several infantry regiments, a flock of hydroplanes, a steam whistle machine, bus and car horns, and all of the city's factory sirens" in an effort re-sound the October Revolution.[40] This description is mostly accurate insofar as it summarizes Avraamov's own account of the symphony, published in the Proletkul't journal *Gorn* one year after the Baku performance. In Baku, however, what actually happened – and what was heard – did not match Avraamov's description. For all its noise on paper, the symphony, according to one "ear"-witness account, was most likely interrupted before it truly began (see chapter 2). This silence speaks to the Soviet Union's imperial legacy and its failure to liberate the colonized spaces of the former Russian Empire. It also suggests that one ought to approach the grandeur and volume of a city symphony's description with skepticism – its scale and volume do not always align with the sounds it makes. As such, paying attention to discrepancies between how a city symphony may have sounded, its composer's conception, other accounts of the sounds of a city symphony's setting, and its historical reception is one of the aims of this book.

In excavating the sounds of the city, city symphonies do not always carefully distinguish between sonic and visual phenomena. They are more interested in the productive confusion of sound and vision than defining them on their own terms or even in terms of each other – as in, for example, visual music or musical vision. This book argues that exploring the fluid boundaries between sound and sight is one of the city symphony's main fascinations. For the most part, I explore these boundaries in terms of three audiovisual figures: noise, vibration, and rhythm. I refer to them as "figures" insofar as they are not discrete phenomena. Noise may be described in terms of vibration or rhythm; rhythm in terms of vibration or noise. These figures embody different ways of grasping the contours of sonic and visual phenomena in urban environments. At the turn of the twentieth century, noise was at the centre of disputes concerning everything from excessively loud sounds to excesses of information. Likewise, a discourse on vibration encompassed everything from sonic frequencies and X-rays to brainwaves and occult stirrings of the ether. Last, rhythm was the subject of debates and experiments regarding the effects of new regimes of mechanized movement (e.g., factory work) on human beings. These figures suggest that the "musical analogy" at the heart of the city symphony participates in various discursive currents surrounding the treatment of audial phenomena as mediated by urban environments.

Space and Time

The city plays an important role in the ideological realm of both communism and capitalism. A sign of industrial progress, the city showcased the ability of both politico-economic systems to deliver on the promise of modernity. Often it functioned as modernism's propaganda, an image of the new, though it could just as often be mined for signs of poverty, alienation, and decay. Over the course of this book, I show how different ideological actors, equal parts artists and urban propagandists, sonically channelled and composed the city's modernizing promise of speed, efficiency, and dynamism. That said, before beginning, a word about this study's geographic and temporal framing is necessary. The reader may have noticed that many of the city symphonies in this study were composed by German or Soviet artists. This is in part due to the intercultural exchanges between Germany and the Soviet Union at the time, as well as the historical legacies of these two countries with respect to the question of how art, politics, and ideology interact. In 1996, these two issues and many others were significantly broached at the "Moscow-Berlin, 1900–1950" exhibit in Berlin. A co-production of the Pushkin Museum of Fine Arts and the Berlinische Galerie, the exhibit followed the overlapping trajectories of German and Soviet art from their shared avant-garde foundations and utopian aspirations to their interaction with totalitarian regimes and their ambivalent relationship to totalitarian politics. This shared history was given renewed significance following the fall of the Berlin Wall and the Soviet Union. Nevertheless, as Oksana Bulgakowa notes, in comparison with its more famous forerunner "Moscow-Paris, 1900–1930" (1981), the "Moscow-Berlin" exhibit has been largely forgotten.[41] Bulgakowa gives a number of reasons for this decline in interest including the proliferation of fake Russian avant-garde works, making art collection difficult, to a rising interest in the art of the 1930s, especially socialist realism.[42] These factors have determined what Bulgakowa calls the "politics of memory" surrounding the 1920s avant-garde.[43]

Despite declining interest, the Moscow-Berlin axis continues to orient discussions of European art and politics in the twentieth and twenty-first centuries. The most recent instance of this orientation, of course, concerns Russia's invasion of Ukraine. As such, this axis is a central focus of my study of the city symphony as a multimedial avant-garde work. At the same time, this book does not restrict itself to the power centres of Moscow and Berlin. Within the Soviet Union, it looks further afield to republics such as Azerbaijan, whose use as the site of a spectacular yet often overlooked city symphony tells part of the colonial story of this artform. This book also explores other European city symphonies, most notably Luigi Russolo's *Awakening of a City*, as well as Jean Vigo's French city symphony film, *À propos de Nice*. In doing so, it orients itself around a

German-Soviet political and cultural axis, while nevertheless remaining cognizant of other power dynamics that determine the sound and shape of the city symphony.

As for this study's temporal frame, it is one that encompasses several important moments in the history of early twentieth-century avant-garde sound art to provide a fuller picture of the city symphony as an audiovisual experiment. These include the advent of "noise music" in the form of Russolo's 1913 *The Art of Noises* and his development of what many consider to be the world's first acoustic synthesizers, the *intonarumori*; the evolution of a medium-specific radio art, particularly in the Weimar Republic, where numerous avant-garde figures including Bertolt Brecht, Rudolf Arnheim, and Hans Flesch took a keen interest in its development; and the anticipation, advent, and widespread adoption of sound film in both Germany and the Soviet Union. Of course, picking an end date for a study is always a somewhat arbitrary decision. History is a continuum; every ending is a new beginning. My book concludes with the date of my final case study, Dziga Vertov's *Enthusiasm: Symphony of the Donbass* (1931), whose contradictions reveal how the avant-garde city symphony struggled to adapt to the changing technological and political conditions of the thirties. While city symphonies continued to be made after 1931, this date marks an important shift insofar as their technology-based aesthetic became less radically new and instead became an object of preservation and reinvention within an avant-garde tradition.

From Concert Hall to Film Strip

This book progresses city symphony by city symphony. Some of these works imagine their cities, others document actual cities, while still others work with the materials of urban environments. In all these cases, sound has played a distinct yet underexamined role. In developing a sound-centred account of the city symphony, this book explores how the city symphony treats and re-mediates the city as a sonic medium, as well as how it engages urban environments in terms of audiovisual ideas such as noise, vibration, and rhythm. It also grasps how city-symphonic and related practices express themselves across media, how they struggle to systematize or gather the materials of urban construction under a single rubric, and the extent to which they encounter resistance from the geographic entities and geological materials they seek to organize.

The challenge of developing such an account confronts the methodology of this book. It may be argued that taking the city symphony out of a strictly cinematic context dilutes it in some way, blurs its borders and undermines its generic definition. Genres and discrete media are historical constructs, to be sure, but they are constructs that make meaningful comparison possible. Without the predefined borders of a specific medium (e.g., cinema), why include certain city symphonies in a study and not others? Why not also focus on city symphony paintings or examine more city symphony novels? My aim, however, is not to account for every single practice that may be defined as a city symphony or to draw comparisons between them just for the sake of drawing comparisons. Rather, I suggest that city symphony films – both "silent" and "sound" – may be usefully re-interpreted through their contemporary sonic and sound-art practices (and vice versa). As such, the first, second, and fourth chapters of this book focus on city symphonies outside the cinema proper ("live" city symphonies and radio city symphonies), while the third and fifth chapters examine "silent" and "sound" city symphony films. Together, these chapters trace the movement of the city symphony from the concert hall to the city and from the airwaves on to film. That said, one should not conceive of this movement as a simple linear progression, but rather as a cross-contamination between different city-symphonic media practices and how they engage, record, and transmit sound. This will reveal the sound at the heart of "silent" city symphonies as well as the silence at the heart of "sonic" ones.

Luigi Russolo's 1913 *Awakening of a City* should be considered the first modern city symphony insofar as it attempts to re-mediate the sounds of urban environments (chapter 1). As such, I examine Russolo's composition as orchestrating a movement from the concert hall to the city proper – the auditorium of the twentieth century. Besides focusing on the noise of Russolo's project, I also focus on its spiritual aims – its attempt to conjure a city of the dead – as well as its attempt to translate sounds into colours, thus evoking a visual world with his music. Visualizing an invisible spiritual world is a fundamental yet overlooked aspect of Russolo's project, and it highlights the importance the vibratory sciences held for his work. Indeed, Russolo's spiritual project and his audiovisual project are two sides of the same coin.

Arseny Avraamov's *Symphony of Sirens* continues the movement of Russolo's city symphony through its attempt to compose the spaces of Baku and Moscow in a musical mass spectacle of the Bolshevik Revolution (chapter 2). Here, the desire to compose a city's sounds collides with the history and geography of specific cities. The *Symphony of Sirens*, I argue, has been the subject of a myth that has gone largely unquestioned in English-language sound and urban-studies scholarship – a myth of overwhelming noise and spectacular scale. Instead of focusing solely on the symphony's dreaded noise, I pay attention to the symphony's silence – to the limits of what can be known about its sounds. Drawing on Avraamov's untranslated writings and personal correspondences, I investigate how the symphony's ideal of proletarian unity founders on the geographic, social, and sonic reality of the cities it sought to compose. In other words, I investigate the ways in which Avraamov's symphony failed to sound. I then explore the roots of the symphony's ideal of unity in Avraamov's personal aesthetic philosophy as well as his idiosyncratic views on the mechanical reproduction of sound. In particular, I analyze how Avraamov sought to apply the principles of sound reproduction and synthesis to structure an aesthetic community.

The connections between the works of composers such as Russolo and Avraamov and the visual dynamics of city symphonies such as Walter Ruttmann's *Berlin, Symphony of a Big City*, Dziga Vertov's *Man with a Movie Camera*, and Jean Vigo's *Apropos de Nice* (1930) manifest themselves through techniques of inaudible sound (chapter 3). These techniques include implied sound, the generation of visual noise through fast editing speeds and motion blur, and the treatment of motion *as* sound. I relate these techniques back to the compositions of previous chapters, as well as converse developments in the field of sound synthesis, specifically the experiments of Avraamov, Oskar Fischinger, and Rudolf Pfenninger. City symphony films, I argue, participate in sonic practices that stem from the rise of noise, vibration, and rhythm as social, aesthetic, and technological problems in the early twentieth century. In sounding the inaudible, these films construct a fluid exchange of the senses that addresses the shifting aesthetic and political implications of sound as a multi-sensory phenomenon in modernity.

If the city symphony film evokes sounds through images, then the radio city symphony evokes images through sounds. A case in point is Walter Ruttmann's radio city symphony *Weekend* (1930) – a composition that was billed as a film without images (chapter 4). This chapter also explores the history of Germany radio through Alfred Döblin's city symphony novel *Berlin, Alexanderplatz* (1929) and its radio adaptation. Already in Avraamov's *Symphony of Sirens* one hears inklings of the radio city symphony. The mass spectacle was conducted from atop a Swedish Mast, a structure used to mount radio antennae.[44] Ruttmann's radio city symphony extends this principle by composing a city symphony on the airwaves. The driving question of this chapter is how radio city symphonies not only took advantage of but also conceived of radio technology as a means to mediate the sounds and spaces of the city. I argue that German experimental radio is in fact rooted in the city symphony tradition, and that Ruttmann's radio experiment engages the question of how to render urban spaces through sound.

Many of the city symphonies in this book push beyond the borders of a particular city. Vertov's *Man with a Movie Camera*, for instance, was a composite of four different cities, thus suggesting a global impulse at the heart of the city symphony film. At the same time, the advent of sound film appeared to challenge this impulse by threatening to balkanize cinema into separate language groups. In response, many avant-garde filmmakers advocated for a contrapuntal approach to film sound, while others, notably Vertov himself, viewed counterpoint as a distraction from the real question of how to record and compose actual, on-location sounds. Both Walter Ruttmann's *Melody of the World* (1930) and Dziga Vertov's *Enthusiasm: Symphony of the Donbass* (1931) reveal how the city symphony entered into this debate (chapter 5). Rather than framing this discussion as a reaction to the advent of sound, I examine it as a question of how to reinvent the techniques for mediating the sounds of the city explored in the previous chapters. It emerges that counterpoint is not a defensive posture, but rather the continuation of a sonic avant-garde practice, one that the city symphony deployed to realize its ambition of moving beyond the borders of the city.

The focus on Ruttmann and Vertov in chapters 3 and 5 – and, to a lesser extent, chapter 4 – is part of the design of this book. It makes it possible to trace the development of the city symphony phenomenon within a more consistent framework of two competing directors, both of whom laid claim to the advent of the city symphony film, as well as to an experimental tradition that went beyond cinema proper. At the same time, I investigate city symphony compositions that originated outside the cinema in the realms of music, mass spectacle, and the novel. In doing so, I reveal how sound manifests itself in the city symphony, how city symphonies mediate urban sounds, and how technologies of mechanical reproduction affect their design and performance.

1

IN THE CONCERT HALL

Luigi Russolo's *The Art of Noises*
and *The Awakening of a City*

At the turn of the twentieth century, orchestral works seeking to render the sounds of city life began to appear with increasing frequency. Many of these compositions – impressionistic tone poems of parks, squares, and streets, peppered with car horns, train whistles, snatches of conversation, and clopping horse hooves – aimed to tell the story of a single city. Inspired by local topographies, they often took their titles directly from the urban centres whose fleeting sounds they sought to compose.[1] Frederick Delius's "Paris: A Song of a Great City" (1899) reimagined the nocturne as a sound-painting of Parisian nightlife; Edward Elgar's "Cockaigne, In London Town" (1900) gave a tour of the British capital through a series of sonic snapshots; Gustave Charpentier's "Paris s'éveille," the prelude to the second act of his opera *Louise* (1900), portrayed the awakening of the French capital; and Charles Ives's "Central Park in the Dark" (1906) layered haunting and dissonant tones to construct a soundscape of New York City bursting with shrieking woodwinds, hammering pianos, and abstract quotations from popular songs such as Joseph E. Howard's "Hello! Ma Baby."

The city-inspired works of Delius, Elgar, Charpentier, and Ives feature many of the motifs and techniques that would later come to define the city symphony film: the awakening of the city; the cries of market vendors; the bustle of night life; day-in-the-life narrative structures; and so on. One may be forgiven, however, for not hearing the nascent rumblings of Futurist noise experiments in these works. With the exception of Ives's "Central Park in the

Dark," many of these compositions may sound quite tame, at least to contemporary ears. Urban-industrial noise is limited to evocative moments; it is not the main subject or material of composition. Yet it is important to keep in mind that the compositions of the sonic avant-garde – works such as Luigi Russolo's *Awakening of a City* (1914), Arseny Avraamov's *Symphony of Sirens* (1922), George Antheil's *Ballet Mécanique* (1925), and Alexander Mosolov's *The Iron Foundry* (1927) – belong to this orchestral tradition of programmatic music, one that stretches back to Hector Berlioz's *Symphonie Fantastique* (1830) and *The Singing of a Train* (1846). Indeed, Futurist composers such as Francesco Balilla Pratella praised the works of Delius, Elgar, and Charpentier – alongside other notables such as Richard Strauss, Claude Debussy, and Modest Moussorgsky – as proto-Futurist, part of the "futurist evolution of music," which the movement in Italy sought to further develop.[2]

Despite their break with the tonal tradition of Western music, their radical conception of microtonal composition, their use of noise as a fundamental aesthetic material, and their reliance on novel noise instruments and everyday noise-making objects, Futurist and avant-garde compositions did not so much break with the romantic tradition of the nineteenth century as exaggerate its Wagnerian tendency to transgress the borders between concert hall and public space. This fact is brought home by their insistence on an alternative relationship between city and symphony. Instead of merely bringing the sounds of the city into the symphony through imitative references to external reality á la Delius, Elgar, Charpentier, and Ives, they attempted to bring the symphony out into the city by creating an urban orchestra. The following two chapters explore the tensions and contradictions of this movement through the works and ideas of two notable avant-garde composers – Luigi Russolo (chapter 1) and Arseny Avraamov (chapter 2). Despite their ideological differences (Avraamov was a lifelong communist; Russolo, an avowed fascist),[3] the two figures have a special relationship, based on not only their mutual interest in noise and microtonal composition but also their shared approach to the city as a sonic and spiritual medium. Both composers sought to channel the occult energies associated with noise into their respective politico-aesthetic projects.

Admittedly, Russolo's 1913 *Art of Noises* was not overtly political in the manner of Avraamov's *Symphony of Sirens*, which, among other things, was a work of Revolutionary propaganda. Mussolini would not found his Fascio d'Azione Rivoluzionaria until December 1914; its first meeting was not held until January 1915. The Futurism of the *Art of Noises* and Italian fascism co-evolved over the course of the 1910s and '20s, embracing each other in terms of an aesthetic that placed enormous stock in the dynamic energy of the occult. Yet the occult as a source of artistic and political inspiration does not inevitably lead to fascism. Ernesto Laclau's insight that fascism's constitutive elements can be, as Slavoj Žižek suggests, "incorporated into a different, non-Fascist, edifice" is brought home by Avraamov's adaptation and radicalization of Russolo's ideas in his city-wide mass spectacle, the *Symphony of Sirens*.[4] There is, in other words, no direct, lawlike correlation between aesthetic, political, and social elements and an overarching political ideology such as fascism or communism. What matters is how these elements are combined and articulated. In the 1910s and early 1920s, the relationship between sonic, technological, occult, and political ideas was very much open to articulation. The different trajectories of Russolo's *Art of Noises* and Avraamov's *Symphony of Sirens* give a sense of this open field while demonstrating the limits and fundamental tensions that it entails.

One of these tensions concerns the channelling and composition of urban-industrial noise. Defining noise, to borrow an analogy from Michel Chion, is like defining the shape of a cloud: both are readily recognizable but resistant to precise description. The main difference consists in the fact that "a cloudy configuration leaves us the time to observe before it changes appearance, whereas observing sounds is like observing clouds that very rapidly stream past and transform."[5] This fact gives us the impression that noises are muddled or confused. Noise may refer to a non-periodic frequency; "spurious or undesirable" information;[6] non-musical, non-linguistic, or otherwise meaningless sounds; or disruptive, unpleasant, and painful sounds. In all these cases, as Paul Hegarty sums up, noise is "unwanted, other, not something ordered. It is negatively defined – i.e., by what it is not, but it is also a negativity," a relation that "helps structure and define its opposite (the world of meaning, law, regulation, goodness, beauty, and so on)."[7]

Over the course of the nineteenth and early twentieth centuries, noise emerged as a pressing problem for industrial society due to the rapid growth of cities and the advancement of sound-transmitting technologies such as the radio and telephone. As Karin Bijsterveld points out, public discussions of "industrial noise, of city traffic noise, of neighborly noise of gramophones and radios, and of aircraft noise" arose in many European cities, leading to various zoning ordinances that attempted to create "'islands of silence' such as parks and neighborhoods with limitations on industry and traffic."[8] Noise-abatement campaigns sprung up across European cities in an attempt to limit and control irritable sounds. At the same time, as the unwanted or threatening sounds of others, noise piqued the interest of avant-garde artists such as Russolo and Avraamov, who marshalled their negativity to disrupt the validity of traditional aesthetic systems. Noise compositions questioned music and language as the primary modes of sonic expression by asserting the radical equivalence between well-tempered notes, human voices, and the sounds of steam engines and tractors.

As Bijsterveld points out, though the chief aim of avant-garde composers – assaulting bourgeois ears – may seem diametrically opposed to that of bourgeois noise-abatement campaigners, their divergent goals nevertheless shared in a desire to control and subjugate unwanted sounds. Whereas noise-abatement campaigners sought to quarantine these sounds, avant-garde composers aimed to harness their disruptive potential through the development of novel instruments and musical frameworks. In doing so, they participated in a dynamic of chaos and control. In *Noise: The Political Economy of Music*, the French economist Jacques Attali locates this dynamic at the heart of not just avant-garde composition but music in general. For him, the relationship between noise and music resembles a dialectical struggle between violence and power. "Since it is a threat of death," Attali writes, "noise is a concern of power; when power founds its legitimacy on the fear it inspires, on its capacity to create social order, on its univocal monopoly of violence, it monopolizes noise." Music, insofar as it structures noise through a progression of dissonance and resolution, "resembles the game of power: monopolize the right to violence; provoke anxiety and then provide a feeling of security; provoke disorder and then propose order; create a problem in order to solve it."[9]

Attali's most controversial claim is that this cathartic dialectic of noise and music is "prophetic" – "social organization echoes music" and not (or not only) the other way around.[10] Sacrificing historical nuance at the altar of grand narrative, he argues that music not only embodies modes of political economy but also prefigures them. While such an idea may not be the best way to account for the history of Western music, it still has traction with contemporary interpretations of Futurist noise experiments in various media, from Umberto Boccioni's *Materia* (painting) to F.T. Marinetti's "Zang Tumb Tumb" (poetry) to Russolo's own compositions. As Christine Poggi points out, for the Futurists, noise embodied the violence inherent in matter; it was a harbinger of revolution, war, and a new mechanical-social order erected on the twin pillars of nationalism and imperialism.[11] "Conceived as an unmediated fragment of the real," Poggi writes, "noise could be incorporated into the work of art as a dissonant element, one that could not be fully integrated into a system of consonant relations suggesting unity and coherence."[12] This element reflected the ceaseless conflict at the heart of both Futurist aesthetics and politics, yet bringing it into the work of art required a certain degree of control; it could not be done haphazardly. To this end, Russolo organized noises into tables, classifying them into six families – rumbles, whistles, whispers, screeches, percussive sounds, and the "voices of animal and people."[13] He devised a new class of instruments, the *intonarumori* (noise-tuners), which served to abstract noises from their material sources – from the spaces and objects that produced them in the first place – thus transforming them into apt materials for composition. With evocative names such as Howlers (*Ululatori*), Roarers (*Rombatori*), Cracklers (*Crepitatori*), Rubbers (*Stropicciatori*), Bursters (*Scoppiatori*), Gurglers (*Gorgoliatori*), Hummers (*Ronzatori*), and Whistlers (*Sibilatori*), these hurdy-gurdy–like contraptions produced and "tuned" noises by accentuating their dominant pitch (figure 1.1). Russolo also developed a notation system that gave the enharmonic (i.e., microtonal) diversity of noises created by these instruments a linear form of representation (figure 1.2).

What Russolo heard in noise was both an eruption of the material world and a chance to dominate it through processes of abstraction. By contrast, for Avraamov, noise was not so much a manifestation of the inherent violence of the material world as a social product of that world's exploitation. It signified the revolutionary energy of the proletariat. To channel this energy, Avraamov devised as special instrument, the *magistral'* (the main

Figure 1.1 / "Nel Laboratorio degli Intonarumori a Milano."

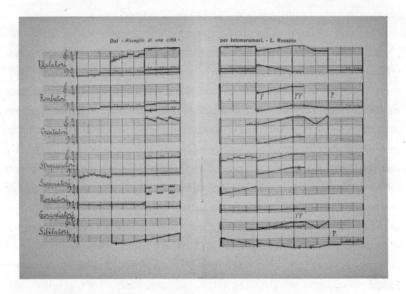

Figure 1.2 / "Risveglio di una città."

line), a steam-whistle machine that would channel the alienated sounds of industrial noise into a common melody – the "Internationale."[14] He may have also attempted to tune the factory sirens of Baku to play the worker's anthem, though this is not certain.

Despite their ideological differences, Russolo and Avraamov both sought to channel the destructive energy of noise through the development of novel compositions and instruments of control – Russolo through the intonarumori; Avraamov through the magistral'. Noise was never noise as such, but a material to be negated, albeit without necessarily negating its acoustic appearance as noise. Such an approach to noise reveals the contradictory impulses that characterize the desire to compose the city. On the one hand, Futurist composers were attracted to the aleatory, chaotic, and destructive quality of urban noise, its ability to slip past rules and standards and break up established codes. On the other, such compositions required a degree of control and abstraction that tamed the very irregularity that attracted composers to noise in the first place. The strictness and precision of noise compositions, performances, and instruments gave the lie to the idea that all noise composers wanted to do was revel in chaos.

That said, it is important to recognize that noise composers did not simply wish to leave the city behind after extracting and processing its noises. Often, avant-garde composers such as Russolo and Avraamov are portrayed as exalting the machine, as being fascinated with noise on account of its ability to express the speed and dynamism of mechanized life. Machine sounds and machine instruments take centre stage as instruments of control, while the city remains a source of material inspiration (i.e., noise). By contrast, I argue that the city played an integral role as a medium, not just for sound but for the often overlooked spiritual and religious strivings of Russolo's and Avraamov's compositions. More than just a celebration of noise, Russolo's *Awakening of a City* was a means of conjuring another realm populated by ectoplasms and astral bodies. Likewise, more than an attempt to embody the sounds of the urban proletariat, Avraamov's *Symphony of Sirens* sought to re-establish a lost unity of art, religion, science, philosophy, and politics. What is more, it was also a love song. These works reveal the multifaceted ways in which the city may be treated as a medium for sound, not only to produce, store, transmit, or resonate sound, but also to access other worlds and emotional states – a sono-spiritual medium. They reveal that the city symphony is more than just an analogy for musical organization; it is rooted in a genuine desire to sacralize the city, thereby bringing the material-urban world in line with an immaterial one. The networks that constitute the city – networks for producing goods, delivering electricity, extracting resources, transporting people, and, of course, transmitting sound – criss-cross and overlap with those that constitute occult and spiritual systems of belief. Listening to this attempt to pluck the strings of the urban network – its successes as well as its failures; its sounds as well as its silences – is the goal of the following two chapters.

The Awakening of a City

Though he began his career as a painter, Luigi Russolo is best known today for his 1913 manifesto *The Art of Noises,* as well as the inventor of a novel set of noise instruments – literally noise-tuners (intonarumori) – for which he composed short musical pieces such as *The Awakening of a City, Meeting of Automobiles and Aeroplanes,* and *Luncheon on the Terrace of the Kursaal Hotel.* Russolo referred to these compositions as "spirals" or "networks of noises," a term that hints at a networked approach to the sounds of the city. In *The Art of Noises*, Russolo remarks on the dialectical relationship between city and symphony, correlating the symphony's increase in volume to the rise of urban noise: "The ear of the Eighteenth Century man would not have been able to withstand the inharmonious intensity of certain chords produced by our orchestra (with three times as many performers as that of the orchestra of his time). But our ear takes pleasure in it, since it is already educated to modern life, so prodigal in different noises."[15] The growth of symphony orchestras over the course of the nineteenth century, for Russolo, was an attempt to keep pace with sounds pressing in from outside, particularly from rapidly developing urban and industrial centres. If the eighteenth-century symphony was performed in the relative quiet of the aristocratic court, and the nineteenth-century symphony expanded in both size and volume to fill the public concert hall, then the twentieth-century orchestra would have to grow to incorporate and ultimately encompass the sounds and spaces of modern life. Part of this expansion meant bringing the sounds of the city into the symphony, a feat already accomplished by the compositions of Delius, Elgar, Charpentier, and Ives; the other meant treating the city as a symphony, as a medium for sonic expression.

Unfortunately, there are no extant recordings of Russolo's compositions for the intonarumori.[16] None of his famed instruments survived past the middle of the twentieth century – many of them having been cannibalized by Russolo himself to build grander inventions such as the *rumorarmonio* (noise harmonium); others lost to the ravages of World War II. As with Avraamov's *Symphony of Sirens*, those seeking to "hear" Russolo's work must rely on ear-witness accounts, as well as the inventor-composer's own manifestos and articles. One such account – written by a correspondent from London's *Pall Mall Gazette* on the occasion of a 1913 trial performance of Russolo's instruments at the Milan home of the Futurist impresario F.T. Marinetti – presents *The Awakening of a City* as a kind of novel program music:

> At first a quiet even murmur was heard. The great city was asleep. Now and again some giant hidden in one of those queer boxes snored protentiously [sic]; and a new-born child cried. Then, the murmur was heard again, a faint noise like breakers on the shore. Presently, a far-away noise rapidly grew into a mighty roar. I fancied it must have been the roar of the huge printing machines of the newspapers.
>
> I was right, as a few seconds later hundreds of vans and motor lorries seemed to be hurrying towards the station, summoned by the shrill whistling of the locomotives. Later, the trains were heard, speeding boisterously away; then, a flood of water seemed to wash the town, children crying and girls laughing under the refreshing shower.
>
> A multitude of doors was next heard to open and shut with a bang, and a procession of receding footsteps intimated that the great army of bread-winners was going to work. Finally, all the noises of the street and factory merged into a gigantic roar, and the music ceased.
>
> I awoke as though from a dream and applauded.[17]

Russolo and his fellow Futurists were in fact less enthralled by the performance. In an oft-repeated complaint, Marinetti lamented "a certain inexperience on the part of the performers, insufficiently prepared by the small number of rehearsals."[18] Russolo would repeat this assessment with respect to subsequent performances, suggesting that to play one of his *intonorumori* required more skill than just the ability to turn a crank. Interestingly, the anonymous correspondent's account reads like a shot list for a future city symphony film. Episodes featuring the sleeping city, printing presses, newspaper vendors, automobiles, speeding trains, office workers, and marching armies of breadwinners would become de rigueur for films such as *Berlin: Symphony of a Great City*. Yet to think of Russolo's compositions – or of city symphony films for that matter – as mere program music would be a mistake.

Accounts like that of the correspondent for the *Pall Mall Gazette* are vague; they reflect the subjective associations of the listener more than the sounds Russolo's instruments may have actually made. That said, most ear-witness accounts hardly describe Russolo's music; they are much more focused on the scandal his instruments caused. On 21 April 1914, Russolo premiered his intonarumori with another performance of his three noise networks – *The Awakening of a City, Luncheon on the Terrace of the Kursaal Hotel*, and *Meeting of Automobiles and Aeroplanes* – at the Dal Verme Theatre in Milan. Ironically, as Poggi notes, the compositions were drowned out by a booing audience. One journalist groused that "many yesterday would have wished to form an opinion on the three spirals of intoned noises composed by Russolo. But they only experienced the sensation of the city's thunderous roar on the evening of Fat Saturday."[19] The noises of the city, which broke into the concert hall in the form of a Futurist-led riot, overpowered the city-inspired noises of Russolo's own compositions.

Such a rowdy reaction on the part of the audience was not uncommon for the time. Compositions such as Igor Stravinsky's *The Right of Spring*, Arnold Schoenberg's *Kammersymphonie*, George Antheil's *Ballet Mécanique*, and many others were frequently met with boos and catcalls. Schoenberg's performance was notably disrupted by audience members jingling their keys. These reactions became, in a certain sense, part of the performance as a kind of mass spectacle.[20] It is curious, however, that, unlike some of his Futurist colleagues, Russolo did not seem to relish the riot and scandal his compositions caused. In fact, Russolo expected his audience to listen quietly to their recital. While the music itself may have been radical, the setting was typical – a bourgeois concert hall,[21] a space defined by the strict separation between performers and audience members. Russolo and his musicians were dressed in black tie; the audience was seated and expected to listen attentively. When they refused, Russolo compared them to wild beasts, animals whose noises he had previously praised in manifestos and articles.[22] Are we then to conclude that Russolo, while seeking to push the limits of what may be called "music" by expanding the realm of musical sound, was content to restrict himself to the confined spaces of the concert hall and the traditional relationships they entailed?

A City of Vibrations

The contrast between Russolo's Milan performance and the ambitions of his noise music is striking when one considers how his description of city sounds seems to call on the listener to leave the dusty confines of the concert hall once and for all. A walk through the city leads to the realization that, far from being "loud and disagreeable to the ear," city noises may be graceful, even delicate, the source of a symphonic experience all their own. In *The Art of Noises*, Russolo writes:

> Let us wander through a great modern city with our ears more alert than our eyes and we shall find pleasure in distinguishing the rushing of water, gas, or air in metal pipes, the purring of motors that breathe and pulsate with indisputable animality, the throbbing of valves, the pounding of pistons, the screeching of mechanical saws, the jolting of trams on their tracks, the cracking of whips, the flapping of curtains and flags. We shall amuse ourselves by creating mental orchestrations of the crashing down of metal shop shutters, the slamming of doors, the bustle and shuffling of crowds, the varied racket of railroad stations, iron foundries, spinning mills, printing plants, subways, and electrical power stations.[23]

Russolo appreciates city noises for their novelty, for their ability to disrupt conventional aesthetic codes, as well as inspire fear and awe in his listeners. At the same time, he appreciates noises for their own unique and subtle resonances. Although at times he gives the impression that, until the Industrial Revolution, the world was largely silent, he actually views urban sounds as existing on a continuum with natural ones, going so far as to justify the aesthetic value of the former though comparisons with the latter. However, insofar as Russolo used his intonarumori to abstract the sounds of the city – and insofar as he argued against the facile imitation of urban noises – it may be argued that the city, for Russolo, played a largely supporting role as the inspiration for his work.

Such a story is complicated by the fact that Russolo was not simply interested in the sounds produced by urban-industrial materials for their novelty, shock value, or ability to express the mechanized spheres of life. He was also interested in how such materials registered and transmitted sonic vibrations, in how they interacted with one another as resonant media. This is evident from Russolo's description of urban materials that are not typically appreciated for their capacity to make noise – materials such as pavement. In and of itself, pavement does not make sound the way pounding pistons, screeching mechanical saws, and jolting trams do. It does not engage in a sound-generating action of its own, but is rather the passive receiver of vibrations from other movements in the city – cars, pedestrians, construction, and so on. Yet it is precisely this fact that attracts Russolo to this relatively ubiquitous and unexciting substance. In "The Noises of Nature and Life," he observes that "in places where continuous noises are produced (much-used streets, factories, etc.) there is always a low, continuous noise, independent to a certain degree of the various rhythm noises that are present. This noise is a continuous low sound that forms a *pedal* to all the other noises."[24] Russolo locates this sound in the "resonating vibrations of the pavement," and cautions that it "should not be confused with the particular noises of different vehicles (the scraping and bouncing of the train on the tracks, of the wheels of carriages and automobiles, the trotting of horses, etc.). It is produced instead by the trembling and vibration of the asphalt as it is overrun by various vehicles."[25]

Russolo, here, is describing an acoustic phenomenon known as sympathetic vibration, the ability of one resonating medium to produce corresponding vibrations in an another – for example, the sound caused by singing into an undamped piano or cranking up the bass near a windowpane. The phenomenon is at the heart of experiments like those of Ernst Chladni, who famously created sound figures by "bowing" a plate of sand-covered metal. Later generations of acousticians such as Hermann von Helmholtz would conduct similar experiments using material such as vulcanized rubber.[26] In *The Art of Noises*, Russolo mentions Chladni and Helmholtz while discussing the variety of vibrations in noises and their ability to produce harmonics and overtones.[27] His approach to urban sounds extends this idea to the city. For Russolo, every street has a pitch – or even multiple pitches – that resonate through its asphalt and other material components. Similar to Chladni's metal plate, the pavement is set in motion by pedestrian and vehicular traffic. Indeed, Russolo goes so far as to claim to be able to discern "perfect triads" and "fifths" in certain streets. Train tracks, trolley wires, and even shuffling crowds function in a similar manner. They not only make noises but also register and resonate the vibrations of other aspects of the city,[28] both on the ground and in the air.

To be sure, the vibratory interactions of a city are far more complicated and irregular than those of a bowed metal plate. Yet it is precisely this complexity that attracts Russolo's interest. While the dominant pitch of a street may be established, it can only be heard through the ever-changing "harmonic and rhythmic modulations" of cars, trams, and trolley wires. This suggests that the networks that compose the city as a Kittlerian medium (see the introduction) – the networks of transport, communication, and so on – have a role to play in Russolo's city symphony that goes beyond simply inspiring the work. These noises are not merely materials to be abstracted, dominated, and transformed into a higher spiritualized form (music); rather, they are the material components of the city as a sonic medium. In this regard, *The Awakening of a City* struggles to reconcile the tension between abstraction and particularity; between the city as presenting sonic materials to be processed and the city as already a symphonic medium in its own right.

Further complicating this struggle is the fact that there is also a spiritual component to Russolo's conception of the city as a sonic medium. Like his fellow Futurists, Russolo was not simply a neo-romantic machine fetishist, nor a brute materialist; rather, he was interested in the overlapping spiritual and technological valences of mechanical media. As Luciano Chessa points out, for the Futurists, the speed, dynamism, and destructive capacity of machines were never ends in themselves; rather, they were means to attain higher spiritual aims. *The Awakening of a City* thus speaks not only to the morning routines of a modern metropolis but also to that metropolis's spiritual awakening – to its greater unification with the cosmos. Like other modernist and avant-garde movements (most notably the Symbolists), the Futurists were fascinated by the occult. More specifically, they were interested in how modern technologies such as the telegraph, radio, telephone, phonograph, photograph, X-ray, and film could materialize occult phenomena such as ectoplasms, astral bodies, thought-forms, and voices of the dead. In this respect, they were part of a movement that Anthony Enns and Shelley Trower call "vibratory modernism."

At the turn of the twentieth century, as Enns and Trower point out, the scientific community was taken with an understanding "of the universe as a vast network of continuous vibrations" – vibrations of ether, matter, energy, sound, light, and mind. This idea had a tremendous impact not only on scientific domains such as physics, optics, acoustics, neurology, and psychiatry, but also modernist literature, art, music, theatre, and philosophy, as well as spiritual practices such as yoga, theosophy, and anthroposophy.[29] The wave theory of light, for instance, which postulated that light consisted of vibrations of the ether, was enormously influential in the development of modernist painting via the idea that the vibrations of visual patterns could stimulate corresponding vibrations of thought. Such notions were useful for explaining the interaction between a host of "invisible" phenomena such as brainwaves, X-rays, radio waves, electricity, magnetism, and radioactivity, all of which fed into occult ideas surrounding the materialization of mental and spiritual phenomena, extrasensory perception, telepathy, communication with the dead, and other forms of non-linguistic communication.

The discourse on vibrations promised to unify the visible and invisible world under a single ontology and epistemology. Matter and motion, heat and energy, smell and touch, sound and sight, spirit and thought, all could be reduced to a universal set of vibratory principles – a prospect that not only explained the ability to photograph bones beneath the flesh (X-ray) but also held out the possibility of photographing smells, thoughts, and even ghosts. Under this rubric, sense and extrasensory perception did not differ in kind but only in degree. The works and theories of Futurists such as F.T. Marinetti, Umberto Boccioni, Giacomo Balla, Francesco Balilla Pratella, Carlo Carrà, and, of course, Russolo himself are, in this respect, experiments with different degrees of vibration. While Marinetti may have envisioned the birth of Futurism in the violence of a car crash, he foresaw its death in the lassitude of idling engines. The successors to Futurism, he wrote, would one day find the Futurists "in the open country, beneath a sad roof drummed by monotonous rains. They'll see us crouched beside our trembling aeroplanes."[30] Marinetti, as Matthew Wraith points out, was as enthralled by this vibratory hum as the thrusting propulsion of the motor that first landed his car in a muddy roadside ditch. This hum spoke to the sympathetic vibrations between human organisms and machines, both of which were subject to the vibratory laws of an entropic universe.

Inspired by a range of philosophical, scientific, and aesthetic ideas including Nietzsche's theory of action, Bergsonian vitalism, Einstein's theory of relativity, and the synesthetic experiments of the French Symbolists, Marinetti explored the overlapping vibrations of organic, mechanic, and spiritual phenomena through his poetry and manifestos.[31] At their heart, these works sought to overcome the Bergsonian division of matter and motion by depicting everything in a state of vibratory flux. The world was in a constant state of transformation, materializing and dematerializing along a spectrum of vibrations that could be captured by a combination of new technologies and aesthetic practices. The poet of the future, Marinetti wrote, will be charged with "metallizing, liquefying, vegetalizing, petryfying, and electrifying the voice, fusing it with the vibrations of matter, themselves expressed by Words-in-Freedom."[32] The radio would further this project of vocal electrification, amplifying and transforming the "vibrations emitted by living beings by living spirits or dead spirits noisedramas about states of mind with no words."[33] It would amplify the "vibrations emitted by matter Just as today we listen to the song of the woods and the sea tomorrow we will be seduced by the vibrations of a diamond or of a flower."[34] Such material-immaterial transformations – here accentuated by the way in which the unpunctuated phrases run into one another – are also the basis for Marinetti's notion of tactilism, the idea that "sight, smell, hearing, touch and taste are modifications of a single, highly perceptive sense: the sense of touch, which splits into different ways and organizes in different points."[35]

For Marinetti, the senses are "more or less arbitrary localizations of that confused total of intertwined senses that constitute the typical forces of the human machine," forces that may "be better observed on the epidermal frontiers of our body."[36] While somewhat privileging the sense of touch, tactilism is primarily concerned with overcoming the arbitrary division of the senses. It aims to facilitate synesthetic links between the senses, links that would provide broader access to the material-spiritual world. Synesthesia was, of course, an obsession of Futurist painters such as Boccioni, Carrà, and the young Russolo, as well as a great many abstract artists such as Wassily Kandinsky, Kazimir Malevich, and Piet Mondrian. In his manifesto on Futurist painting, Carrà argues that "sounds, noises, and smells are none other than different forms and intensities of vibration," and that "any continued series of sounds, noises[,] and smells imprints on the mind an arabesque of form and color."[37] For this reason, Futurist notions such as the "wireless imagination, words-in-freedom, the systematic use of onomatopoeia, antigraceful music ... , and the art of noises are all derived from the same Futurist sensibility."[38] – a sensibility that is attuned to different vibrations of the universe.

Such ideas also extended to the realm of thought and emotion. As Enns points out, at the turn of the twentieth century, abstract artists were especially influenced by the theosophical writings of Annie Besant and C.W. Leadbeater, themselves inspired by scientific experiments in thought photography, the early neurological practice of capturing brainwaves on photographic plates.[39] In their 1901 book *Thought-forms*, Besant and Leadbeater claimed that "every thought gives rise to a set of correlated vibrations ... accompanied with a marvelous play of color, like that in the spray of a water fall as the sunlight strikes it, raised to the nth degree of color and vivid delicacy."[40] These vibrations emanate from the body of the thinking subject and may come into contact with other bodies, thus accounting for non-verbal thought transference. Associating psychic states with colours, Besant and Leadbeater produced a series of colour plates, drawn by various artists, that purported to document their emotions at different times of day.

Boccioni, as Chessa points out, makes clear reference to these colour plates in his paintings and writings. In a 1911 lecture on the future of art, Boccioni prophesies:

> There will come a time when a painting will no longer be enough. Its immobility will be an archaism when compared with the vertiginous movement of human life. The eye of man will perceive colors *like feelings in themselves*. Multiplied colors will have no need of forms to be understood, and pictorial works will be whirling musical compositions of enormous colored gases, which on the scene of a free horizon, will move and electrify the complex soul of a crowd that we cannot yet imagine.

Synesthesia, in other words, was not simply about painting sounds and smells, but about painting "feelings themselves." Like the electrified voice of the radio carrying Words-in-Freedom, synesthetic forms would radiate outward, arousing sympathetic vibrations in the crowd. Boccioni put such Besant and Leadbeater–inspired ideas into practice in paintings such as *The City Arises* (*Città che sale*, 1910–11), which depicts two horses rendered in enormous clouds of red and white clashing against the backdrop of a city under construction (figure 1.3). Although the painting does not entirely abandon figure, it nevertheless places the emphasis on the combatting swirls of colour, which move in multiple directions in a manner reminiscent of Russolo's description of noise.

In *The Art of Noises*, Russolo describes noise as the product of "secondary vibrations" that are "more numerous than those that usually produces a sound."[41] He illustrates this idea with a visual example: "If I launch a rowboat in still water, I will make a wave which, starting from the rowboat, will expand regularly. But if instead of launching it gently, I also shake it a little, I will make a wave but no longer just one. Other waves will be formed which will be partly superimposed on the first, different from it but still expanding regularly from the point of agitation."[42] Such a description also fits the directions of brush strokes and colour forms in Boccioni's painting, albeit with the added complication that these forms emerge from multiple points of agitation. Indeed, it is a fitting description for many

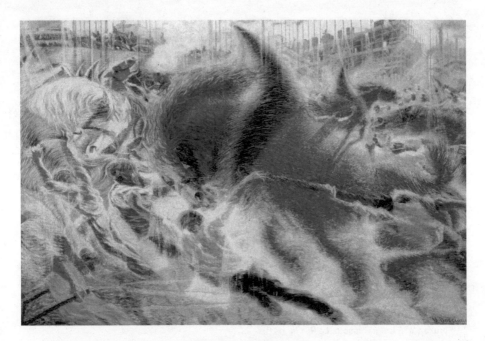

Figure 1.3 / Umberto Boccioni, *Città che sale* (1910–11).

paintings that Carrà mentions in his manifesto as examples of the painting of sights, smells, and sounds. These include Carrà's own *The Funeral of the Anarchist Galli* (1910–11) and *Jolts of a Taxicab* (1911), Boccioni's *States of Mind* (1911) and *Forces of a Street* (1911), Gino Severini's *Pan-Pan* (1909–11), and Russolo's *Revolt* (1911), all of which were shown together in 1912 at the first Futurist exhibition in Paris.

The Revolt is itself a kind of city symphony. It depicts a bright-red mob outlined in yellow charging toward a city composed of uniform blue buildings with dark-red roofs (figure 1.4). The mob's violent energy is rendered through a series of crisp chevrons radiating from the crowd in yellow and red. Like the sound waves of some tremendous blast, these chevrons overrun the city, tilting it at an angle parallel to their force, as if bending the city to the mob's will. Such a composition in which sonic forms evoke the vibratory energy of crowds, violence, and creativity (and vice versa) are typical of Russolo's paintings in the early 1910s, many of which are suffused with occult themes that Russolo would take

Figure 1.4 / Luigi Russolo, *La Rivolta* (1911).

up more fully later in life, particularly in his *Al di là materia*, which set forth his occult philosophy. As Chessa points out, "most of [Russolo's] canvases are laden with symbols of death, skeletons, skulls, globes of fire; supernatural, hallucinatory, ethereal, and residual images; and synesthetic representations – in short, all the *caravanserai* of icons typically associated with the occult."[43] These themes reflect a variety of influences including Bergson, the French Symbolists (especially painters associated with the *Salon de la Rose+Croix*), Wasily Kandinsky and *Die Blaue Reiter* circle, as well as Besant and Leadbeater.

To see such themes mixed with Russolo's synesthetic interests in painting sound, one need look no further than a painting such as *Linee-forza della folgore* (1912; figure 1.5). The painting depicts two lightning bolts traversing the city sky at night. Towering dark-blue buildings loom over the implicit viewer, framing the lightning bolts, which radiate blue, yellow, and pink. One also "hears" the sounds of thunder, which take the form of triangular shockwaves that burst from the flash and resound through the city, causing the buildings to undulate. As Chessa points out, Besant and

Figure 1.5 / Luigi Russolo, *Linee-froza della folgore* (1912).

Leadbeater's *Thought-forms* was most likely the inspiration for this painting. He finds a striking parallel between the triangular shockwave emanating from the flash and plates 22 and 23 of *Thought-forms*, which resemble a narrow triangle and flash of lighting shooting from a cloud. There is also a marked similarity between the shockwaves and Leadbetter's description of "sound forms" in another theosophical text titled *The Hidden Side of Things*: "The majestic role of a thunderstorm creates usually a vast flowing band of colour, while the deafening crash often calls into temporary existence an arrangement of irregular radiations ... or sometimes a huge irregular sphere with spikes projecting in all directions.'[44] Many of these sonic elements are found in Russolo's painting, thus hinting at the mystic potentialities of light and sound to manifest occult phenomena such as astral bodies (the topic of Leadbeater's description).

Another important painting that blends sonic and visual elements into a mystical experience is Russolo's *La Musica* (1912). The painting depicts a demonic, silhouetted figure playing the piano, his multiple hands occupying several positions along the keyboard, as though he were photographed using a time-lapse technique. Blue concentric circles radiate from his head, growing darker as they expand, while a carnival of variegated tragicomic masks stream toward him from the edges of the frame. Last, a blue ribbon of sound, the melodic line, winds its way from the keyboard to the upper-right corner of the painting, as if moving onward to a space beyond the image. The concentric circles and the ribbon evoke the sounds of the piano both spatially and temporally, while the masks harken back to Besant and Leabeater–inspired forms of Russolo's *Maschere* (1907–8), which here take the form of muses or spiritual manifestations of sonically-inspired ideas. They may also serve as the artist's etheric doubles insofar as they appear to resemble the pianist at times, or they may manifest the spirit of dead composers as Lista has argued.[45] In the latter case, the painting presents the artist as a spiritual medium, capable of amassing and materializing the energies of the dead.

Enharmony

While spiritual and synesthetic concerns are typically acknowledged as influencing Russolo's painting, as well as the Futurist movement in general, few, with the exception Chessa, have given these concerns much credit in the development of Russolo's *Art of Noises* and *Awakening of a City*, not to mention his noise instruments. But why shouldn't a Futurist sensibility attuned to a universe of vibrations not extend to these sonic works and inventions as well? Here, the concept of enharmony is crucial to understanding the relationship between Futurist painting and *The Art of Noises*. The Futurists used this term in a very specific sense. It did not simply designate an equal value placed on all notes of the well-tempered scale (i.e., chromaticism); but an equal value placed on all tones – whole, half, and any fraction thereof (1/4, 1/8, etc.). "Whereas chromaticism," wrote Pratella, "only lets us take advantage of all the sounds contained in a scale that is divided into minor and major semitones, enharmony contemplates still more minute subdivisions of a tone; and hence it not only furnishes our renewed sensibilities with a maximum number of specifiable combinable sounds, but also new and more varied relations among chords and timbres."[46] Enharmony liberated the tones *between* well-tempered gradations of the traditional Western scale, and even the tones contained within a single note. E-sharp and F, Russolo points out, are in fact two different tones, rendered equivalent by the well-tempered system's artificial division of the octave into twelve equal parts. In a non-tempered system, "a single note could have up to four different intonations (that is, could be represented by four different ratios of vibration)"; while in the well-tempered system, this note would be "always identical with itself."[47] Expressing this non-identity – i.e., expressing the microtonal variety of pitches within a natural octave – was the goal of enharmony. It sought to open up all possible tone-expressions as elements of composition.

In explaining the advantages of enharmonicism, and the deficiencies of the well-tempered system, Russolo drew explicit comparisons with painting.

> A tempered harmonic system can be compared in a sense to a system of painting that abolishes all the [infinite] gradations of the seven colors ... and accepts only their type color, having only one yellow, one green, one red, and so on. A kind of painting that was ignorant of the different *tonalities* of the same color would have no rose, no scarlet lake, no bright yellow, no dark yellow. This kind of painting would be comparable to the sounds of the tempered diatonic scale. With the addition of five gradations, it might produce what is our chromatic scale. It is obvious how limited in means and deprived of coloristic sensations such painting would be. The present tempered system is in the very same state as this kind of painting.[48]

In this respect, enharmonicism was concerned with the expression of different gradations of tonality, of harmonic and microtonal variation, in a manner analogous to painting with different shades of colour. Painting, however, was not intended only as an analogy. As Carrà notes, the devices of Futurist painting – acute angles, oblique lines, subjective perspective, polyphonic and polyrhythmic construction, continuity and simultaneity – "correspond to the necessity for an internal *enharmonic* relation which we Futurist painters believe to be indispensable for pictorial sensibility."[49] This enharmonic relation sprung from the infinite gradations between not just colour, angle, and form, but between sights, sounds, and even smells – all of which corresponded to different frequencies of vibration. Enharmony – whether of sound, colour, or visual form – was a touchstone of Futurist art. Given the Futurist's vibratory conception of the universe, one may safely assume that this concept was not bound by any single visual or sonic medium; rather, it extended to all the vibratory gradations of thought, spirit, and the cosmos.

To see how enharmony connected the material world of sound to the spiritual world of the occult one need look no further than Russolo's *Art of Noises* and *Awakening of a City*. Russolo valued noise as a source of enharmonic possibilities. Noise had the power to disrupt traditional aesthetic systems. For Russolo, this power was not nihilistic; rather, it was constructive, a way to build a new aesthetic system based on the principle of enharmony. One already sees this principle in a painting such as *La Musica*, where it is represented by the continuously flowing blue ribbon, the simultaneity of the outwardly expanding concentric circles, and the infinite keys of the keyboard.[50]

In many respects, the principle of enharmony is derived from the appearance of sounds in the real world. The noises of the world, both natural and mechanical, are always enharmonic. Russolo writes:

> All the sounds and noises that are produced in nature, if they are susceptible to variation of pitch (that is, if they are sounds and noises of a certain duration) change pitch *by enharmonic gradations and never by leaps of pitch*. For example, the howling of the wind produces complete scales in rising and falling. These scales are neither diatonic nor

chromatic, they are *enharmonic*. Likewise, if we move from natural noises in the infinitely richer world of machine noises, we find here also that all noises produced by rotary motion are constantly enharmonic in the rising and falling of their pitch. This rising or falling of pitch is naturally in direct proportion to the increasing or decreasing speed. Example: dynamos and electric motors.[51]

If nature and machinery proceed by enharmonic gradations, then why not music as well? Russolo contends that even the average human ear can discern differences in pitch down to 1/8 of a tone, so why not compose music that fully takes advantage of this capacity? As an element of composition, noise, in this regard, is valued for two reasons. First, it changes pitch enharmonically as in the example of dynamos and motors, as well as the whistling of the wind. Second, it is "very rich in harmonics, stronger and more audible than they are in sounds properly so called and commonly used."[52] A noise is not a single, clear vibration like that produced by a tuning fork, but multiple vibrations through which one often perceives a dominant pitch. (Recall Russolo's example of the rocking sailboat.) These overtonal vibrations, themselves outside the traditional well-tempered system, create a great degree of variety that Futurist music seeks to composes with enharmonic instruments. In other words, it is not just that noise changes pitch by the enharmonic gradations that attracts Russolo to it; it is that, like the pianist's hands in *La Musica*, noise expresses multiple positions along the sonic spectrum simultaneously.

To generate and compose noises, Russolo invented a new class of instruments, the *intonarumori*, or noise-tuners. One may think of these instruments biographically in connection with Russolo's father's profession as a tuner and church organist. They reflect his heritage both as a technician and a musician. In their construction, the intonarumori resembled hurdy-gurdies. A lever atop a rectangular wooden box controlled the pitch of a noise-making mechanism such as a string attached to a drum skin–like membrane. A hand crank on the side of the box – or sometimes a small battery – sustained or interrupted the noise. Last, the sound generated by the combined action of the lever and hand crank (or battery) was amplified by a trumpetlike horn at the front of the box. "The noise instruments,"

Russolo wrote, "are played by gripping the lever with the left hand and turning the handle, or pressing the button, with the right. By adjusting the lever, the pitch is changed as desired, with any possibility of change – not only leaps of tones and semitones but also gradual enharmonic passages between one pitch and another."[53] Russolo also devised a notation system to represent these leaps of tone and enharmonic passages. While retaining the traditional musical staff, Russolo replaced the system of dotted notes (whole, half, quarter) with a single line that could represent all the enharmonic possibilities of his instruments (see figure 1.2). "The length of this line," he wrote, "enclosed between vertical lines, will give us the length or duration of the sound itself. Its absence will indicate rests, likewise limited by vertical lines according to their duration."[54] Such a system brings musical notation closer to drawing (as opposed to writing). "Indicating the unfolding of one or more sounds, these lines form an arabesque that immediately describes the typical physiognomy of a given composition, making its reading easy and rapid."[55] Such a linear system of musical representation would represent the "dynamic continuity" of Russolo's enharmonic noise instruments.[56]

In his introduction to Russolo's *Art of Noises*, Barclay Brown describes the intonarumori as the world's first synthesizers insofar they point to the future ability of synthesizers to play any sound and pitch whatsoever. Their primary aim, however, is not sound synthesis per se, but rather occult transformation, akin in many respects to Marinetti's Words-in-Freedom. "To understand the intonarumori," Marinetti wrote, "one needs ... religion."[57] More precisely, one needs an almost religious belief in the transformative powers of enharmony. For Brown, Russolo's emphasis on enharmony and microtonality was largely a consequence (as opposed to the cause) of the manner in which his instruments were constructed. "Whether by chance or intent," writes Brown, "the mechanism that Russolo selected to vary the pitch of his noises produced a continuous change or tension rather than discrete steps or stages. As a result, Russolo was forced to take account of microtones in his new music."[58] Such an explanation puts the cart before the horse. It is rather due to the fact that Russolo already had an interest in enharmony – one that stemmed from a broader interest in the vibrations of material and occult phenomena – that Russolo built the intonarumori, as well as other instruments like the *rumoramonio* and the enharmonic bow.

"*Dynamic continuity*," Russolo writes, "is the essence of Enharmonicism. This is what distinguishes it from the music of the diatonic-chromatic system, which might be called rather, *Intermittent dynamicism*, or more exactly, *Fragmentary dynamicism*." To hear a Futurist such as Russolo criticize a traditional aesthetic system as "fragmentary" may sound strange to contemporary ears, especially those used to associating Futurism with an aesthetics of fragmentation and disruption. In the Futurist self-conception, however, the case is rather the opposite. These signifiers of seeming fragmentation, be they multiple perspectives or disruptive noises, are in fact markers of continuity, of a single continuous universe of vibration. As Russolo points out, the enharmony of noise is not so much intended to disrupt the traditional musical system as fill in its gaps.

> It should be borne in mind that Enharmonicism, as a total system and as produced by the noise instruments, has the characteristic possibility not only of dividing the interval of the whole tone into a given number of smaller intervals but also of producing the *change* from one tone to another, the shading, so to speak, that the tone makes in moving to the tone immediately above or below. This transition is not logically divisible, just as the shading of a colour from light to dark is not divisible. It can be defined as stages of steps, that is, by quarters, eighths, and so on, of a tone; but in doing so the *dynamic continuity* of the pitch will be broken.[59]

What Russolo heard in the enharmonic potential of noise and his noise instruments is akin to what he and other Futurists saw in abstract painting or time-motion photography – the ability to represent continuity, whether that be the continuous passage of time or the continuous vibrations of sights, sounds, smells, and thoughts. Such an understanding of noise was part of a greater Futurist sensibility.

Given all this emphasis on continuity, one may rightly ask what happened to the noises of the city? More specifically, what happened to those everyday objects that actually produce noise in the first place – the purring of motors, the throbbing of valves, the screeching of mechanical saws, and so on? The answer to this question is complicated by the fact that Russolo was simultaneously inspired by city and industrial noises and afraid of appearing to slavishly imitate them – an accusation that was frequently lobbied against him.[60] In fact, Russolo was not so much interested in the everyday objects that made noise as harnessing the types of noises these objects made to draw closer to the spiritual world.

> Stir the senses and you will also stir the brain! Stir the senses with the unexpected, the mysterious, the unknown, and you will truly move the soul, intensely and profoundly! Here lies the destined and absolute necessity of borrowing the timbres of sound directly from the timbres of the noises of life. Here – with the sole exception of the meagerness of orchestral timbres – lies the unbounded richness of the timbres of noises.
>
> But it is necessary that these noise timbres become *abstract material* for works of art to be formed from them. *As it comes to us from life*, in fact, noise immediately reminds us of life itself, making us think of the the things that produce the noises that we are hearing. This reminder of life has the character of an impressionistic and fragmentary episode of life itself. And as I conceive it, *The Art of Noises* would certainly not limit itself to an impressionistic and fragmentary reproduction of the noises of life. Thus, the ear must hear these noises mastered, servile, completely controlled, conquered and constrained to become elements of art ... Noise must become a prime element to mould into the work of art. That is, it has to lose its accidental character in order to become an element sufficiently abstract to achieve the necessary transformation of any prime element into an abstract element of art.

In this passage, Russolo hedges against an interpretation of *The Art of Noises* as mere program music – the kind of music that uses urban-inspired sounds to animate a street scene. The irony, of course, is that Russolo's music was interpreted in precisely this manner, as the reaction of the correspondent for the *Pall Mall Gazette* attests. Nevertheless, it is important to note that there is in fact a tension between Russolo's avoidance of the indexical quality of noises – their tendency to point toward their sources, to the machines that make them – and his high estimation of abstraction. Namely, while Russolo seeks to channel city and industrial noises, he also strives to obscure their sources, going so far as to build a set of instruments that do not so much reproduce these noises as vaguely reference them (Cracklers, Hummers, Howlers, etc.). This tension manifests itself as a dialectic between chaos (noise) and control (abstraction) – the dialectic outlined by Attali. However, when taking Russolo's spiritual concerns into account, it becomes clear that this description oversimplifies *The Art of Noises*. Russolo's musical project is not simply a means to generate a cathartic response, a game of power between tension and resolution; rather, it is a means to attain a higher spiritual unity that is irreducibly contradictory – a unity of the cosmos that is firmly grounded in the material noises of the world.

It is this tension that animates Russolo's *Awakening of a City*. Chessa reads this short city symphony as the culmination of a three-stage process, one that he fruitfully compares to an alchemical experiment.[61] In the first stage, the noises of the world are abstracted from their sources using the intonarumori. Here, noise is characterized as "raw matter," which must be spiritualized by a process of "enharmonic transformation." In the second stage, the noises of the intonarumori are brought together (synthesized) in dynamic simultaneity – that is, in an orchestral work. In his 1910 "Outline to a New Aesthetics of Music," Ferruccio Busoni provides an account of what this dynamic simultaneity might sound/look like.

> *Everything resounds* ... and all the beats are a single thing, a whole ...
> And now the *sound* is heard! Innumerable are its voices; compared to them the whisper of harps is a din, the blare of a thousand trombones a chirping.
> All, all the melodies heard before and unheard, all of them none excluded resound together at the same time, they transport you, linger upon you, brush against you ... they themselves are the souls of millions of beings of millions of epochs. Bring one of these melodies close to your eye, and you will see how it is connected with others, combined with all the rhythms, colored by all the colors, accompanied by all the harmonies, down to the bottom of every depth, up to the arch of every vault of the heavens.

Now you all understand how planets and hearts together unite into one, and never and nowhere could there be an end, nowhere could there be a boundary. Now you all understand that, in the spirit of the being, the infinite lives complete and undivided; that every thing is at the same time infinitely large and infinitely small; and that light, sound, motion, energy are identical, and the each of them itself, all joined together, are life.[62]

Both Busoni and Russolo shared an interest in microtonality and novel instruments. Busoni was particularly taken with Thaddeus Cahill's Telharmonium, an early electric organ. In this passage, the dynamic simultaneity of noise – of all sounds all at once – opens up a world of continuous vibrations. The passage reprises a number of Futurist-occult themes. One "sees" melodies and is awakened to the spirits of the dead. The universe is revealed in its fundamental unity on all scales and spectrums of vibration.

Russolo's occult interests, his paintings, and his belief that the dynamic simultaneity of noises was a way to awaken the brain and the soul points to a shared cosmogenic conception of noise. As a simultaneous expression of sound, *The Art of Noises* was an exercise in bringing the material and spiritual worlds into alignment. Such a conception of *The Art of Noises* deepens our understanding of Russolo's descriptions of city sounds. Russolo's invitation to walk "through a great modern city with our ears more alert than our eyes" appears now less as an exercise in active listening and more as an experiment in dynamic simultaneity. The listener hears all at once "the throbbing of valves, the pounding of pistons, the screeching of mechanical saws, the jolting of trams on their tracks, the cracking of whips, the flapping of curtains and flags," and so on. Moreover, if we return to Russolo's account of the sonic qualities of pavement – that is, his account of the city as a medium in which sound-producing and resonating materials vibrate in sympathy with each other – we can see, too, that such a quality is an expression of the dynamic simultaneity of sound as it makes its way through the city. It is akin to Boccioni's description of dynamism as "the lyric conception of forms interpreted in the infinite manifesting of their relativity between absolute motion and relative motion, between environment and object, until they shape the apparition of a whole: *environment + object*."⁶³ Boccioni is speaking in painterly terms, yet the idea is the same: there are no gaps, everything reflects or resounds everything else, every breakdown or deformation of form or tone unleashes dynamic possibilities.

Russolo's *Awakening of a City* is not a sonic portrait of a city; its intention (if not its actual effect on the listener) is far from the description given by the correspondent for the *Pall Mall Gazette*. Rather, *The Awakening of a City* is an attempt to construct an entirely new city in sound at the spiritual level, one where spiritual forms are materialized. In other words, if at the first level noises are spiritualized via the intonarumori and at the second level noises are synthesized in concert, then at the third level the spiritual world is materialized through these noises. This takes the form of an awakening, not of people living in a city but of the dead awaiting reincarnation. Russolo hinted at such a process with respect to the materialization of etheric doubles in his late theosophical work, *Al di là materia*, as well as his early self-portrait in which he figures his double alongside himself. These two works reflect Russolo's lifelong interest in the occult – an interest he maintained not just in his artwork but also his enthusiastic participation in seances throughout the 1910s and '20s.⁶⁴

This image of Russolo the inventor-conductor-composer *as* spiritual medium is sustained by Russolo's close friend, Paulo Buzzi, who, in a poem lionizing the composer, described Russolo as follows: "Luigi, the *ululatore* is the oracle / Of the God who inspires you and who will render you justice. / The abyss, our illustrious Relative, is grateful to you. / I hear the only true musics: those / That the dead hear, / Over their heads, under our feet. / The future City awakens / In an explosion that invites / The cemeteries to masked balls of power and desire."⁶⁵ Buzzi later developed this poem into a novel with Russolo as the protagonist. In the above excerpt, Russolo appears as one of his own noise-making machines, the *ululatore*, and as an oracle of a violent God – a God of Justice. Russolo the noise-maker/oracle connects the spiritual world with the material one through a music whose explosive power – its dynamic simultaneity – awakens the dead. *The Awakening of a City* is not presented in its typical city-symphonic guise, the washing of streets, the opening of shop shutters, and so on; rather, it manifests itself as a noisy explosion through which the dead materialize. This might explain why Russolo insisted on silence at his concerts: he was essentially conducting a seance.

A Futurist aesthetics of death and desire pervades this seance; yet what is perhaps most interesting is how the above passage accords with Russolo's own conception of his musical works. Russolo referred to his compositions as networks, and then, a short while later, as spirals of noises. The term *network*, which derives from Marinetti, emphasizes simultaneity, whether of images or sound – a type of fusion that grasps "all that is most fleeting and elusive in matter."[66] The term *spiral* gives this idea an occult intonation, reminiscent of the spiral of sound that traverses Russolo's painting *La Musica*. As a network of noise, *The Awakening of a City* is a combination and synthesis of sounds generated by the intonarumori, one that causes sympathetic vibrations in the spiritual world, causing the dead to arise. In this respect, the composition is similar to Marinetti's conception of "La Radia" (quoted above) as an "interception amplification and transfiguration of vibrations emitted by living beings by living spirits or dead spirits noise-dramas about states of mind with no words."[67] In *The Awakening of a City*, the noises of living beings are spiritualized through abstraction and combination. They generate a network that – like Words-in-Freedom, automatic writing, or even a simple Ouija board – allows the composer/medium to connect and manifest the vibrations of the spiritual world.

City Symphony as Noise Network

The central problematic of Russolo's city symphony concerns a tension between the materiality and indexicality of terrestrial noise – of urban and industrial noise – and the vibrations of another world – a spiritual world beyond the audible and visible, but not beyond the vibratory. How to tune the former to the latter, using the tools of enharmony and the intonarumori, is the task of *The Art of Noises* generally and *The Awakening of a City* in particular. Russolo's compositions are rooted in the tradition of program music, of symphonies and sinfoniettas such as Elgar's "Cockaigne, In London Town" (1900); yet they are also a departure from such works insofar as they do not aim to evoke and sustain an image of a modern industrial center. Instead,

The Awakening of a City sought to harness the dynamic simultaneity of urban-industrial noise through a process of abstraction and spiritualization – one that led to the conjuring of an entirely different city – a city of the dead. Russolo was not attracted to noise simply as an expression of mechanized life. He was not seeking to disrupt conventional aesthetic systems simply for the sake of disruption. Rather, he was aiming to construct a new aesthetic system based on the shared vibratory and occult fascinations of the Italian Futurists. In this respect, the city as a space of dynamic and simultaneous sympathetic vibrations – as a network in which one material medium (e.g., tramways) may cause another to vibrate (e.g., the pavement) – became a model for a spiritual network of noises.

The Attalian dialectic of chaos (noise) and control (musical organization) does not adequately describe *The Art of Noises*. As Russolo points out, noise is not chaotic, only complex – a layering of tonal and overtonal vibrations centred around a dominant pitch. Although he argues for the need to harness the power of noises – to render them servile through a process of abstraction – this process is not primarily concerned with limiting noise's chaos – its opposition to all systems of meaning and communication. In other words, Russolo's goals do not really align with those of environmental anti-noise campaigners, even when the two are viewed as complimentary opposites. Russolo was instead concerned with limiting the indexicality of noises – of limiting their ability to point back to the objects that made them. In and of themselves, the indexical noises of street cars and mechanical saws were not problematic; they were aesthetically pleasing and inspirational. Nevertheless, they required an abstract transformation to put them in contact with an occult world of vibratory forms. One cannot harness the power of purring motors to communicate with the other world when their noise is a constant reminder of actual motors. To make contact with the other world requires a process not of imitation but of abstraction, of gleaning the essential principle (enharmony) that joins all earthly noises and reproducing it through a set of spiritual machines (the intonarumori).

Russolo's *Art of Noises* and *The Awakening of a City* underscore the city symphony's treatment of the city as a sonic medium, a treatment based in sonic and synesthetic experimentation. The city symphony does not simply draw on music as an analogy for form, visual or otherwise; rather, it treats the city as a material network, a medium whose infrastructure can generate and resonate sound. Instead of simply acknowledging that the city produces pleasing, exciting, and dynamic sounds, the city symphony seeks to compose these sounds, tuning them to one another, matching their rhythms. To be sure, Russolo's *Awakening of a City* falls short of explicitly realizing this goal. It does not directly compose the city in the manner of Avraamov's *Symphony of Sirens*, which, as we see in the following chapter, comes closest to realizing some of Russolo's most radical ideas. Instead, *The Awakening of a City* abandons the terrestrial metropolis in search of a city of the dead – a city of spiritual thought-forms and astral bodies. It abstracts and spiritualizes urban noise in search of another city. Despite this abandonment, the composition is still very much inspired by a conception of the city as a networked sonic medium whose noises are not meaningless but rather resonant vibrations filled with spiritual possibilities. It points the way forward to compositions such as Avraamov's in which the spiritual and transcendent aims of a vibratory conception of the universe collide with the ideological and logistical problems of restructuring an actual city.

2

ON THE STREET
The Sound and Silence of Arseny Avraamov's *Symphony of Sirens* in Baku (1922) and Moscow (1923)

On 7 November 1922, vessels from the Caspian flotilla assembled in the harbour of Baku, a port city on the Caspian Sea in what is now the Republic of Azerbaijan, to partake in a mass spectacle commemorating the fifth anniversary of the October Revolution. Composed and conducted by the Proletkul't composer Arseny Avraamov (1886–1944), the *Symphony of Sirens*, as the mass spectacle was called, constructed a montage-like interaction of military, industrial, and human sounds taken from across Baku's ethnically diverse districts, docks, factories, and squares.[1] These sounds included those of ship cannons, machine guns, artillery batteries, hydroplanes, factory sirens, crowds of spectators, and a specially designed steam-whistle machine (the *magistral'*) capable of belting out "The Internationale" or "La Marseillaise" (figure 2.1). The symphony levelled the distinction between its listeners and participants, radically altering Baku's industrial and oil-derricked landscape into both orchestra and auditorium. Its deafening and awe-inspiring noise rearranged the spatiality and temporality of the city, transforming the oftentimes fraught relationship between its religiously and ethnically divided working classes – consisting of Azerbaijanis, Armenians, and Russians – into a symbol of proletarian unity and Soviet power.

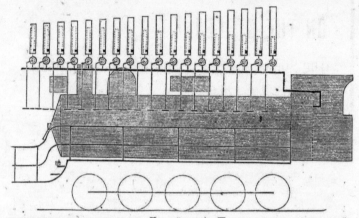

Figure 2.1 / An idealized sketch of the steam-whistle machine (*magistral'*).

In many respects, the *Symphony of Sirens* attempts to fulfill Russolo's vision of a day when "the motors and the machines of our industrial cities will ... be able to be consciously attuned, so that every factory will be made an intoxicating orchestra of noises."[2] How the symphony in fact sounded is far from clear. What is known about Avraamov's symphony comes primarily by way of a reproduction of the symphony's "score" – a set of military-like instructions originally published in three Baku newspapers, the *Baku Worker*, *Labor*, and *Communist* (the latter in Turkish).[3] These instructions were republished in a 1923 article Avraamov wrote for the Proletkul't journal *Gorn* (the title is a pun on the Russian word for "bugle" and "blast furnace"). According to this article, Avraamov conducted the symphony via semaphore and telephone from atop a Swedish Mast. Using these devices, Avraamov signalled cannon fire from the battleship *Dostoinyi* parked in Baku's harbour, which in turn signalled specific sonic events across the city.

Although somewhat lengthy, a reproduction of this score will provide the reader with a fuller picture of the intended scope and scale of Avraamov's composition. The *Gorn* text reads as follows:[4]

For the 5th anniversary of the October Revolution. Instructions for the "Symphony of Sirens."

On the morning of the 5th Anniversary on 7 November, all vessels of Gocasp, Voenflot, and Uzbekcasp, including smaller ships and boats, concentrate near the railroad pier by seven o'clock a.m. Every vessel will receive written instructions and a group of musicians. Then each will take a designated place in the vicinity of the custom's pier. The destroyer Dostoyny [Worthy] with the steam-whistle machine and small vessels will be anchored ahead opposite the tower.

By 9:00 the entire fleet should be in place.

All available shuttle engines, local and armoured trains, and repaired steam engines will arrive at the same time.

Cadets of the Fourth Armavir courses of the higher party school, students of Azgoconservatory, and all professional musicians should be at the pier no later than 8:30.

At no later than 10:30, the signalers take their place at the [regional, dock, and railroad sirens.]

The **noon canon is cancelled**.

The first artillery salute signals the sirens of Zykh, Bely Gorod [White Town], Bibi-Eibat,[5] and Baylov to sound thunderously from the road.[6]

The fifth gun signals the first and second districts of Chernyi Gorod [Black Town].

The tenth – sirens of Azneft trade offices and the Docks.

The fifteenth – mountain district, [hydroplanes] take off. [Bells] ring.

The eighteenth – sirens from the [railroad] depot and [remaining engines at the station].

(At the same time, the first company of the [fourth] Armavir courses headed by a joint brass orchestra and "Varashavanka" marches off the square toward the piers.)

Alarm reaches its climax and terminates by the twenty-fifth canon.

Pause

Tri-chord from the sirens. "Hurrah" from the piers.

Termination signal from the steam-whistle machine.

"Internationale" (four times).

On the second half verse, a joint brass orchestra and automobile chorus enters with the "Marseillaise." At the second repetition the whole square as a chorus joins in the celebratory singing.

At the end of the fourth verse, cadets and the infantry return to the square where they are met with a "Hurrah."

Finale – general festive chord of all steam whistles and sirens lasting three minutes accompanied by a ringing bell.

Termination signal from the steam-whistle machine.

Ceremonial March.

Artillery, fleet, autotransport, and machine guns receive their signals directly from the conductor's tower. Red on white background – battery; yellow and blue – sirens; four-colored – machine guns; red – solo ships, steam engines, and automobile chorus.

On the battery's signal, "The Internationale" repeats two more times during the final procession.

Stoking of the furnaces is obligatory wherever there is a signalling siren.

All the above is for the leadership and irrevocable execution under the responsibility of the leading establishments: military authorities, Azneft, Gocasp, and related educational institutions. Every performer must have these instructions on him during the celebration.

The chairman of TSOK [Central Organizing Committee] is P. Chagin.

Symphony of Sirens organizer is Ars. Avraamov.[7]

Avraamov's symphony was not designed simply to produce the maximum amount of noise. The cannon fire functioned as a pacing mechanism; each round signalled a specific, symbolically-laden sonic event. The fifth gun signalled the sirens of the first and second districts of Black Town, a neighbourhood named for the oil that gushed from its derricks;[8] the tenth gun signalled the sirens of the Azneft trade offices, the seat of the Azerbaijani Oil Administration; the fifteenth gun signalled the sirens of the "mountain district," also known as Armenian Village and the site of sporadic ethnic violence in the internecine Azeri-Armenian feud; the eighteenth gun signalled the sirens of the railroad depot, an essential component of Azerbaijan's oil-export economy. The noise of the symphony reached its climax with the sounding of the twenty-fifth cannon, followed by a brief pause that marked the transformation of the previous sounds – coded as sounds of alarm and continuous battle – into those of proletarian solidarity. What were initially the threatening sounds of capitalist oppression and the struggle against capitalism now became those of a worker's anthem. Crowds near the harbour began singing the "Internationale" and the "Marseillaise," accompanied by the steam-whistle machine, which literally channelled the alienated sounds of industry into the melody of the worker's movement. The symphony's grand finale – a "general festive chord of all steam whistles and sirens lasting three minutes," followed by a ceremonial march and an uproar of celebratory artillery fire, wailing sirens, an automobile chorus, machine guns, steam engines, and two more repetitions of the "Internationale" – marked the eruption of an era of inter-ethnic harmony. A new center was announced; not Petersburg or Moscow, but Baku – a capital in which the proletarians of the West were unified with the formerly oppressed toilers of the East.

With the mild sarcasm of scare quotes, the Bolshevik chronicler René Fueloep-Miller wrote that the "music" of Avraaamov's symphony "could be heard far beyond the walls of the town"; it was intended to "remind the proletariat of its real home, the factory."[9] Fueloep-Miller's assessment implied that Avraamov's celebration of proletarian freedom was in fact an inauguration of a new kind of slavery. This was not the noise of liberation but of a novel repressive regime. Contemporary critics, on the other hand, have viewed the city symphony in a more favourable light, part of an innovative period of avant-garde experimentation surrounding the October Revolution. That said, they have not shied away from calling attention to its authoritarian overtones – for example, the fact that the symphony is structured on an authorial principle of follow the leader.[10] Although not entirely new (the symphony recalls the mass spectacles following the French Revolution), Avraamov's composition was nevertheless revolutionary in its use of noise as a means not only to break traditional aesthetic codes but also actually level the distinctions that separated an ethnically divided working class. Noise as the Other of systems of beauty and meaning is often presented as a kind of uncolonized territory – a material to be subjugated, spiritualized, and transformed into the music.[11] This is certainly an accusation that can be levelled against the Italian Futurists. Avraamov's symphony, by contrast, appears to do quite the opposite. It uses industrial noise as part of a Soviet decolonizing project – however flawed, misguided, and misleading its conception – one in which the struggle against Russian oppression in places such as Azerbaijan is folded into an international worker's movement as part of a multi-ethnic, multi-national worker's empire (the Soviet Union).

In this chapter, I further complicate this account of Avraamov's symphony by arguing that the mass spectacle may not in fact have been as noisy as contemporary scholars suggest. Indeed, Avraamov's symphony may have barely made any sound at all. Such an analysis highlights an important yet overlooked aspect of the city symphony phenomenon – its engagement with (and avoidance of) silence, as well as its colonial dynamics and ambitions. In what follows, I aim to temper the myth of the Baku Symphony's awe-inspiring sound and scale – one that has been largely unquestioned in English-language sound and urban-studies scholarship on Avraamov's mass spectacle.[12] Instead of focussing solely on the symphony's dreaded noise, I pay attention to its lack of sound – to the limits of what can be known about its noises. Drawing on Avraamov's untranslated writings and personal correspondences, as well as an ear-witness account, I wish to question the "fact" of the Baku Symphony's successful performance – its attempt to harness the noise of industry as a way of sounding the Revolution. In doing so, I investigate how the symphony's cosmogenic ideal of unity collides with the geographic, social, and sonic particularity of the city it sought to compose.

Thus far, I have been arguing that the city symphony uses sound in more complex and varied ways than the narrow conception of the musical analogy at its purported center allows. Russolo's *Awakening of a City* experimented with abstract noises to construct an occult city of the dead – of doppelgängers, thought-forms, and etheric doubles; it did not just seek to evoke the sounds and sights of a modern city. At the same time, in composing such a city, Russolo's city symphony insisted on a strict separation between performers and audience members. Nothing was to disturb the seance. By contrast, Avraamov's city symphony sought to overcome this separation in accordance with a Soviet-Taylorist aesthetics that derived the principles of artistic creation from those of mechanical industry. Of course, this does not mean that spiritual striving and occult yearnings disappear from Avraamov's symphony – far from it; they only shift registers. The same vibratory principles and cosmogenic aspirations that we find in Russolo's paintings and compositions can be found at work in the *Symphony of Sirens*, albeit geared toward a Bolshevik-inflected unity of politics and art. The first part of this chapter examines this ideal of unity in terms of Avraamov's work as cultural organizer in the Caucasus, thereby exploring its engagement with the Bolshevik's troubled attempts to reach out to the subjugated peoples of the former Russian Empire. The second part outlines the reasons for questioning the success of the symphony's performance in Baku and explores how this failure complicates the symphony's colonial dynamic. The third part digs deeper into the personal philosophy behind Avraamov's ideal of unity and the spiritual aspirations of the *Symphony of Sirens* through the failed Moscow Symphony. Finally, the fourth part traces this ideal's connection to Avraamov's idiosyncratic views on mechanical reproduction and understanding of the science of vibration. What emerges is an account of the symphony as an attempt to reproduce the spirit of the October Revolution in terms of an urban framework in which the networks for waging war, extracting resources, colonizing space, and transmitting sound make use of overlapping channels. However noisy it may appear on paper, such a reproduction most likely fell silent soon after the performance began.

Global Petrograd

Like many in the Russian avant-garde, Arseny Avraamov was fond of pseudonyms and wordplay. As a young revolutionary Cossack, he was Arseny Krasnokutsky (Russian *Krasnyi* = red); as a commissar for the arts stationed in Dagestan he was Arslan Ibrahim-ogli Adamov (Hebrew

Adam = red); last, as a composer and music theorist he was simply *A*rs (Latin *Ars* = art), a.k.a. *Revarsavr* (the *R*evolutionary *A*rseny *Avr*aamov).[13] These names expressed a fundamental unity. "Avraamov" invokes the idea of Abraham, the Father of monotheism. His monicker *Ars* harkens to the overarching unity of all arts. His play on translations of *red* points to the unity of all peoples in the communist idea. As such, with a twist of a word a revolutionary Don Cossack became a Muslim. Likewise, with the felicitous first three letters of his first name, a composer inscribed himself in the middle of an artistic revolution (Rev*ars*avr) and cemented an identity between himself and Art.

Avraamov's many names embody the "universalist-cosmogonic aspirations" of his musical practice in all its theoretical, aesthetic, and political manifestations from his early, Scriabin-inspired writings on microtonality to his invention of a forty-eight-tone Universal Tone System (Weltonsystem) to his ethnomusicological studies and his experiments in sound synthesis and sound film.[14] These universalist tendencies, as Nikolai Izvolov suggests, were characteristic of the avant-garde artistic movements of the 1910s.[15] What poets such as Aleksei Khruchenykh and Velimir Khlebnikov sought to do for the word – that is, create a trans-rational language (*zaum*) that would facilitate universal expression – Avraamov sought to do for the tone by de-tempering the well-tempered scale. As it was for Russolo, microtonality was the frequent subject of Avraamov's articles for *Muzikal'nyi Sovremennik* and *Letopis'*, two journals he co-edited with the composer Nikolai Roslavets from 1914 to 1916, in which he explored the mathematical, religious, physiological, and social foundations of music. In a similar vein, in the 1930s, Avraamov's experiments in sound synthesis (alongside those of Evgeny Sholpo, Boris Yankovsky, and Nikolai Voinov) sought to create a universal language of geometric figures (circles, triangles, squares) that could, in principle, produce any sound whatsoever, be it the sounds of nature, human speech, traditional instruments, or never-before-heard whoops and bleeps (figure 2.2). Meticulously drawn by hand and then photographed onto a film strip, the combination of these shapes promised not only to bring about the music of the future but also to one day annul time itself – for example, by resurrecting Lenin's voice.[16] More practically, they allowed for the direct expression of a composer's idea by

Профиль синтетического кларнета: имеет 3, 5, 7, 9 и 11-й обертоны, причем амплитуды у всех одинаковые. Синтез Б. Янковского—в 1935 г. Зазвучал в 1938 г.

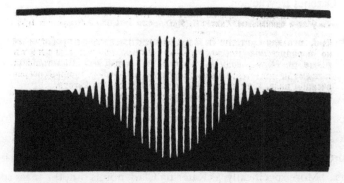

Тембр, наиболее контрастный синусоидальному, состоит из 5 высших обертонов, без низших, что придает ему резкий и яркий характер колокола или трубы с сурдиной (в зависимости от разного извлечения звука)

Figure 2.2 / Examples of drawn sound from Arseny Avraamov's article "Synthetic Music."

giving him control, in Avraamov's words, of a "universal 'super-orchestra, conducted by the composer himself.'"[17] According to Sholpo, such an orchestra would make the neuromuscular "acrobatics of miserable conservatory students" obsolete.[18]

Performed in part by ostensibly miserable conservatory students (amassed aboard the battleship *Dostoinyi*), the *Symphony of Sirens* embodied the same universal spirit as Avraamov's ideas on microtonality and sound synthesis. Echoing the words of the Taylorist poet Alexei Gastev (1882–1939), Avraamov explained that the symphony sought to convert the "call of slavery" – i.e., the "chaotic industrial roar" of factory sirens under the alienated conditions of capitalism – into a collective "song of the future."[19] Instruments such as the steam-whistle machine symbolically embodied this idea by channelling the industrial noise of alienated workers into a common melody (the "Internationale"). As an epigraph to a 1924 article for the journal *Artist and Viewer*, Avraamov quoted Mayakovsky's 1918 "Orders for the Army of Art:" "Enough of penny truisms / Erase the old from your heart / The streets are our brushes / The squares are our palettes."[20] The symphony attempted to literalize these lines using the streets and squares (as well as oil refineries and factory sirens) of Baku as instruments in a "universal super orchestra" capable of synthesizing, as it were, the sounds of the October Revolution.

Avraamov's symphony belongs to a tradition of Soviet festivals that sought to literally bring the masses into culture through the application of Futurist and Soviet-Taylorist ideas concerning the fusion of art, labor, industry, and urban planning with modes of audience participation.[21] The roots of this tradition go back to Jean-Jacques Rousseau's ideas on theatre, particularly his proclamation that the "entertainments appropriate to a republic are those in which the citizen, participating in his own person, is reinforced in the sentiment of his own being and in his relation to his fellow beings."[22] More specifically, as Katerina Clark points out, the mass spectacle derived "from a German dream of Greek wholeness"[23] found mutatis mutandis in the works of G.W. Hegel, Nietzsche, and Wagner and carried over into Russia by philologists such as Vyacheslav Ivanov and Tadeusz Stefan Zieliński. The universalist ambitions of this dream found fertile soil in civil war–era Petrograd. In the eyes of Petersburg intellectuals such as Avraamov, "Petrograd, as a 'commune,' was ... a sort of modern socialistic version of the old city-state. The next step – the move to a world commune – would entail expanding that model to embrace the entire world."[24]

The *Symphony of Sirens* follows this trajectory. Avraamov first attempted to stage the symphony in 1918 in Petrograd, followed by a technically flawed performance in Nizhny Novgorod (1919) that employed a flotilla of small torpedo boats.[25] The next performance sought to export the Petrogradian ideal to the world using Baku as a "gateway" to the East – an idea that had been recently championed in speeches and celebrations at Baku's 1920 First Congress of the Peoples of the East.[26] As D.D.B. Wendel points out, the Congress was itself a kind of mass spectacle. Held in Baku during the first week of September, the Congress combined solemn speeches, agitprop trains, negotiations and conferences, street parades, volunteer activities, and other types of pageantry to send a message of international proletarian solidarity. Fanfares of the "Internationale" played after dramatic pauses in almost every speech, effigies of Lloyd George and Woodrow Wilson were burned in the streets, and people dressed in traditional garb and brandishing exotic weapons made overt displays of camaraderie in what H.G. Wells sarcastically described as a "quite wonderful accumulation of white, black, brown, and yellow people, Asiatic costumes and astonishing weapons."[27]

The transition from Petrograd commune to global city-state was, of course, far from smooth. The political climate in which the *Symphony of Sirens* was performed was characterized by a colonial dynamic of mutual suspicion and distrust between the Bolsheviks and the "formerly colonized" subjects of the Russian Empire. The rights of oppressed nations to self-determination was a major sticking point in Bolshevik policy throughout the early 1920s. While skeptical of nationalism and nationalist movements, and generally dismissive of the Caucasus as "backward," the Bolsheviks nonetheless sought to present themselves as guarantors of national liberation by promoting ethnic particularism and positive discrimination in the domains of language, culture, education, and local government.[28] As Terry Martin argues, in positioning themselves as guarantors of these rights, the Bolsheviks hoped to stave off a resurgence of pre-Soviet power dynamics under the cover of formal legal equality and state neutrality.[29]

Considered in this light, Avraamov's cultural projects in the Caucasus appear as an instance of what Lenin at times decried: the persistence of Russian chauvinism in the guise of ostensibly egalitarian relations between workers.[30] The story of Avraamov's Islamic name provides insight into this dynamic. After the October Revolution, Avraamov became the head of the Musical Department of Proletkul't, the Proletarian Culture Movement, as well as a Commissar of Arts for Narkompros, the People's Commissariat of Enlightenment. In 1921, his work as a cultural curator for the Red Army sent him to Dagestan where, following an expedition to collect folksongs, he was expelled from the party for impersonating and aggravating the Muslim population. What is known about Avraamov's expulsion comes by way of an unsent 1943 letter to the Central Committee of the Communist Party in which the composer petitions to be reinstated as a member.[31] According to this letter, Avraamov came into conflict with the chair of the Dagestan Soviet, the Lak and Russian writer Saïd Ibragimovich Gabiev (1882–1963), concerning Avraamov's attempt to commandeer pianos from wealthy residents to build a music school. In Petersburg, Avraamov argued, one simply stuck a Nagant (a typical Red Army revolver) to the side of a person's head and commandeered what was needed by the state. In response, Gabiev accused Avraamov of being a *Tsentrovik*, an interloper from the center, who knew nothing about "Eastern Politics." He then threatened to send the composer back to Russia, to which Avraamov replied, "But I am in Russia, am I not?"[32]

Following their dispute, Avraamov set off on an excursion to collect folksongs, during which, as one might imagine, his interaction with locals did not improve. Forced to bring him folksingers, local militiamen in the town of Gubden provided him with tuneless prisoners instead. What is worse, there was nothing to eat: "Not only did [the locals] not treat me [to a meal]; they wouldn't even sell me any [food]."[33] One vendor, Avraamov reports, went so far as to pour a pail of milk on to the street rather than sell him a cup. Frustrated and hungry, Avraamov arrived in the town of Gunib (about 80 kilometres away), where he and a communist schoolteacher hit upon a plan. They went to a sympathetic local mullah who, apparently moved by Avraamov's story, wrote a letter stating that "the bearer of this document, one Arslan Ibrahim-ogli Adamov, had been born a Muslim, but, having been raised in Russia, had forgotten the local language and customs." For this reason, it is "necessary to teach and help him with everything he does not understand."[34] The mullah and schoolteacher then shaved Avraamov's head, dressed him in a traditional chokha, and outfitted him with a khanjali knife and astrakhan hat.

Avraamov's new outfit and mandate, he reports, "worked miracles." The locals "received me as a welcome guest; they sat me in a place of honor, fed me, gave me drink, sang songs and danced for me; they even forced their women to sing and dance and play the harmonica (for some reason with them this is a female instrument)."[35] Thrilled by his success, he wrote a full report for the first party purge detailing the story of his Islamic identity and how he used it to further Bolshevik propaganda efforts, going so far as to sign the report with his pseudonym. Bolshevik officials, however, were not impressed. He was accused of "double-dealing" and summarily expelled from the party. Shortly after the failure of his appeal, he arrived in Baku and – after working at an oil refinery and a high school – began organizing the *Symphony of Sirens*.

Despite having been expelled from the Party, a well-connected artist such as Avraamov could continue to count on the support of sympathetic cultural organizers for his ideas. To a certain degree, he could also rely on the support of cultural organizations such as Proletkul't, which, since they predated the Revolution, were only loosely affiliated with the Bolshevik Party and state. Even after Lenin ordered Proletkul't's reorganization and subordination to Narkompros (the People's Commissariat of Enlightenment) in 1920, Proletkul't continued to play a role in organizing and sponsoring artists regardless of party membership.[36] That said, following Lenin's decree, the organization's power and independence were severely restricted, and Futurist artists – party and non-party members alike – could no longer count on the state's support so long as they presented themselves as Futurists. This state of affairs may explain the lack of organization surrounding Avraamov's two final performances of the *Symphony of Sirens* in Baku and Moscow (discussed below). The symphony occurred after the alliance between avant-garde artists, the Bolshevik Party, and the state had begun to unravel. The new socio-economic organization of society that took its place – the New Economic Policy (NEP) – treated avant-garde artists as one of a variety of acts in the artistic marketplace. Nevertheless, during this transition, and throughout the 1920s, a party card was not necessary to perform cultural work in the name of the state. Many important cultural figures at this time were not party members.

Avraamov's symphony echoes the contradictions of his attempt to collect folksongs in the Caucasus. It offers a vision for the socialist reconstruction of post-imperial space that inadvertently reproduces the colonial relationships characteristic of that space. The universal principles that the symphony embodies mask the colonial dynamics that make the expression of these principles possible. This is apparent in the role that Baku's history of resource extraction plays in the symphony's composition. No factor contributed more to the sonic profile of Avraamov's mass spectacle than the oil rush of the 1870s.[37] As Audrey L. Altstadt points out, during this period and in its wake, scores of Russian and Armenian workers arrived in Baku to work in Nobel and Rothschild refineries. In the 1890s, "Russian peasants came by the thousands for jobs in the oil fields. By the early twentieth century, they would be the largest ethnic group in Baku. Armenians flocked to the city for commerce and oil. Iranian Azerbaijanis similarly came as oil workers, taking the worst unskilled jobs."[38] By the turn of the twentieth century, Baku was producing more oil than all U.S. refineries combined, roughly 200,000 barrels per day.[39] This material wealth largely flowed away from the city. "Of the 54 oil firms engaged in the extraction of oil in Baku in 1888, only two major companies were Azerbaijani owned."[40]

As the oil flowed out, the landscape, too, began to change. While Azerbaijanis "continued to live in homogenous *mahalle* (quarters) or villages," Russians and Armenians began filling the working-class and oil-producing districts of the cities.[41] From 1897 to 1913, the population of Baku doubled from 111,904 to 214,672, while the population of Azerbaijani Turks remained constant.[42] This displacement evoked resentment that often boiled over into ethnic violence, dashing socialist hopes of organizing the working class. From 6 to 9 February 1905, "several areas [of Baku] were engulfed in bloody battles between Azerbaijani and Armenian populations."[43] A general strike in August of the same year quickly degenerated "into another round of the Azerbaijani-Armenian feud that ended with the burning of vast sections of the oil districts."[44] Such eruptions of violence continued in the Bolshevik era, undermining the attempt to build a unified labour movement. The most famous of these, the March and September Days, which surrounded the formation of the 1918 Baku Commune, saw the slaughter of 12,000 Azerbaijanis and 15,000 Armenians just four years before the staging of Avraamov's symphony.[45]

Like many of Baku's residents at the turn of the twentieth century, the *Symphony of Sirens* was a transplant, grafted on to a city that had undergone seismic levels of industrial expansion. The mass spectacle tapped into Baku's already existing networks of colonialism and resource extraction – the Transcaucasian Railroad Depot, the offices of the Azerbaijani Oil Administration (Azneft), the shipping docks, and the industrial and oil districts of Zykh, Black Town, Armenian Village, White Town, and Bibi-Eibat – in an attempt to make them sing the melody of the October Revolution. In doing so, as D.D.B. Wendel suggests, the symphony sought to unify these spaces, overcoming years of ethnic division through the interconnected sounds of labour and transforming Baku into a symbol of inter-ethnic proletarian solidarity.[46] At the same time, by not acknowledging the inequities amid Baku's working-class population, the symphony reproduced them in its "song of the future." Its logic of Petrogradian universal unity was expressed by a collective noise making that drowned out all distinctions. The multi-ethnic population that made it possible for the symphony to express this Petrogradian ideal was the result of colonization. The same goes for the industrialization of the spaces the symphony connected. The sounds theses spaces produced were primarily those of a colonizing workforce. As such, like Avraamov himself, the mass spectacle was a kind of *Tsentrovik*, a symphony from the center. Its universalist ambitions ended up treating all space as, in effect, Russian space.

Baku

Further complicating the colonial dynamics of Avraamov's mass spectacle is the potential failure of the symphony itself, a fact that has been typically overlooked given the rush of some scholars to treat Avraamov's account of events as historically accurate. Due to an increasing interest in the phenomenon of noise over the course of the last half of the twentieth century, sound and urban-studies scholars have sought to tune their historical ears to noisy events such as the *Symphony of Sirens*.[47] Similarly, reacting to the Eurocentrism of avant-garde studies, they have sought to recover avant-garde events on the "non-European" periphery. These scholars primarily rely on Avraamov's *Gorn* article and instructions as a faithful representation of events in Baku. In their 2012 preliminary remarks to a new translation of the *Gorn* instructions, Marina Frolova-Walker and Jonathan Walker write that "although published in 1923, [the instructions] are entirely an account of events that took place in 1922 ... They document a successful performance of Avraamov's *Symphony of Sirens* in Baku."[48] Mel Gordon's 1994 translation of the *Gorn* instructions also creates the impression of a fully realized performance. Based on Gordon's translation, Wendel has gone so far as to provide a meticulous "spatial reconstruction" of the symphony by charting its movements across a 1913 map of Baku,[49] as well as offering some speculations on how the natural acoustics of the city's harbour facilitated the performance.[50] In her opinion, Baku's ethnic composition had "a profound impact, not only on the choice to site the symphony in the Azerbaijani city, but also on the logistical success of the complex performance and its intended outward symbolism."[51]

Such accounts and reconstructions manifest a misplaced desire to turn the symphony into a definitive sonic event – one in which every sound has its place – despite limited documentation of the event. Yet there are reasons to doubt that the performance in Baku was an unequivocal success. First, the *Gorn* article is a limited document. It can tell us much about Avraamov's concept for the mass spectacle but comparatively little about how it sounded. As Sergei Rumiantsev points out, there are, in fact, discrepancies between the reproduction of instructions in *Gorn* and the extant originals published in the *Baku Worker*.[52] The instructions in the *Baku Worker* feature many of the same of events as those in *Gorn*, albeit in a different order. In *Gorn*, the tenth gun signals the sirens of the Azneft trade offices and the docks; in the *Baku Worker*, it signals the second and third factory groups of Black Town. In *Gorn*, the fifteenth gun signals the sirens of the mountain district (Armenian Village), hydroplanes, and bells; in the *Baku Worker*, it signals Group 1 of Black Town, the sirens of the Caspian Flotilla, and a recital of the "Warszawianka" by a joint brass orchestra.

Such differences persist to the end of the symphony, altering not just the location and timing of certain sounds, but also their significance. This chiefly concerns the placement of a series of sounds, conducted directly via semaphore, around the pause following the twenty-fifth cannon – the moment when the chaotic sounds of slavery, alarm, and battle give way to the "Internationale," played on the steam-whistle machine. The *Baku Worker* places a portion of the *Gorn* "finale" – a burst of rifle salvoes, machine-gun fire, sirens, and an automobile chorus – *ahead* of the pause, thus determining these sounds as noises of fear and anxiety, rather than those of victory.

Second, there is a general lack of ear-witness accounts of the symphony's success.[53] Avraamov himself appears to have been aware of this problem. In a letter dated 13 October 1923, Avraamov asked his lover Revecca Zhiv, whom he met as a piano teacher in Rostov-na-Dony and with whom he maintained a correspondence in the run-up to the Moscow performance, to send him materials related to the Baku Symphony.

> By the way, please send one typed "instructions" [of the *Symphony of Sirens*], one blank [text-note] of the 'Internationale,' my article from *Don Labor*, the notice in 'Southern Soviet,' the mandate from the *TsK AKP* [Central Committee of the Azerbaijan Communist Party], and the article written by A. Borodin. These will give me a better chance of winning the battle with the Central Committee. Otherwise I do not have any "evidence" of the Baku experiment. Please also send my tuning key.[54]

Avraamov wrote this letter before the failed 1923 Moscow performance of the symphony, suggesting that he needed to convince authorities in Moscow of not just the importance of the Baku experiment but also its very existence. The evidence that he asks for, however, is rather scant: the symphony's instructions (perhaps those from the *Baku Worker*); the text-notes to the "Internationale" (figure 2.3); an article that Avraamov himself wrote; a notice (most likely announcing the symphony's performance); and a mandate from the Azerbaijan Communist Party giving Avraamov permission to perform.[55] Little of this evidence concerns the Baku performance itself – for example, how it sounded or how audiences reacted. As Rumiantsev points out, "except for Avraamov and the invisible A. Borodin, no one wrote anything about the Baku Symphony, while in Moscow they only knew about it from the words of its organizer-initiator."[56] What is more, A. Borodin appears to reference the Georgian composer Alexander Porfiryevich Borodin (1833–1887), leading Rumianstev to suspect that Avraamov may have used the name as another pseudonym.

A final reason for skepticism is the possibility that Avraamov's lack of evidence is a result of the symphony's failure to sound. One reason to think this might be the case is an ear-witness account from Lydia Ivanova (1896–1985), the daughter of the Symbolist poet, Vyacheslav Ivanov. Ivanova had been living in Baku since 1920, where her father held the university chair in classical philology. In her memoirs, she dedicates three paragraphs to Avraamov.

ТЕКСТОНОТЫ ИНТЕРНАЦИОНАЛА.

Вста 4	вай 2 3 про	клять ем за клей	млен 2 3 4	ный 2 3
весь	мир 2 3 го	лод ных и ра	бов 2 3 4	1 2
Ки 4	пит 2 3 наш	ра зум воз му	щен 2 3 4	ный и в смерт
ный	бой 2 вс 4	сти 2 го 4	тов 2 3 4	1 —
Ве — сь	мир 2 3 на	силья мы раз	ру 2 3 4	шим до ос
но	ва 2 3 нья	а 2 3 за	тем 2 3 4	1 —
Мы 4	наш 2 3 мы	но вый мир по	стро 2 3 4	им кто был
ни	чем 2 тот 4	ста 2 нет 4	всем 2 3 4	1 —
Э то	есть 2 3 4	наш 2 3 по	след 2 3 4	ний 2
И ре	ши 2 3 4	тель 2 ный 4	бой 2 3 4	1 —
С ни 4	тер 2 3 4	на 2 ци о	на 2 3 4	лом 2 3
вос	пря 2 3 нет	род 2 люд 4	ской 2 3 4	1 —
Э то	есть 2 3 4	наш 2 3 по	след 2 3 4	ний 2
И ре	ши 2 3 4	тель 2 ный 4	бой 2 3 4	1 —
С ин 4	тер 2 3 4	на 2 ци о	на 2 3 4	лом 2
Вос 4	пря 2 3 нет	род 2 люд 4	ской 2 3 4	1 —

Подчеркнута партия гудка „соль".

РИТМОНОТЫ ИНТЕРНАЦИОНАЛА.

(и т. д., подчеркнута партия гудка „до").

Ноты должны быть напечатаны на удобном по форме, плотном картоне: может быть дурная погода, ветер, дождь.

Figure 2.3 / Text-notes to the "Internationale."

There arrived in Baku a musician – Avraamov. He was a lanky, red-haired enthusiast with a starved look. Everyone pitied him, fed him, listened to his theories. Then came one of the largest civil celebrations and Avraamov hit upon the idea of observing it with an immense, never-before-seen symphony of all peoples. The sirens of all oil refineries surrounding Baku would create a tremendous organ which would play the melody of the "Internationale." Each siren would be responsible for playing one note of the melody. Small siren boats in the harbour would assemble into groups, composing chords for accompaniment. Avraamov was supposed to conduct this whole symphony himself, standing on a battery and signaling the artillery to shoot from a cannon in the port. At the same time, in each oil refinery [the workers] knew which siren to play after each cannon shot. Avraamov was able to get money and permission from the corresponding institutions. Preparations lasted a very long time and were very complicated.

At the fated hour a large group of people gathered to listen, but the symphony suffered an utter collapse [*poterpela krakh*]. A cannon sounded, a siren, another cannon, another siren – then the cannon went silent. The sirens, too, went silent; then each began wailing at random, at first one by one, then roaring all together. It seems that on the horizon a vessel appeared; the authorities aboard forbade the cannon from firing. Avraamov announced that, despite this setback, never in his life did he feel more powerful than when he was conducting a 60-verst orchestra.

Avraamov lived a little longer in Baku on money he received for his symphony. Then, after borrowing as much as he could from acquaintances, he disappeared from the city, leaving his wife, whom he was quick enough to marry in his short time there. Spiteful tongues said that he systematically roamed from city to city, leaving behind debts and a local wife.[57]

Ivanova's account presents Avraamov as part ecstatic avant-garde artist, part Soviet trickster. That the symphony was cut short – and that the sirens failed to sound the "Internationale" – explains the lack of ear-witness accounts. While some of Baku's residents may have heard a cannon firing into the harbour, they did not necessarily realize that they were listening to the sounds of a symphony. Of course, this does not prove that the symphony was a complete failure. Nevertheless, it suggests that scholars do not have a mandate for declaring the symphony an audible success, let alone treating the *Gorn* instructions as a precise record of sounds and movements.

This potential failure changes the colonial dynamics of the symphony. Rather than a propaganda effort to foster inter-ethnic harmony, Avraamov's "symphony of all peoples" appears largely as promotional material for a repeat performance. In fact, the *Gorn* article is explicit about this goal: "For the Sixth Anniversary [of the October Revolution], we want every town with at least ten boilers to organize a well-deserved 'accompaniment' for the revolutionary festivities, and here we present a manual for organizing the *Symphony of Sirens* applicable to various local conditions."[58] In this regard, the *Gorn* article finalized post hoc the significance and theoretical groundwork of the mass spectacle. It lent the ostensible events in Baku the legitimacy of objective fact, not just to ensure a repeat performance in Moscow, but to promote and serve as a model for similar performances in other major cities. Indeed, in a letter to Zhiv, Avraamov suggests that performances of the symphony in German cities would signal a revolution in Germany.[59]

Avraamov's Baku Symphony highlights the difficulties the city symphony encounters in seeking to compose city space. City symphonies do not always realize the full scope of their ambitions; the material sounds and spaces they seek to compose resist arrangement. Like many in the avant-garde, city symphony composers such as Russolo and Avraamov treated real-world sounds and spaces not only as phenomena to be documented but also as materials to be transformed through creative labor, whether abstractly (Russolo) or literally (Avraamov). Their works sought to overcome the alterity of the material world through compositions that assimilated its concrete manifestations to creative expression. Noises were never just noises, the Other of musical sound and human speech. For Russolo, they had to be systematized according to tables, reduced to linear representation, and moulded into musical forms. For Avraamov, they had to be forced to play the "Internationale," thereby expressing the dialectical history of the material world as the object of labor. Similarly, Vertov (as we see below) sought to negate the negativity of noises by showing that, in fact, there were no such things as noises per se, only musical sounds to which the ear was not yet attuned.

Avraamov's city symphony channelled the material world through processes of negation and assimilation. Techniques such as montage, cross-section, and call and response gathered a manifold of sights and sounds into a single creative whole, organized according to correspondences of sound, rhythm, and movement. The city symphony's treatment of urban sounds and spaces as materials echoes a shift in the philosophical understanding of materialism that dates back to Karl Marx and Friedrich Engels. "Old materialism," Engels wrote, "looked upon all previous history as a crude heap of irrationality and violence; modern materialism sees in it the process of evolution of humanity, and aims at discovering the laws thereof."[60] This idea goes under the heading "dialectical materialism," though, as Pheng Cheah points out, Marx and Engels never used the term; rather, it was popularized by Georgi Plekhanov to "distinguish the Marxist approach to the sociohistorical process ... from the teleological view of history in Hegelian idealism."[61] Dialectical materialism conceived of "material existence as something created through the purposive mediation of human corporeal activity." Labor, in this regard, was a form of negativity. As a "process of actualization," it negated given reality or matter "through the imposition of a purposive form."[62] This idea was famously adapted to aesthetics by the Frankfurt School. Theodor Adorno, for instance, elaborated on the "labor of the negative" in terms of music. He called music a "system of the domination of nature" – an idea reprised in Attali's conception of music as the domination of noise. Music, according to Adorno, "answers to a longing arising out of the primordial age of the bourgeoisie: to seize all that sounds in a regulatory grasp and dissolve the magic of music in human reason ... Conscious disposal over the musical material is both the emancipation of the human being from the constraint of nature in music and the subordination of nature to human purposes."[63]

Adorno's conception of music as the domination of nature is taken to its literal extreme in the *Symphony of Sirens*. The city symphony not only documents the subjugation of nature to human purposes (Baku's oil industry); it actively participates in it. It gathers up the excess of this subjugation – its noise – and uses it as material to be assimilated into creative labor. What is interesting about this dynamic is how Avraamov's city symphony *fails* to subjugate – how its organizational schemes are undermined by its chosen materials and the social environment in which they are embedded. In the *Symphony of Sirens*, spaces fraught with histories of ethnic tension and religious strife could not be incorporated into a harmonious musical whole. Local authorities were not aligned with (nor perhaps informed of) Avraamov's musical celebration. This failure may have been a matter of chance, and the symphony could have succeeded (just as Soviet internationalism could have succeeded in genuinely reconciling ethnic nationalism and Bolshevism); nevertheless, its failure is suggestive, for it reveals the limits of attempting to organize urban society and material according to musical principles.

These limits remain somewhat hidden when one watches city symphony films, which have the advantage of taking place in contained architectural settings where there are more or less defined norms of spectatorship. Expanding the theatre to the size of a city, by contrast, encounters problems of scale: Where will audience members listen? How will the symphony deliver a relatively uniform acoustic experience? From what position will its juxtaposition of urban spaces make sense? Avraamov's symphony does not appear to provide satisfying answers to these questions.[64] In *Gorn*, he hardly raises them. Although he conceived a new kind of performance, Avraamov did not conceive a new kind of space. Instead, the symphony assumes the uniformity of acoustic space and experience, as if Baku were just another auditorium. No matter where one stands – and no matter whether one is a member of the colonizing or colonized proletariat – the sounds of the symphony are supposed to be the same.

Moscow

In *Modern Epic: The World System from Goethe to García Marquez*, Franco Moretti argues that works such as J.W. von Goethe's *Faust*, Herman Melville's *Moby Dick*, and James Joyce's *Ulysses* are semi-failures insofar as they struggle to develop a unifying form or narrative structure that embraces the fragmentary multiplicity of modernity. Modern epics "reveal a kind of antagonism between the noun [epic] and the adjective [modern]: a discrepancy between the totalizing will of the epic and the subdivided reality of the modern world."[65] Avraamov's city symphony reveals a similar antagonism between the spatially and temporally heterogeneous spaces of the city and the unifying and harmonizing impulses of the symphony. The city is often the subject of modern epics such as Joyce's *Ulysses*, Andrei Bely's *Petersburg*, and Alfred Döblin's *Berlin, Alexanderplatz*, works that may be considered city symphonies in their own right. It is the space in which the contradictions of the modern world play out and struggle to find form. Avraamov's city symphony takes a more literal approach to these contradictions than the epic. It represents a radicalization of the epic by applying the epic's gathering/totalizing principles to actual city spaces, networks, and raw materials. As Vivian Sobchack points out, classical urbanism tends to consider "the city as an 'object' distinct from the subjects who inhabit it."[66] The same may be said of Avraamov's treatment of city space (streets and squares) as literal material for artistic construction (brushes and palettes). The problems Avraamov's symphony faced serves as a reminder that the city is not an object; rather, it is something that emerges from the interaction between its inhabitants and their material, social, and political surroundings. In attempting to structure these relations into a work of art, Avraamov encountered their resistance. The city could not be played like an orchestra.

In the *Symphony of Sirens*, the work done by epic narrative and action finds its geographic and sonic counterpart. Moretti conceives of the "totalizing will of the epic" in Hegelian terms as embodying an ethical community through the action of a hero. "In Homer," Moretti points out, "even the hero's *inactivity* – Achilles in his tent – produces practical consequences of great importance: it is, in its own way, action." This feature, according to Moretti, poses a problem for the epic in modern times since the role of the hero is usurped by that of the state. "Once 'State life' becomes established, the unity of universal and individual dissolves: 'the ethical and the right' cease to 'depend exclusively upon individuals' and become objectified in laws and the state apparatus."[67] The desire to unify a community in heroic action – and the inability to do so – is the locus of the modern epic's failure.

"Digressions," as Marjorie Perloff puts it, "become the main purpose of the epic action. The construction of national identity is no longer temporal or historical, as in classical epic, but geographical."[68] Faust wanders the world in search of humanity yet manages only to seduce Gretchen and narrowly avoid being killed by her brother (two actions that do not necessarily require demonic intervention).[69] In *Berlin, Alexanderplatz*, Franz Biberkopf wanders the streets of the German capital in the hopes of unifying his fractured personality only to be physically dismembered in the process after losing his arm in a failed robbery.

On the one hand, in the *Symphony of Sirens*, the place of the epic hero is taken up by the geographic construct of the polis. This gives a fuller sense to the idea that the city in the city symphony is itself a protagonist. The city symphony's radical geographic construction exacerbates the latent tensions of the modern epic. Its attempt to unify that which was formerly held together in a single personality leads to tensions that are neither resolved nor successfully managed. When Avraamov's city symphony fails, it does so in a way that points to modes of art that go beyond heroic action, nation, personality, and cult. It points to an engagement with the material world – the sounds and spaces of the city – that is not, in Cheah's words, "complicit with idealism" but rather defies the negation of matter as that which gives form (composes) material existence.[70] On the other hand, it is important not to forget just how complicit with idealism Avraamov's city symphony and its ideal of unity actually are. This complicity is brought out in the failure of the Moscow performance of the *Symphony of Sirens*. The ideal of unity behind this performance enfolds the symphony's goal of a multi-ethnic proletarian community in a philosophy of romantic love.

In a certain sense, the true audience of the *Symphony of Sirens* was not in Baku, but rather in Moscow. Similar to scholars today, this audience "heard" the symphony by reading about it in *Gorn*. By contrast, with respect to the 1923 Moscow performance, the verdicts of the critics were unambiguous. One journalist reported that the music critic and composer Mikhail Gnesin (1883–1957) "considered the Symphony unsuccessful on account of its overly-complicated melody."[71] Another critic, A. Uglov, reported that

Симфония гудков в Москве 7 ноября 1923 г. Гудки за работой.

Figure 2.4 / The steam-whistle machine (*magistral'*) at the 1923 Moscow *Symphony of Sirens*.

the strength of several pipes sounding together was so staggering [*potriasaiushchii*], in the literal sense of the word, that not everyone was left standing. It helped little to stuff cotton in one's ears. Likewise, during the performance, a few of the steam whistles did not give off the same sound as they did during the trial run. Attempts to adjust the melody of the "symphony" were not successful ... The failure of this first experiment should not embarrass anyone; it follows that the second should be approached in a more experienced way.[72]

Responding to such criticisms, Avraamov eventually acknowledged some of the Moscow Symphony's problems. In his 1924 article for *Artist and Viewer*, he blamed the excessively difficult harmonization of the "Internationale" and the "Warszawianka" for the steam-whistle machine's technical difficulties. In contrast to Uglov, however, he argued that the symphony was not too loud, but rather not loud enough. The steam-whistle machine (figure 2.4) had been misplaced "in the courtyard of the Moscow

Hydroelectric Station (instead of on its roof as had been initially planned.)" There was thus "not enough sound for the Moscow auditorium."[73] Similarly, in his correspondence with Zhiv, Avraamov complained about the lack of sound: "in all, there were only twenty-seven cannon shots! That's supposed to be a big drum! And there *weren't any* machine guns ... only rifle salutes! At the same time, twenty airplanes were buzzing over Red Square as we were sounding off."[74]

Few scholars discuss the Moscow Symphony except to say that it was a failure. In doing so, they overlook key elements of Avraamov's correspondence and philosophy that provide insight into the symphony's ideal of unity. As it turns out, this ideal is more spiritual and personal than Avraamov's articles would lead one to suspect. A Taylorist *Gesamtkunstwerk*, the Moscow Symphony was, in a certain sense, also a love song – one that confirms, to a degree, Ivanova's characterization of Avraamov as a kind of Soviet Casanova. This "love song" reveals the continuity between Avraamov's aim of reorganizing proletarian communal life in terms of revolutionary music and his romantic philosophy. The two are two sides of the same coin, a fact hidden in the symphony's curious alternative title. This title appears in a 1923 appeal to Moscow factory committees just days before the performance: "For the sixth anniversary of the October Revolution, the 'Symphony *La*' will be performed on the *magistral'* [steam-whistle machine] and the factory sirens of the Zam[oskvoretskii] district and railway stations."[75] The "Symphony *La*" refers to the sixth of solfeggio (do re mi fa so *la* ti da); it also refers to Avraamov's complicated romantic history. In a letter to Zhiv, written just before the Moscow performance, Avraamov explains that the title *"La"* incorporates both her and his wife Olga into the structure of the composition. "The *theme* of the symphony is yours," he writes, "the *tonality* is hers. The thing is, the children and I always called her *La* ... Hence, let it be *La*, the theme's concluding chord – the tonic of the entire symphony."[76]

Though he soon denounced the Moscow mass spectacle as a failure, Avraamov initially considered this conceit a great success. (One wonders how Avraamov may have portrayed the Moscow performance had there not been so many critics listening.) Immediately following the symphony's recital, he wrote to Zhiv on a piece of tracing paper: "It happened

... Everything happened! ReveccA [sic] sounded over Moscow – and will sound once more on the night of the 12th at 11 pm ... You both stood with me there on the heights ... Not my hands but yours and 'La's' raised the banner of the *Symphony of Sirens* over the Kremlin and were given an artillery salute."[77] A symphony that converts the alienated sounds of work into a song of proletarian unity thus performed another kind of transformation – from a symphony of labour to a polyamorous love song. Indeed, a few weeks after the performance, Avraamov wrote a letter to Zhiv's mother, Sofia Veniaminovna, proposing a union between Revecca, his wife Olga, and two other lovers – Eva and Lilya Segal.[78]

The concluding chord of the Moscow Symphony is not merely a romantic conceit; it is a fundamental element of the symphony's composition. Love is an active principle in Avraamov's philosophy of art, one that is reminiscent of the nineteenth-century philosopher Vladimir Solovyov's philosophy of love.[79] Not surprisingly, the most striking summation of this principle is found in his correspondence with Zhiv. In a letter dated "Year Six of the First Century,"[80] Avraamov details a program for the unification of all creative drives – a program he calls LIR (*Liubov'*, *Isskustvo*, *Revoliutsiia* – Love, Art, Revolution) as in the Russian words for lyre and lyric. LIR in fact encompasses six creative drives – love, art, religion, science, philosophy, and revolution. Although equal to one another, these drives are in constant conflict, which Avraamov illustrates in terms of world-historical figures: "Science vs. Religion (Newton, Copernicus); Religion vs. Art (Savonarola, Luther, Nikon), Art vs. Science ('Mozart and Salieri')"; and so on. Likewise, he arranges these drives with arrows pointing toward an empty inner circle and poses the problem of their infighting in biblical terms: "six irreconcilably hostile figures I see now on this great historical crossroads, on the threshold of the New World ... The legend of the Tower of Babel and its builders resurrects itself – a terrible legend, all the more terrifying since it is being born out in life, in reality."[81]

The Tower is a stock trope of the Russian avant-garde, one that manifests itself in projects such as Vladimir Tatlin's "Monument to the Third International," a three-tiered structure in which each rotating level corresponds to the cycles of year, month, and day. Clark has noted the similarity between Tatlin's tower and mass spectacles in general, arguing that "both these products of revolutionary utopianism entail the sacerdotalization of space and highly ritualized movement through it."[82] As an attempt to reconcile all creative drives through the unification of art (music, performance), science (industrial technology), religion (communism), revolution (October), and eventually love (Revecca and Olga), Avraamov's symphony goes one step further by seeking to construct its tower in sound. The empty inner circle at the center of Avraamov's sketch outlines the tower as a non-place – a utopia. Its sonic corollary is the silence that follows the sounding of the twenty-fifth cannon, which marks the moment when the chaotic and conflicting noises of alienated labour are miraculously transformed into a song of unity. Like the empty inner circle, the moment of silence is a non-place; it is outside the spatial and sonic dynamics of both the city and the symphony. In Baku and Moscow, this non-place clashes with actual city space; the result is a chaotic and disorganized din.

The Moscow performance shows that Avraamov's symphony's engagement with the city's "streets and squares" as materials for aesthetic and social construction concerns a metaphysical space that is far removed from the city. It is an attempt to impose a romantic idealism on the sociomaterial constraints of an industrial city. By emphasizing love in his art, Avraamov hedges against the possibility that this non-place will not be realized through his projects on earth. In the same letter, he writes that he and Zhiv must choose between two paths: The first – the path of avowed love – demands that Zhiv break all ties with her past life and join Avraamov in the construction of a new world. This world would be the "real" materialization of utopia on earth. The second "no less sublime" path – that of secret love – requires that neither Avraamov nor Zhiv speak of their love but instead reap the rewards of its sublimation in art. "Let the fruits of our love speak for us," Avraamov writes, "our immortal children. You will be their *father* – I, their mother. I will find the strength to forget the nightmare that surrounds us and create, create – give birth without end."[83]

In the path of secret love, that Revecca will be forever unattainable allows Avraamov to usurp her reproductive role, using his longing as a means to create ad infinitum. The path of avowal holds that utopia can be achieved – Avraamov can build his Tower of Babel just as he can realize his love. The path of secret love, by contrast, holds that one must defer utopia to keep dreaming it. Avraamov, here, may give birth to works of art – his "immortal children" – so long as he ignores the limitations of the real world – the "nightmare that surrounds."[84] As such, for Avraamov, love as a principle serves to reconcile the contradictions of utopian construction, not to mention those of the city symphony. Operating behind his symphony is a mechanism that wishes to simultaneously engage and flee the world; to bring about utopia in reality and yet defer its arrival by dreaming. This twofold desire is hidden in the concluding chord of the Moscow *Symphony of Sirens*.

Mechanical Reproduction

As pointed out in chapter 1, the vibratory sciences of the nineteenth and twentieth centuries were a significant part of the cultural backdrop to the city symphony. These sciences made it possible to understand an array of disparate phenomena – sound, light, thought, spirit – as expressing a fundamental unity. Each one of these existed along a spectrum of vibrations that could in principle be recorded by new technologies of mechanical reproduction – the phonograph, photograph, X-ray, and so on. Avraamov was, of course, no stranger to theories of vibration. Most of his creative output – consisting primarily of articles on microtonality, music history and theory, instrument design, and experiments in sound synthesis – aimed to ground the mathematical, physical, social, and spiritual properties of music in the vibratory properties of sound. In principle, as Avraamov argued in these articles, not only could sound be flawlessly mechanically reproduced, so could the context surrounding its production – its "creative ecstasy," as he called it, or what Benjamin might term its "aura," its "here and now." A better understanding of vibration would make it possible to transform the sounds of brass into strings, and strings into woodwinds – all while directly reproducing the genius of the composer without the need for pesky conservatory students and musicians.[85] From the composer's mind directly to the listener's ears – such an understanding of vibration was at the heart of Avraamov's *Symphony of Sirens*, even if it did rely on human performers.

The era of ludic Petrograd-inspired mass spectacles came to an end shortly after the Moscow Symphony. Out of work, Avraamov lived a meagre existence around the Pegasus Stall, a Futurist café in Moscow. His next major project was the soundtrack for the first Soviet sound film *Piatiletka: The Plan of Great Works*, followed by his pioneering experiments in sound synthesis.[86] Yet even in the harsh cultural climate of the 1930s, Avraamov never gave up dreaming about the *Symphony of Sirens*. In 1933, he conceived of resurrecting the symphony as a piece of synthetic music composed of drawn sounds: "The *Symphony of Sirens* is being constructed out of right triangles, and it will be more harmonious and more powerful than my 'documentary' siren symphonies, performed in Moscow and Baku ... For the 'International' we especially like the timbre of squares and rectangles – no natural recording could produce such singular and forceful sounds. Trapezoids and isosceles triangles produce softer, more 'lyrical' colors: they will be used in the 'Funeral March.'"[87] Sound synthesis at this time consisted in meticulously drawing sound figures by hand, then photographing them onto the soundtrack portion of the film strip – hence the idea of a symphony of right triangles, squares, and trapezoids (see figure 2.2). Similar to Rudolph Pfenninger, Avraamov conceived of sound synthesis on the basis of a linguistic analogy – as an alphabet of sounds-shapes whose combination could produce any sound whatsoever.[88] A *Symphony of Sirens* composed in this manner would have no need of musicians, nor listener-participants.[89] This, of course, drastically changes the ethos of Avraamov's composition. The synthesized *Symphony of Sirens* would be closer in spirit to Russolo's *Awakening of a City* – a re-sounding of the October Revolution, to be sure, but one that relies on a strict separation not only between composer and audience, but also between noise-sound (the product of synthetic instruments) and noise-making object. Although arguably a reflection of the more conservative politics and aesthetics of the 1930s, such a conception nevertheless implies that, for Avraamov, neither audience participation nor real "documentary" sounds were essential components of the *Symphony of Sirens*. But then what was an essential component? On what basis could such a synthetic composition merit the same title as Avraamov's earlier mass spectacle?

Until the above proposal, Avraamov also envisioned broadcasting the *Symphony of Sirens* from airplanes using electro-acoustic instruments: "And if the sound of sirens is not powerful and qualitative enough, what could we dream about? Clearly: about the devices of Theremin or Rzhevkin installed on aeroplanes, flying above Moscow! An Aerosymphony!"[90] Here, the nonplace of Avraamov's symphony is resurrected in the airborne thundering of electronic instruments and the abstract geometry of sound synthesis. These dreams point to a crucial yet overlooked aspect of Avraamov's mass spectacle – its reliance on an idiosyncratic conception of mechanical reproduction. This conception of mechanical reproduction, I suggest, is the essential component of Avraamov's symphony. It is what makes the "live" and "synthetic" versions of the *Symphony of Sirens* part of the same project.[91]

Avraamov did not share his contemporaries' anxieties about new technologies such as the gramophone and the movie camera. In a 1916 article titled "The Coming Musical Science and the New Era in Music History," he recalls a debate with a friend about the possibility of creating an exact copy of the Venus de Milo.[92] The friend argues that it is "impossible to re-create the Venus de Milo, that even the most ideal copy would be dead, even if its material and form were flawlessly and mathematically reproduced." Avraamov replies that he's not so sure: "I admit that the feeling one experiences contemplating the original might be a special one, related, for example, to that sacred trembling which accompanies the examination of an authentic Bach manuscript. However, in the case of this feeling, a trick is certainly possible – if I do not suspect anything, I will look upon a forgery with no less a feeling of 'sacred trembling.'"[93] The idea of "sacred trembling" recalls Walter Benjamin's notion of aura, an artwork's unique time and place. For Benjamin, mechanical reproducibility spelled the decay of aura. The works of the Soviet avant-garde, he believed, were uniquely positioned to take advantage of this decay in the service of a politicized aesthetics. By contrast, Avraamov believed that aura – the feeling of awe in the presence of the original – *must* be mechanically reproducible to ensure the possibility of politicized mass art. If it were not, he writes, then every single person in search of "authentic aesthetic enjoyment" would have "to make a pilgrimage to the Louvre or the Vatican."[94] Against such an absurdity he proposes making exact copies of the Venus de Milo and placing them in the squares of every major city.

This conception of mechanical reproduction is another instance of Avraamov's ideal of unity – the unity of original and copy. The *Symphony of Sirens* is inspired by the desire to replicate the Venus de Milo and place it in every city square. According to this principle, the spirit of the October Revolution, if it could be flawlessly mechanically reproduced, could be replicated in every single city. Just before his discussion of the famous statue, Avraamov considers such an idea with respect not to the would-be music of the Revolution but to the music of great Russian composers. "Let us suppose," he writes, "that once a year (to dream of any more is frightening), all the major works of our great masters were compulsorily performed in all our cities, or at least in all the regional capitals – wouldn't that be utopia?"[95] This proto–*Symphony of Sirens* would be played city-wide for the masses, as opposed to in a concert hall for a restricted audience. Technologies of mechanical reproduction – gramophones and megaphones – would be instrumental in realizing this idea, a way of giving Russian audience's "their" music. Such an idea is adapted to the exigencies of re-sounding the October Revolution through the materials of Avraamov's mass spectacle. As Wendel points out, the Swedish Mast from which Avraamov ostensibly conducted the symphony in Baku was a type of tower used to mount radio antennae (figure 2.5). In *Artist and Viewer*, Avraamov suggests that such technologies would resolve "the social problem in music" through the "active engagement of the broad masses with musical creativity (the socialization of music) and the perfection of its hitherto archaic *material* technology (the electrification of music)." The first solution he characterized as a movement "from the village to the city; the second – from the city to the village."[96] Electrified music would create a collective aesthetic experience in cities similar to the kind that already existed in villages.

In creating a mass electric village, the *Symphony of Sirens* essentially flips the conventional understanding of mechanical reproducibility on its head: not a multitude of recorded copies sent out to individual homes, but one central copy delivered en masse to an entire city;[97] not the decay of aura, but its preservation and democratization. Interestingly, this idea of flawless mechanical reproduction has it roots in a pre-Revolutionary search

Figure 2.5 / Artist's rendering of the *Symphony of Sirens* in Baku.

for authentic Russian music. In the same discussion of mass performances, Avraamov writes, "Not long ago, we had [*u nas*] Taneev and Scriabin ... Who had them [*u kogo*]? Where is this 'ours' [*gde eto 'u nas'*]? In Moscow? In Petrograd? Even in the Grand Duchy of Kiev they only know Scriabin on the basis of a few tours, and the great works of Taneev – even in Kiev – have never been played at all."[98] How is it possible to say these are Russian composers if so few Russians have actually heard them? As Avraamov poses it, the question "To whom does a particular form of music belong?" becomes a question about where this music resides – *"gde eto u nas?"* The phonograph provides the answer: it resides in the community of listeners who hear it, who bear its imprint, and on whom it is inscribed.

For Avraamov, music inheres in people in a material sense. When a great pianist plays, he argued, the pressure of his fingers on the keys causes unique vibrations in the strings. If we can perfectly capture these vibrations, then "we have in our hands nothing less than a *negative of creative ecstasy.*" If we re-create these very same vibrations – e.g., using recording technology – then we'll have a "positive image – authentic creative ecstasy."[99] A phonograph record does not just register vibrating airwaves but the very pressure in the pianist's fingers that bear the creativity of his performance. By extension, the listener who hears this recorded performance experiences these same vibrations. Each stage of the process – from the ecstasy of the performer to the plane of the phonograph to the ears of the listener – is a lossless reflection of an integral whole.

This utopian faith in recording technology expresses the logic of a vibratory universe discussed in chapter 1. It hearkens to the first uses of the phonograph to record Russian and Ukrainian folksongs. Here, for instance, is Evgeniia Lineva, the first person in Russia to record peasant music with a phonograph: "What had seemed impossible was now a fact. Songs, echoing somewhere in space – filling the fields, forests, and villages, unconquerable, uncatchable – could now be captured on the cylinder made of delicate resin, carried over onto paper in the same whimsical form which flowed from the poet's mouth – from the mouth of the people – and preserved for posterity for many years to come."[100] In this quotation, Lineva whimsically elides a rather complicated process. Peasant songs were recorded on resin cylinders, but they did not magically appear on the page. Nor were these recordings meant for the general public. Instead, they were analyzed by an expert musicologist, then transferred to paper using graphic notation, then approximated using standard musical notation, and finally published in song books such as Lineva's *Folk Songs of the Ukraine.*[101] This great chain that connects sounds echoing through the fields to posterity is in fact broken in many places, yet Lineva suggests that the final product maintains the integrity of the original melody. With the ear as opposed to the eye, she is happy to follow, to borrow Benjamin's famous phrase, "a mountain range on the horizon or a branch that casts its shadow on the beholder," confident that her phonograph will capture the music that resonates through these spaces.[102]

Similarly, Avraamov's notions of "sacred trembling" and "creative ecstasy" describe a seamless connection between artist, artwork, and audience facilitated by recording technology. In the West European and North

American context of *The Audible Past*, Jonathan Sterne traces the origins of this faith in recording technology in terms of a discourse on sound fidelity. This discourse, Sterne argues, "is much more about faith in the social function and organization of machines than it is about the relation of a sound to its 'source.'" It is a kind of story told to "staple separate pieces of sonic reality together."[103] Lineva and Avraamov's conception of the power of the copy works in a similar fashion. Their faith in the phonograph serves a distinct social function. It staples separate pieces of Russian/Soviet sonic reality together in accordance with a desire to create an ideal community of artists and listeners. This community takes the form of an unbroken chain that stretches from the sonic and spiritual sources of music (the peasantry; the mouth of the people; great Russian composers) to present and future generations of listeners.

Such a logic of the exact copy pervades Avraamov's mass spectacle. The symphony is a way of transmitting and reproducing the sounds of the October Revolution. In this regard, pace Kittler, it treats the city as a medium for bearing the sonic imprint of this momentous event. It reinscribes this event in the networks of the city, in the flows of industry, people, and traffic. Avraamov's symphony rewires and reconnects the networks of the city based on a utopian conception of mechanical reproduction as part of a new sonic reality in which noise is no longer the alienated byproduct of industrial labour but the sound of a victorious working class. The symphony is structured according to a logic of signal and receiver. An unbroken chain connects Avraamov in his tower to crowds of listeners and performers via semaphore, cannon fire, and wailing sirens. The city's material infrastructure serves as a conduit for transmitting the "creative ecstasy" of the composer. Listeners experience the "sacred trembling" of the October Revolution through the thundering sounds that literally shake their streets. This is a way of giving the people "their" music, albeit in proletarian (as opposed to Russian) terms – their music as workers. Instead of bringing the artwork to the city, the symphony transforms the city into a work of art. Instead of bringing the Venus de Milo, it brings the Revolution. In this manner, all peoples, from Petersburg to Baku (and on to Berlin) could experience the aura of the same world-historical event.

Between Sound and Silence

Vsevolod Pudovkin's first sound film, *Deserter* (1933), opens with a scene reminiscent of the *Symphony of Sirens*. The "symphony of siren calls," as Pudovkin calls it (wittingly or unwittingly referring to Avraamov's composition), is composed of "six steamers playing in the space of a mile and a half in the port of Leningrad. They sounded their sirens to a prescribed plan and we worked at night in order to have quiet."[104] On the one hand, this scene gives a sense of what Avraamov's composition may have sounded like – noisy yet organized, patterned to give a sense of structure and rhythm. On the other, it suggests the difficulty of performing such a spectacle for a live audience – one that is, moreover, engaged in other festivities. Noise music of the kind Pudovkin was making required silence; hence the need to work at night. Avraamov's composition, by contrast, may have been drowned out by the noise of the city (as was the case in Moscow), or it may have been unceremoniously cut short (as was perhaps the case in Baku).

In this regard, the *Symphony of Sirens* hovers between sound and silence, tantalizingly close to our ears and yet echoing from an unbridgeable distance. Quite possibly, the symphony was a siren song of Avraamov's own making – one that seduces scholars today with its scale, noise, and colonial ambition. Like Avraamov, we, too, have a desire to hear and reproduce the original. Yet it is the failure of the symphony that tells the more interesting story. This failure reveals the underlying dreams of unity at the heart of the symphony's construction – the unity of all peoples (regardless of race, religion, or ethnicity); the unity of all creative drives (love, art, science, philosophy, art, and revolution); and the unity of original and copy (of flawless mechanical reproduction). It also underscores the resistance of urban spaces to such dreams. Playing the Revolution through a city's material infrastructure does not replicate its creative ecstasy any more than a copy of the Venus de Milo re-creates the presence of the original. In Baku, the political, ethnic, and material makeup of the city most likely rejected the Petrogradian ideal of the *Symphony of Sirens*. In Moscow, it was distorted through the mistuned sounds of a broken steam-whistle and overpowered by the rumblings of an airshow. The aero and synthetic *Symphony of Sirens* never materialized; however, as attempts to re-sound the Revolution through an urban infrastructure, they would have most likely shared the same fate.

The *Symphony of Sirens* reveals the limitations of the city symphony, of the desire to compose city space according to musical principles. It is also an important forerunner and accompaniment to the city symphony films of the 1920s. As we see in the next chapter, these so-called silent films were not silent at all. Their visual dynamics are an audible expression of ideas already heard in Russolo and Avraamov's compositions.

3

ON THE SCREEN

Sounding the Inaudible in the City Symphonies of Walter Ruttmann and Dziga Vertov

The *Symphony of Sirens* was a city-wide mass spectacle whose seemingly overwhelming noise hid a much larger silence. By contrast, the apparent silence of city symphony films covers up an abundance of sound. City symphony films of the 1920s fused the documentary and avant-garde impulses of the cinema. On the one hand, these films sought to record urban reality – to capture people living their everyday lives. In doing so, they aimed to fulfill cinema's promise of granting access to the real. On the other hand, these films sought to re-create and even accelerate the speed and dynamism of urban life. They sought not only to record urban reality but also to embody its mode of perception. In this respect, they relied on a number of filming and editing techniques that fall under the rubric of the musical analogy – the idea that shots and sequences may be treated like musical notes (see the introduction).

Cinema scholars have long acknowledged how silent city symphony films organize the visual elements of urban experience – the movements of people, machines, traffic, and crowds – according to musical techniques such as rhythm and counterpoint.[1] Less attention, however, has been paid to the parallel ability, namely, how these films manage the aural elements of urban experience – the sounds of trains, whistles, telephones, and typewriters – through visual techniques such as fast editing speeds and motion blur.[2] The goal of this chapter is to hear the sound of these visual techniques in two of the most famous city symphony films – the German director Walter Ruttmann's *Berlin, Symphony of a Great City* (1927) and the Soviet filmmaker Dziga Vertov's *Man with a Movie Camera* (1929). I contextualize these films in terms of the sonic experiments of Luigi Russolo (chapter 1) and Arseny Avraamov (chapter 2), alongside the projects of other members of the sonic avant-garde such as Rudolf Pfenninger and Oskar Fischinger. Ruttmann's and Vertov's films, I argue, sound the inaudible: their visual tracks contain aural elements that go beyond the standard description of these films as "organizing moving images of city life ... according to musical guidelines."[3] Exploring these aural components reveals the influence of the twentieth-century sonic avant-garde on the visual dynamics of city symphony films.

Music in the city symphony is more than just a significant historical analogy for film form. It is more than a way for directors to ennoble cinema as a high art or combat the idea that cinema, to quote Bordwell once more, is the "art of the real."[4] Taking inspiration from recent re-evaluations of the role of the musical analogy in both absolute and narrative films, I argue instead that the musical analogy is the site of a fluid exchange between aural and visual faculties and technologies in the early twentieth century.[5] The musical analogy concerns audial and technological developments that sought to destabilize Western music's fixed notation system and also revolutionize the way in which Western culture thought about sound. Sonic experiments entirely outside the cinema inflected the practice of the cinematic city symphony. Here, many of the developments that influenced Russolo and Avraamov's work – namely, the rise of noise as a social, aesthetic, and technological problem, alongside the evolution of technologies that facilitated the inscription, reproduction, and transmission of sound – figure prominently.

The incorporation of these practices into musical compositions is typically considered the sonic legacy of the Futurist movement. The contradictions of this legacy – at once aesthetically revolutionary and politically reactionary, chaotic and controlling, decadent and ascetic – fundamentally transformed the understanding of sound and music in the early twentieth century. This chapter traces the influence of this audial legacy on the visual dynamics of silent film. It focuses on three interrelated techniques of inaudible sound: visual noise (the first part); the treatment of motion *as* sound (the second part); and audiovisual rhythm (the third part).[6] Together, these techniques and practices allow for a fundamental rethinking of the city symphony's musical analogy. More than a metaphor for formal aesthetic structures, the musical analogy continues a tradition of Futurist and avant-garde composers, such as Russolo and Avraamov, who sought to tap into sonically marginalized yet increasingly pervasive spheres of mechanical existence in order to exert influence on social and political life. In this respect, the musical qualities of the city symphony films in this chapter are an inaudible manifestation of sound.

Noise

1

In 1916, while a student at Vladimir Bekhterev's Neurological Institute in St. Petersburg, the soon-to-be filmmaker David Kaufman (a.k.a. Dziga Vertov) embarked on the creation of a notation system for representing the seemingly indistinguishable continuum of real-world sounds. This "system" consisted largely of onomatopoeic experiments in Futurist poetry – experiments that very much resembled those of other Futurist poets such as Aleksei Kruchenykh and Velimir Khlebnikov. Vertov called the room where he worked the "Laboratory of Hearing." Here, he pursued his goal using a combination of verbal and musical symbols, but grew frustrated due to the "absence of a device by means of which [he] could record and analyse these sounds."[7] This lack, according to a 1940 diary entry, led Vertov to abandon the laboratory and pick up a film camera instead.

> Once in the spring of 1918 – returning from a train station there lingered in my ears the signs and rumble of the departing train ... someone's curses...a kiss...someone's sobbing ... laughter, a whistle, voices, the ringing of the station's bell, the puffing of the locomotive ... whispers, cries, farewells ... And I thought to myself while walking: I must get an apparatus that won't describe but will record, photograph these sounds. Otherwise it's impossible to organize, to edit them. They rush past, like time. The movie camera perhaps?

Record the visible ... Organize not the audible, but the visible world. Perhaps that's the way out?[8]

Vertov's reminiscences recall the 1937 words of John Cage, who, writing in the wake of the advent of optical-sound film, envisioned a new sound art that would come to be known as musique concrète: "The sound of a truck at fifty miles per hour. Static between the stations. Rain. We want to capture and control these sounds, to use them not as sound effects but as musical instruments."[9] Vertov's interest in filmmaking emerged from a similar desire to photograph, as it were, the audial world; the end result, however, was a practice that amplified the visual one. In 1918, mobile camera technology was more advanced than mobile recording technology, which often served as little more than a convenient notebook for ethnomusicologists. Likewise, technology for editing images together (montage) was far more advanced than technology for editing sounds; the latter would have to wait for the advent of optical-sound film. Vertov's interest in the ostensibly visual practice of filmmaking thus emerged from a then-impossible desire to edit and organize sounds that escaped traditional notation systems of music and language – that is, noises. He aimed to photograph audible phenomena; as a result, he ended up amplifying visual ones.

Vertov referred to his cinematic practice as *Kinochestvo* – "the art of organizing the necessary movements of objects in space as a rhythmical artistic whole, in harmony with the properties of the material and the internal rhythm of each object."[10] Yet far from "cleaning *Kinochestvo* of foreign matter – of music, literature, and theatre," Vertov sought his own unique rhythm not in recording the visible but in capturing an audiovisual world in which sights could be heard and sounds could be seen. Rail against traditionally defined music he did; but Vertov did not banish music entirely – certainly not the music of street sounds; nor did he seek to define his cinematic practice in purely visual terms in accordance with a tyrannical conception of medium specificity, as some have claimed.[11] Rather, his silent films – especially *Man with a Movie Camera* – anticipate the sound montage that would characterize proto–musique concrète compositions such as Walter Ruttmann's *Weekend* (1930; chapter 4). By in large, silent city symphony films, too, share in this desire to edit sounds, be they those of music, language, or seemingly unclassifiable noises – a desire that, as we have seen with respect to the compositions of Russolo and Avraamov, stems not only from a need to control noise as the Other of music and speech but also from a deeper spiritual longing to compose the city into an expression of unity. Noise's ability to transcend boundaries has the power to disrupt and challenge the validity of traditional aesthetic systems. For Russolo, noise heralded the dawning of a new mechanical era through the pain and fear it wrought on the bodies of listeners. This physical sense of cataclysm yielded ecstatic visions of men fused with machines, of the body transformed into metal, of the violence inherent in matter and the cosmos, but also of the occult unity of the material and spiritual world under the rubric of a vibratory universe. Soviet avant-garde composers such as Alexander Mosolov and Avraamov, who were part of the same artistic sphere as Vertov, composed works for industrial orchestras that embraced noise as a means of embodying the revolutionary and political spirit of the proletariat – a spirit that Avraamov conceived as embodying all aspects of material and spiritual life. Both movements led to the questioning of music as the primary mode of sonic expression by asserting a radical equivalence between the well-tempered notes of scales and the sounds of steam engines and tractors. At the same time, in the sphere of acoustics, noise became a central problem for the burgeoning technologies of telephony and sound reproduction. In this sphere, noise was defined as a "non-periodic frequency" or as "spurious and undesirable" information. Here, noise appeared as disorder that endangered order, particularly as a form of excess. Noise was not too little information, but too much – an overload of audible data that mitigated the communication of a useful signal.

Not simply something loud or unharmonious, noise is an excess that threatens a distinction or border, whether social (uncivilized/civilized), aesthetic (non-musical/musical), or technological (noise/signal). City symphony films take advantage of this dynamic at a visual level. These films generate noise through an excess of visual information that correlates to the noisy sounds implied on screen. In this regard, Ruttmann's *Berlin, Symphony of a Great City* (hence: *Berlin*) is an excellent example. Ruttmann described the film in musical terms, writing that, in it, "the most delicate pianissimo had to be consistently moved toward fortissimo. Major and minor had to be logically transformed into, or sharply contrasted with, one another. A counterpoint had to emerge out of the rhythm of man and machine."[12] The film follows the city of Berlin in five acts that evoke the rhythms and pacing of daily life, from the awakening of the city at dawn to its evening entertainments. The standard account of the film relates its compositional methods to Ruttmann's earlier abstract animations, *Lichtspiel: Opus I–V* (1921–25). Based on an analogy of "absolute music," these "light plays" (*Lichtspiele*) sought to compose shapes, colour, and light into an absolute film.

That said, in *Berlin*, these forms serve more than just an "absolute" function; they in fact amplify the implied sounds of the film, allowing them to reverberate into the film's editing. *Berlin's* image track refers to a number of such implied urban sounds including those of organ grinders, telephone operators, industrial machinery, and typewriter keys. Repeated close-ups of these objects are a constitutive element of the film's soundscape, serving to remind viewers of the continuous presence of sound in this seemingly mute universe.[13] As Michel Chion argues, silent cinema placed a high value on the representation and suggestion of aural phenomena, leading him to suggest that so-called silent cinema is better construed as "deaf." Characters in silent films often speak "even more than they would ... in a sound film, since they [have] to make visible the activity of speaking."[14] Repeated "refrain" shots of foot stomps, door knocks, ringing bells, and bellowing horns abound throughout the silent era evoking the continuous presence of sound in this seemingly mute universe. Oftentimes, these refrain shots are used to structure entire scenes, as in the case of Eisenstein's *Strike*, in which a workers' revolt is structured around a refrain shot of a factory whistle, which, in Avraamovesque fashion, also serves as a wake-up call for the proletariat.

City symphonies often depend on such refrains, structuring a scene around a motif of a particular sound, sonic practice, or sonic feature of urban life – for example, an organ grinder (*Berlin*); a wine-glass harmonium (Georges Lacombe's *La Zone*, 1928); a spoon-based percussion section (*Man with a Movie Camera*); a gramophone (Robert Siodmak and Edgar G. Ulmer's *People on a Sunday*, 1930; *La Zone*); jazz bands and nightlife (Corrado D'Errico's *Stramilano*, 1929; *Berlin*); the sounds of carnival (Jean Vigo and

Boris Kaufman's *Apropos de Nice*, 1930; Henri Storck's *Images d'Ostende*, 1929); the clacking of typewriter keys (*Berlin*); the telephone and telegraph (*Berlin*; *Man with a Movie Camera*; Rudolf Rex Lustig's *Sao Paulo, Metropolitan Symphony*, 1930), and so on. City symphonies create a montage of these sounds as part of a sonic spectrum. In Vertovian fashion, they use the silent camera as a device to photograph and organize these sounds.

One may get a better sense of how the editing of a film can amplify these implied sounds through a closer look at some scenes from *Berlin*. *Berlin's* editing makes use of fast intercutting, superimposition, and motion blur to amplify implied sounds, thereby generating the visual equivalent of their aural manifestations. Ruttmann deploys this inaudible sound technique in the amplification of the staccato-like clacking of typewriter keys. In a sequence that takes us into the offices of a large firm, we see young secretaries sitting in organized rows methodically yet speedily typing up memos. Shots of their hands alternate quickly with those of hammering type-bars, round placid faces, and circular keys, emphasizing the click-clack of a typewriter with every rapid change of frame. As the sequence progresses, the pace of the montage quickens: close-ups of keys (J, K, L) are superimposed on one another and begin to swirl, blurring and distorting until their circular motion breaks the frame rate. This motion then gives way (through a match cut) to the spinning figure of a roto-relief. Moving laterally along the theme of communication, the next sequence depicts businessmen rapidly picking up and slamming down telephone receivers. The montage then juxtaposes these shots with those of rotary dials, yelling telephone operators, telephone switchboards, barking dogs, and shrieking monkeys. The menagerie marks the cacophonous climax and abrupt conclusion of act 2 (figure 3.1).

In this scene, noise manifests itself in several ways that evoke its social, aesthetic, and technological conceptions. First, it appears as the scene's main focus – the sounds of communication. In this regard, it elides the border between human and animal sounds. Speech is presented as just another form of animal noise, thereby blurring the distinction between socially accepted and unaccepted forms of communication. The unwanted, threatening, or incomprehensible sounds of dogs and monkeys are presented as equal to those "comprehensible" sounds of men, while the

Figure 3.1 / The visual sound of typewriters.

sounds of seemingly important suit-wearing men are reduced to those of animals.[15] It is unclear who should be less flattered by the comparison. This radical likeness of social sounds is also a matter of aesthetic significance. Ruttmann's camera is attracted to noisy environments – and not just because modern life is noisy. Rather, the choice of which sounds to depict is often just as important in *Berlin* as the choice of visuals. In the above scene, it is not merely the formal, visual structure of typewriters, telephones, and switchboards that is important, but the actual sounds they make. These sounds, in turn, influence the editing. Fast cuts, for instance, emphasize the clacking of keys or the ringing of telephones. Like the noises of Futurist compositions, the filming and editing of these sounds undermines the distinction between the musical and the non-musical, as well as the distinction between the audial and the visual. In doing so, they question the primacy of traditional modes of sonic expression, thereby fulfilling a central objective of Russolo's 1913 *The Art of Noises*. Indeed, Edmund Meisels's score for Ruttmann's film relied on a number of Russoloesque noisemakers to generate sound effects.[16]

Unlike Russolo's *Awakening of a City*, Ruttmann's *Berlin* received a largely warm reception. Audiences "listened" to his film in precisely the sort of respectful, even reverent silence for which Russolo had hoped. Paradoxically, this difference in reception may be explained by the fact that, in the cinema, the traditional relationship between audience and performer is partially overturned. Instead of being treated to the rather comic and contradictory spectacle of black-tied musicians cranking music boxes (as was the case with Russolo's performance), *Berlin's* audience saw "performers" – i.e., the real people in the film – who largely resembled themselves. What is more, the audience did not have to make the conceptual leap from the sound of a wooden box (Russolo's *intonarumori*) to that of a passing train, an association that Russolo would have wanted to avoid. Rather, they could see the train accompanied by a corresponding sound or visual technique that mimicked its passing. In this manner, Ruttmann's film could both undo the typical audience-performer relationship on one level (the separation between audience member and performer), while preserving it on another (the separation between audience member and what occurs on screen).

Besides offering a Russoloesque noise performance that breaks the boundaries between audial and visual, Ruttmann's *Berlin* also presents noise in terms of its technical conception. In the above scene of secretaries and businessmen, repeated references to telephones and switchboards emphasize the material aspect of communicating a signal. The visual structure of the scene connotes a conception of noise associated with these

Figure 3.2 / Financial rollercoaster.

modes of communication. In this sequence, significant and insignificant audial information cannot be distinguished. The editing underscores this fact by presenting more visual information than the eye can handle. As such, the editing becomes a direct expression of the noise on screen, not simply as the ceaseless buzz of the office but as the overload of information generated by proliferating telephone lines.

A further instance of noise in *Berlin's* editing appears in its treatment of motion. Throughout the film one is made to feel as if one were on an amusement park ride. Indeed, such an attraction is the basis of an important scene in the film in which, after experiencing a series of flashing newspaper headlines ("crisis," "murder," "stock market," "marriage," followed by "money" six times in rapid succession), the camera suddenly shifts to a POV shot of a rollercoaster. We find ourselves flying down a hill, its tracks blurring to match the impression of streaming newspaper print. Here, we see the same alteration of shapes (lines, circles, squares) in the movement of the rollercoaster whose ups and downs give a physical sense to the inflation Germany experienced in the early 1920s (figure 3.2).

This visual motion is not merely analogous to noise. It is in fact sensed by the same inner-ear vestibular mechanism that registers both motion sickness and noise as a non-periodic frequency – namely, the sacculus. In the rollercoaster scene, noise as sound meets noise as nausea. In English, the two words share a common etymological root – the Greek *naus*, or ship – that stretches back, in evolutionary terms, to the time when "fish gill arches became inner-ear bones, and integrated balance with vibratory sensation."[17] In German, the word for noise (*Geräusch*) brings to mind another etymological connection – that of intoxication (*Rausch*), which originally signified unstable or unbalanced movement.[18] For Ruttmann, *Berlin* was akin to this feeling of drunkenness. It allowed the audience to experience the "intoxication of movement without knowing precisely where their intoxication stems from."[19] The etymological connection between intoxication, movement, and noise (Geräusch) suggests that *Berlin's* aim of generating this inebriated state has as much to do with its manipulation of sound as it does with its manipulation of sight.

2

Far from empty forms arranged musically, *Berlin's* editing reflects a concern with sound, particularly noise conceived as a phenomenon that blurs borders and distinctions. In the city symphony film canon, such a conception is apparent in scenes depicting pedestrians and traffic, as well as sequences of work and industry. Yet it is important to keep in mind that such urban-industrial scenes focused on the mechanized pace of modern life are not the only sources of noise. Noise, in other words, is not always threatening and dystopic. Often, in the city symphony, it is the product of youthful exuberance and rebellion; it communicates a kind of joyous energy, a chaotic and ludic atmosphere of carnival. The latter pervades some particularly noisy episodes from Vertov's *Man with a Movie Camera* (MMC) and Jean Vigo's *À propos de Nice*, two films related not only by their cameramen (Vertov's brother Mikhail Kaufman was the cameraman for MMC; his other brother Boris was the cameraman on *À propos de Nice*), but also by their themes and subject matter.

Perhaps the greatest city symphony of all time, MMC follows the adventures of a cameraman as he records images from four Soviet cities – Moscow, Odesa, Kharkiv, and Kyiv. The cities are never announced, though they are recognizable by their landmarks, such as the famous *Izvestia* building in Moscow or the beaches in Odesa. The film is noted for its self-aware, constructivist aesthetic – its use of canted camera angles, split screens, superimposition, freeze frames, slow motion, and reverse motion as building blocks to construct an image of the revolutionary optimism and breakneck modernization of Soviet life. The film is also lauded for baring the apparatus of filmmaking itself – not just the camera but the editing and screening process, which are successfully incorporated into the film's mise-en-abîme structure. Less well known is that the film most likely began not as project designed to showcase industry and the pace of modern life, but as a vacation film, putting it in good company with other leisure city symphonies such as Storck's *Images d'Ostende* and Vigo's *À propos de Nice*. As John MacKay argues, the notes to MMC suggest that the film began with the idea of a cameraman's holiday, a fact that is apparent in the beach scene where Mikhail Kaufman can be seen bathing alongside his tripod-mounted Le Parvo.[20]

Connections between industry and leisure as well as work and play make for fruitful comparisons when considering forms of noise that are not primarily the products of industrialization. One such scene in MMC features workers listening to the radio at a Lenin worker's club. The scene begins with a famed image of an ear superimposed on a radio receiver, an allusion to the invisible sound that permeates the club (figure 3.3). This ear is listening to images of the piano, accordion, and voice, which are superimposed over the speaker/ear. As the music pours into the club, the film cuts back and forth between shots of workers playing checkers, the instruments, and shots of hands playing spoons and bottles – an allusion to the noise orchestras promoted by the Proletarian Cultural Organization, Proletkul't,[21] of which Avraamov was a driving member. While the "traditional" music plays, the workers continue to play checkers, all but ignoring the radio. The sound of the spoons, on the other hand, appears to catch their attention. Shots of curious and smiling peasants enter the montage, alternating with close-ups of feet dancing a foxtrot and laughing women whispering jokes to one another. These images further drive home the point of the sequence – the idea that noise, laughter, and traditional music (music composed with scales and played on instruments) are parts of a sonic spectrum, each of which has an equal right to representation through composition. Such composition facilitates the understanding of the sonic environments of others, realizing one of Vertov's oft-stated goals for the cinema – the construction of a vast community of the senses, which John MacKay has called Vertov's "sensory agora."[22] As the music grows to a climax, the frantic pace of the montage increases, amplifying the sounds

Figure 3.3 / A radio-ear.

depicted on screen, until they erupt in an exuberant superimposed display of spoons, accordions, and dancing feet.

In this scene, noise manifests a power that the philosopher and literary critic Mikhail Bakhtin ascribed to laughter. For Bakhtin, laughter "not only destroys traditional connections and abolishes idealized strata; it also brings out the crude, unmediated connections between things that people otherwise seek to keep separate, in pharisaical error."[23] Here, Vertov utilizes noise to abolish not only traditional aesthetic distinctions but also the boundaries between social classes. The idealized strata, to use Bakhtin's terms, are those which seek in pharisaical error to keep noise separate from music and working-class listeners separate from bourgeois listeners. Vertov transforms the so-called noise of bottles and spoons into the collective artistic expression of the urban proletariat – an artistic expression in which they themselves participate by dancing and clapping along. Furthermore, the montage, whose fast cuts approximate the mixture of sounds emerging from the speaker, overcomes yet another social stratification – that between the proletariat and the peasantry – by bringing together images of both in its cacophonous construction. The result is a bacchanal, in which musicians participate alongside listeners as part of a collective. Indeed, it is not surprising that this scene follows immediately after the cameraman's trip to a local pub. The connotation is clear: exuberant and joyful proletarian dance should replace alcohol as a way for workers to express their dionysian urges.

On the one hand, this scene reflects the elevation of workers and peasants following the end of the New Economic Policy. On the other, it elevates these workers and peasants in terms of an aesthetic that the policies of the NEP and the First Five-Year Plan would both reject. As pointed out in chapter 2, the NEP sought to distance itself from the aims and aesthetics of avant-garde organizations such as Proletkul't, going so far as to curtail its independence. Under the NEP, the avant-garde was just one of many trends on the art market. That many avant-garde artists were hostile to the NEP does not mean that they were embraced by the new cultural order inaugurated by the Five-Year Plan and its radical break with the past – far from it. To the extent that Vertov propagandizes the plan in MMC, he does so in a cinematic idiom that accords with the aesthetic currents of the avant-garde. The elevation of workers and peasants in terms of a collective noise making that overcomes the distinctions of traditional music rejects the policies of the NEP and, to a certain extent, is in accord with the aims of the Five-Year Plan; yet it is far from embracing the top-down aesthetic and political logic of Stalinism.

In this regard, in the above scene, Vertov faced a similar problem to that of his contemporary, Avraamov. Like MMC, the *Symphony of Sirens* sought to fuse the aesthetic aims of noise (unseating traditional forms of music) with its political aims (embodying the sounds of the proletariat). In harnessing noise's power to bring together these separate social strata, however, Avraamov encountered a problem – namely, how to shape noise into a composition that was worthy of the proletariat's heroic striving. While the levelling power of noise broke down social and aesthetic barriers, it still required direction, particularly one that was aligned with the goals of the party. As we see in chapter 2, Avraamov provided such direction by a curious device – a steam engine outfitted with pipes (the *magistral'*) tuned to play "La Marseillaise" and "The Internationale." In this manner, the worker's "noise" – the sound of steam whistles – could be channelled into a melody that represented the goals of the revolution, thereby achieving a curious marriage between the spontaneous energy of the workers and the conscious direction of the Party.

Avoiding a simplistic solution like Avraamov's, Vertov utilizes the camera to achieve this kind of control. The above scene from MMC does not so much dispel traditional distinctions between musical and non-musical sounds as displace them. Initially considered a chaotic mess, here noise becomes the site of increasingly nuanced and refined classifications – spoon noise, bottle noise, feet-tapping noise, etc. – that the cinematic apparatus organizes. Noise leads paradoxically back to the very discontinuity that its indistinguishable continuity threatened. Just as Avraamov relies on the steam-whistle machine to transform workers' noise into discrete sounds, so Vertov, in accordance with the stated aims of his "Laboratory of Hearing," uses the cataloguing power of the cinematic apparatus to isolate each noise from the continuum of sound, thereby making it fitting material for composition. Initially a means to undo distinctions, noise itself becomes the locus of further distinctions.

This dialectic is also present in Vigo's *À propos de Nice*. On the surface, aside from the fact that its cameraman was Vertov's youngest brother, the film may appear to have little in common with *Man with a Movie Camera*. It belongs to a particular subgenre of leisure city symphonies (most notably Storck's *Images d'Ostende*), films marked by their fascination with the rhythms of seaside towns and the tourists who flock to their shores. (One of the first images of *À propos de Nice*, just after the fireworks display, is of two puppet tourist dolls being raked up by an unseen croupier.) Like *Images d'Ostende*, Vigo's film is heavily influenced by surrealism – from which it borrows trick effects reminiscent of sequences from René Claire's *Entr'acte* (1924) – and French Impressionist cinema – from which it takes its dreamy fascination with water. As its title suggests, the film follows a day in the life of Nice, a resort city in the south of France, taking the viewer on a tour of its beaches, hotels, streets, and markets. The first half of the film is punctuated by a tension between idle tourists (representing the bourgeois order) and the city's proletarian and underclasses (workers, child-laborers, beggars, gypsies, and lepers). Lounging in their deck chairs, the former are often shown fending off the latter.

This tension comes to a head in the second part of the film, which is marked by a carnival procession complete with life-size papier-mâché dolls, can-canning dancers, and drunken revellers. Here, the noisy images of carnival – dancing, music, laughter, shouting – filmed at alternating fast and slow frame rates function as refrain shots in Chion's sense. They are reminders of the raucous atmosphere that has suddenly descended on Nice, disrupting its usual rhythms and social distinctions. In this respect, scenes of carnival – especially a slow-motion shot of dancing young women revealing their legs and undergarments – are juxtaposed with images of the establishment – police officers, warships, clergy, an epauletted doorman, and an older bourgeois lady. On the one hand, as Michael Temple points out, this juxtaposition may signify the revolutionary potential of popular entertainments – a dance whose joyous violence has the power to purify, to bring down the established order. On the other, it may be just another instance of "bread and circuses," a steam release for revolutionary energy and popular discontent. The film ends without resolving this tension in either direction.[24]

As we see in chapter 2, a ludic atmosphere of carnival pervades Avraamov's *Symphony of Sirens*, which came on the heels of the 1920 First Congress of the Peoples of the East. Such an atmosphere was characteristic of early mass spectacles in the Soviet Union before they took on a more solemn and regimented form. Vertov's film is also characterized by a carnival-like atmosphere, especially toward the end, where traditional distinctions and temporalities are abolished in a celebratory explosion of Revolutionary energy (all grasped by the Kino-Eye). The noisiness of these scenes may be thought of in two ways. First, there is the implied noise of the celebratory images – shots of laughing, dancing, percussion, shouting, and so on. These shots are often edited in such a way that the montage or the camera's movement mimics or complements their noise. Second, there is the goal that such scenes seek to accomplish. That is to say, they aim to undermine a border or distinction in a manner characteristic of Attali's description of noise or Bakhtin's characterization of laughter, both of which are strikingly similar in this context.

The dialectic between noise and order – undoing distinctions and establishing new ones – is also present in *Berlin*, albeit with less of an emphasis on the ludic violence of carnival, and more of an emphasis on re-establishing the harmonious order of a symphony. The film catalogues sounds the same way it catalogues images. Each noise is rendered discrete, a compositional element unto itself. The aim is not simply to undo distinctions – e.g., between speech and noise – but to create new ones by means of a device that, in principle, could isolate any sound whatsoever. In this regard, both Ruttmann's inaudible sound techniques reveal a concern with the management of noise and aural environments – a concern he shares with Futurist and avant-garde composers such as Russolo and Avraamov, as well as twentieth century noise-abatement campaigners. Far from simply liberating noise, these composers sought different ways of controlling and cataloguing it by designing an arsenal of new musical instruments, notational systems, and compositional methods. Rather than isolate and get rid of noise, they sought to isolate and incorporate it into new modes of composition. Similarly, for Ruttmann, Vertov, and Vigo the paradox of noise provided both opportunities and stumbling blocks for socially minded compositions. On the one hand, noise's otherness made it useful to uphold traditional social and aesthetic distinctions; on the other, this very otherness, revealed their porousness. Finally, the attempt to harness noise's power to undo differences led, ultimately, to attempts to develop newer and more precise distinctions.

Motion

In *Noise, Water, Meat*, Douglas Kahn makes the playful suggestion that the line is the meeting point of *"audio* ('I hear') and *video* ('I see')."[25] The suggestion captures the ethos of vibratory modernism – the idea, as discussed in chapter 1, that all phenomena, from sight to thought and beyond, are expressions of different frequencies of vibration and therefore amenable to graphic representation. The two moments – audio and video – run through the history of sound, from the earliest vibrations of the "single string of the Pythagorean monochord" – the basis for Western musical intervals – to the drawn sound (phono-graphic) experiments of Ernst Chladni, Édouard-Leon Scott, and Thomas Edison. Such experiments helped visualize, for the first time, the movement of airwaves as frequencies. They made, in Kahn's words, the "invisible visible."

In *Gramophone, Film, Typewriter,* Friedrich Kittler makes a similar point in describing a paradigm shift from the Pythagorean logic of intervals – the fourth, the fifth, the octave – to a physics of frequencies.[26] Formerly conceived as a ratio whose relations expressed the harmony of celestial spheres, sound became over the course of the nineteenth and twentieth centuries a field of investigation for the science of acoustics. The line, in turn, proved to be more than just a passive trace, a remnant of something that has already occurred; instead, it produced sound – from the purest tones to the harshest noises – that could be drawn directly onto vinyl or tape. This active trace manifests itself in the second way that city symphonies sound the inaudible. This takes the form of a dynamic inscription through bodies and motions. Vertov's and Ruttmann's films draw sound, as it were, onto the celluloid of their film strips using the figures of the city. Motion, in their films, is a manifestation of sound; it makes the inaudible audible.

Nowhere is the audible line more apparent than in Vertov's famed theory of the movement interval. For Vertov, the mere representation of movement is not, in and of itself, the basis for cinema's powerful effects. Instead, "the material – the elements of the art of movement – is composed of the *intervals* (the transition from one movement to another) and by no means of the movements themselves. It is they (the intervals) that draw the action to a kinetic resolution."[27] Much has been written about what precisely Vertov means by "interval."[28] In the introduction to the English translation of Vertov's writings, for instance, Annette Michelson writes that this term refers to the "movement between frames and the proportion of these pieces as they relate to one another."[29] Alexander Graf, by contrast, has criticized Michelson for writing "frames" when she should have written shots, thereby mistaking the mere technical aspect of montage – one isolated frame following another – for the creative possibility of editing shots together.[30] In fact, whether the movement interval occurs between frames or shots is not important, given Vertov's modular conception of the interval. One can always subdivide and create finer intervals – until one reaches the frame rate – or create larger intervals between shots. Vertov's intervals are not well tempered – they exist along a continuum. This is the point of numerous sequences throughout MMC in which the film stops and analyzes movement – e.g., of a running horse – frame by frame, or in which it contextualizes movement in the production of the film as a whole – e.g., in filming the film strip itself.

More importantly, these debates over the meaning of the interval miss the full implications of the musical analogy, which places Vertov's film practice in the context of the history of drawn sound. In tonal terms, the movement interval expresses the relationship between movements as notes – say C and F-sharp – organized along a frequency spectrum. In his manifesto, Vertov builds these movements into phrases and calls for the development of graphic "cine-scales" to notate not just their rhythm but their direction as well.[31] In doing so, he draws a historical connection between the theory of the movement interval and experiments in graphic or drawn sound. Here, it is important to recognize these experiments as existing along an audiovisual continuum that emerged out of technologically enhanced means of representing sound and motion – for example, the phonograph and photograph. At the visual pole of this continuum, figures such as theatre director Vsevolod Meyerhold took inspiration from the time-motion experiments of Étienne Jules-Marey and Edweard Muybridge to create a music-like notation system for dance movements. At the audial pole, Russolo and Avraamov – along with now-forgotten composers such as Evgeny Sholpo, Nikolai Voinov, and Boris Yankovsky – developed graphic notation systems that reflected the plurality of microtones – that is, frequencies – between notes.[32] Proliferating throughout the 1920s and '30s, these experiments gave rise to modes of representation that not only resemble but are also in fact a form of abstract film. In the 1930s, for instance, Avraamov and Yankovsky drew ornamental soundtracks that were photographed and played back as films by a projector and loudspeaker (figure 3.4).[33]

These synthetic sound films presented visual motion *as* audible sound in the form of abstract or representative patterns similar to those found in Ruttmann's *Opus* animations. One film, for instance, shows a series of waxing and waning triangles, semicircles, waves, and bars; another amplifies

Figure 3.4 / Ornamental soundtracks drawn by Arseny Avraamov. *Left* image (1930); *right* image (1931).

a series of alternating black and white faces. Treating movement as sound, Vertov approaches these experiments from the other direction, as it were: not from movement to sound, but from sound to movement. The movement interval is not a representation of audible phenomena but the conception of movement *as* an audible phenomenon. More than a musical analogy, it is part of a historical moment that considered the boundaries between sound and sight as malleable.

The visual forms of Ruttmann's *Berlin* have similar audible echoes that may be heard in the film's opening sequence. Here, an image of water – one that recurs throughout the city symphony canon in films such as Joris Ivens's *Rain* (1929), Vigo's *À propos de Nice*, László Moholy-Nagy's *Marseiller Haffen* (1929), Storck's *Images d'Ostende*, and Marcel Carné *Nogent: Eldorado du Dimanche* (1929) – serves as the film's Ur-form. This image is reminiscent of noise in terms of what Douglas Kahn calls "all sound." For Kahn, all sound is the result of the phonograph's incursion into the world of music: the phonograph's ability to hear and record everything makes any frequency whatsoever a possible basis for composition.[34] Just as noise contains such a heterogeneous number of frequencies that no single one of them can be distinguished – hence implying all sounds – so water contains such a great number of potential shapes that no single figure can be discerned. It holds out the promise – as Christa Blümlinger points out paraphrasing Gilles Deleuze – "of an extended human perception,"[35] one that finds expression in impressionist city symphonies such as Henri Chomette's *Jeux des reflets et de la vitesse* (1925), which tracks the flow of Parisian railways and waterways. From *Berlin*'s opening liquid image of all shapes, three particular ones emerge: the line, the circle, and the square. Together they amount to a graphic trichord, a statement of the film's visual tonality. These three forms alternate at an increasingly rapid tempo until they begin to vibrate, giving way (through a match dissolve) to a pair of falling railroad crossbars. The sequence that follows is a jarring one, emblematic of the shock, pace, and dislocation associated with machinery and modernity. A speeding train nearly runs over the camera. As the train advances toward Berlin, we see the same graphic elements repeated in the swift alteration of wheels (circle), tracks (square), and power lines (line). These shapes continue to repeat themselves throughout the film in the guise of revolving doors, windows, traffic signals, rollercoaster rides, and so on (figure 3.5).[36]

In composing with shapes derived from a fluid image of all possible figures, Ruttmann's *Berlin*, like Vertov's ммс, also finds a place in the tradition of drawn sound. The film operates according to principles that, not three years after its release, would guide the synthetic sound experiments of Rudolf Pfenninger and Oskar Fischinger. Indeed, there is a sense in which Ruttmann's film contains elements of both Pfenninger's and Fischinger's approaches to drawing, photographing, and projecting sound. Fischinger, as Thomas Y. Levin notes, was intrigued by the possibility of acoustic-visual isomorphism. Suspecting that "there was more than an accidental relationship between the physical shape of an object and its auditory manifestation," Fischinger embarked on a search for a "deep and previously inaccessible common structural logic that governs both

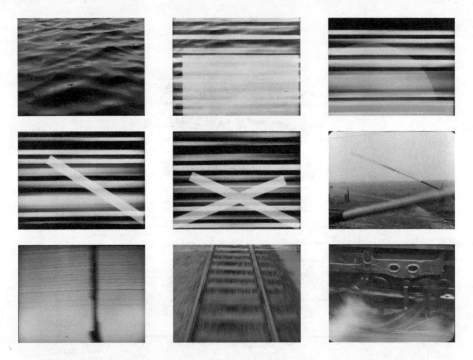

Figure 3.5 / Elementary shapes emerging from water.

the most prevalent ornamental practices of a given society and its dominant auditory patterns."[37] As one rightly suspects, this search had its nationalist and colonialist overtones. Fischinger argued that acoustic-visual ornaments manifested "'personal, national and characteristic traits' akin to a kind of cultural 'mouthwriting'" (as opposed to handwriting).[38] He thus recommended investigating "the [visual] ornaments of primitive tribes in terms of their tonal character."[39] With these concerns in mind, Fischinger in his experiments typically focuses on the sonic manifestations of the visual ornament (figure 3.6).

By contrast, Pfenninger's experiments were closer in spirit to those of Soviet sound engineers such as Nikolai Voinov, Aleksandr Ivanov, and Avraamov. Rather than concentrate on the aesthetics of the ornament as a manifestation of culture, Pfenninger aimed to develop a new graphic-sound language composed of discrete sound curves, each representing a different sound. "Despite the potential visual appeal of their sine-wave

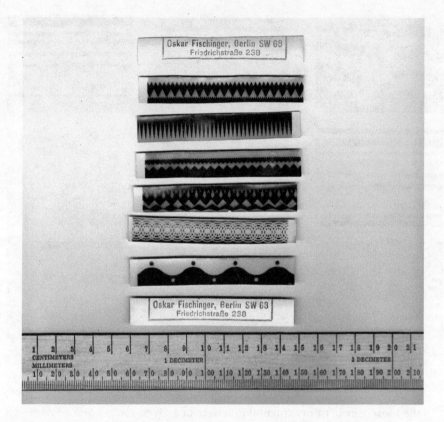

Figure 3.6 / Examples of original strips used in Oskar Fischinger's *Ornament Sound* experiments.

forms," Levin notes, the curves "are decidedly not ornaments but are rather ... 'templates or print-types'; that is, semiotic entities that can be combined to produce sounds in a linguistic – which is to say, thoroughly technical and rule-governed – manner."[40] In creating such sound templates, Pfenninger's goal was to break free from traditional musical instruments and conventional notation, thereby ushering in an era of composition that had all possible frequencies at its disposal. Perhaps the most important distinction to draw between this project and Fischinger's is that, as Levin points out, the latter still operates according to a logic of acoustic indexicality, while Pfenninger's essentially undermines such a logic. Fischinger's sounds always point back to their respective graphic traces and vice versa.

He thus composes a "proleptic musique concrete" with already existing graphic forms.[41] Pfenninger, on the other hand, anticipates the sound synthesis of electronic music – he creates sounds that are not intended as the indexical markers of their respective wave structures. His curves "depend, strictly speaking, on only the particular – and in the last analysis, arbitrary – properties of the selenium cell that is the basis of the particular optical cinema sound system he used to produce his sonic graphematics."[42] If Fischinger is intrigued by the graphic manifestation of sound as ornament and (culturally determined) mouth-writing, then Pfenninger is interested in graphic sound as sign system and typewriter.

Besides being indebted to the same absolute film practice from which Ruttmann draws inspiration, both Pfenninger's and Fischinger's approaches to drawn sound are contained embryonically, as it were, in Ruttmann's film. The opening sequence of sound shapes, for instance, anticipates Pfenninger's semantic experiments with graphic forms. Ruttmann's film is not about the sounds that lines, circles, and squares make; rather he uses these to evoke a myriad of different urban sounds. These shapes form a rule-governed graphic musical system that is, to a certain extent, arbitrary in the same way that the signs of a given language are arbitrary markers of the concepts they represent. How a square or circular shape complements an implied sound on screen is determined by its use in the film. At the same time, Ruttmann's film never strays far from the sounds that actual things make. Its circles, squares, and lines are a way of sounding the real-world objects from which they are derived. In this regard, as Nora M. Alter notes, the film, like Fischinger's experiments, prefigures "in certain ways what would decades later be realized as concrete music."[43] Ruttmann, in other words, is not concerned with new never-before-heard, non-indexical sounds. Instead, his film uses a visual sound notation to bring the sounds of the street to life.

Ruttmann's shapes also function in a third musical manner: they serve to regulate the emotional energy of his film. Varying according to different tempos and combinations, these figures form motifs that evoke the diverse and conflicting temporalities of the city including awakening, work, leisure, and rest. In doing so, they touch on a number of social themes including migration and class difference. The interaction between these shapes – particularly that between linearity and circularity – regulates *Berlin*'s composition, with each shape taking on different culturally determined associations. As Sabine Hake notes, in *Berlin*, "the principle of forward movement is usually associated with activity, directness, energy, and power."

> Throughout the film, linearity signifies control. By contrast, loss of control and surrender to the attractions of the metropolis are visualized through the principle of spirality or circularity. The appearance of the spiral indicates extremely subjective perspectives, as during the roller-coaster ride, or it prepares the ground for a complete reinterpretation of the visible world, as in the animated sequences ... With these associations, circularity stands for the city's more dangerous and disturbing aspects: repetition, emptiness, chaos, frenzy, vertigo, madness.[44]

More than just an organizing structure for the film, this dialectic implies a philosophical and scientific conception of forms as active principles that regulate growth. Such an idea is present, for instance, in Goethe's later writings on plants in which he conceives of plant development in terms of two opposing tendencies – the spiral and the vertical. For Goethe, as Sabine Mainberger neatly summarizes, the "spiral tendency of vegetation" manifests itself in "spiral forms/growth of plants, and when this form binds itself to a vertical form, the resulting whole is associated with both sexes: the spiralled tendency acquires a feminine connotation and the vertical tendency a masculine connotation."[45] In *Berlin*, as Hake points out, the spiral and vertical are similarly coded according to gender. Episodes of circular motion tend to follow female characters such as the secretaries typing up memos or the woman in the suicide sequence. Episodes of linear motion, on the other hand, tend to follow masculine professions – police officers and firefighters. Like a healthy plant, Ruttmann's *Berlin* is the product of a balance between these tendencies – the circular motion of the spiral channelled into the linear striving and directness of the vertical. Such a notion has an echo in the idea of cinema itself – the linear film strip on the circular reel.

Rhythm

1

"In silent film," Michel Chion suggests, "all movement, such as the shimmering water behind Janet Gaynor in the rowboat in Murnau's *Sunrise* (1927)" – or, for that matter, the opening image of water in Ruttmann's *Berlin* – "is automatically suggestive of sound: there is a continuity between the (noisy) whistle of the steam locomotive and the (silent) smoke of a cigarette."[46] In this sense, the dynamic range of sound in a silent film is greater than that of a sound film. Water (as in Ruttmann's *Berlin*, Ivens's *Rain*, and Kaufman's *Les Halles*); the play of light on reflective surfaces (as in Henri Chomette's *Jeux des reflets et de la vitesse*); or the traces of wind on sand and sea foam (Storck's *Images d'Ostende*); all play an important sonic role in city symphony films. These images are not only evocative of sound, but are directly tied to new practices of sound storage and transmission that bridge the audial and the visual. They operate along the meeting place of "I see" and "I hear."

This meeting place – the line – is also integral to the study of rhythm – a phenomenon that bridges sight, movement, and sound. In the nineteenth and twentieth centuries, scientific advances that made it possible to visualize, trace, and materialize sound also made it possible to track the movement of bodies in time and space. Étienne Jules-Marey's chronotographic gun (1882) and Edweard Muybridge's motion photography (1886) became the basis not just for cinema but for the time-motion studies of Frank and Lilian Gilbreth, pioneers, along with Frederick Winslow Taylor, of scientific management.[47] As Michael Cowan points out, the main axis around which these debates and experiments revolved was a conflict between "natural-biological" and "artificial-technological" rhythms.[48] Conservative philosophers such as Ludwig Klages, for instance, sought to drive a hard-and-fast distinction between these two poles, going so far as to declare that the latter (technological rhythm) was not a form of rhythm at all. Klages, according to Cowan, "insisted on the absolute dissociation of rhythm from anything resembling the movement of a machine."[49] Echoing Bergson, he argued that mechanical movements lacked continuity; like the camera, they cut into the fabric of time, creating artificial divisions and boundaries.

Derived from the Greek verb for *flow*, true rhythm was vital, irrational, and non-identical; it was impossible to systematize. It manifested itself in the ebb and flow of waves, the phases of the moon, the "alteration of waking and sleeping states, energy and fatigue, hunger and satiation, thirst and the aversion to fluids."[50]

Klages's conception of rhythm, as the linguist Émile Benveniste would point out, is based on a false etymology. In his famous essay "The Notion of 'Rhythm' in its Linguistic Expression," Benveniste argues that "it was not in contemplating the play of waves on the shore that the primitive Hellene discovered 'rhythm;' it is, on the contrary, we who are making metaphors today when we speak of the rhythm of the waves."[51] There is no evidence, according to Benveniste, of a semantic connection between *rhytmos* (rhythm) and *rhein* (flow) via the pounding of waves in Greek literature. Instead, tracing the term through the writings of Luecippus, Democritus, Herodotus, Plato and Aristotle, Benveniste suggests that *rhythmos* originally meant form, albeit in a very specific sense. Unlike *schema*, which defines a "fixed form," *rhythmos* "designates the form in the instant that it is assumed by what is moving, mobile and fluid, the form of that which does not have organic consistency; it fits the pattern of a fluid element, of a letter arbitrarily shaped, of a robe which one arranges at one's will, of a particular state of character or mood. It is the form as improvised, momentary, changeable."[52] Rhythm, in other words, was not derived from the pulsations of the ocean; rather, it was a term that could be applied to fix any "fluid" situation – a meaning that, two millennia later, would be technically realized by photography, film, and the gramophone. The musical conception of rhythm was first formulated by Plato, who tied *rhythmos* as "'distinctive form, disposition, [and] proportion'" to ideas of metre, harmony, and bodily movement, thereby solidifying the contemporary definition of rhythm as "a configuration of movements organized in time."[53]

Klages, as Cowan points out, had difficulty maintaining a hard-and-fast distinction between organic and mechanical rhythms, particularly when considering the effects of certain mechanical rhythms on human beings. Faced with the fact that trains often put passengers to sleep, Klages argued that it was not the rhythm of the wheels that was responsible for this soporific effect, but rather the continuous forward motion of the train.

Yet, if Benveniste's etymology is correct, it is in fact Klages who is mistakenly making an arbitrary distinction between mechanic and organic rhythms based on a romanticized conception of the meaning the term held for the Greeks. By contrast, though they still partially subscribed to an artificial dichotomy of mechanic and organic rhythms, theorists such as Georg Simmel, György Lukács, and Émile Jacques-Dalcroze (the founder of rhythmic gymnastics) sought different ways of reconciling humans and machine rhythms in domains ranging from economics to literature. One of the most important influences on these figures was the economist Karl Bücher, whose now-forgotten 1897 study *Labor and Rhythm* (*Arbeit und Rhythmus*) postulated that rhythm emerged, in the words of John MacKay, from "the need to labor collectively, to amass and apply the energy of a group." For Bücher, MacKay continues, rhythm was "a mode of corporeal communication" that united "workers 'organically,' rather than through the imposition of some external disciplinary schema.[54]" What concerned Bücher and other theorists of his ilk was not drawing a distinction between human and machine rhythms, but rather fusing the two together in a "higher rhythmic unity" that would overcome the alienation of factory work in industrial society.[55]

From this context yet another interpretation of the city symphony (in general) emerges. The city symphony experimented with different – and at times violent – ways of fusing organic and mechanic rhythms. This fascination with the rhythms of the city dates back to the nineteenth century, manifesting itself prominently in works such as Adalbert Stifter's "Vom Sankt-Stephansturme" and E.T.A Hoffmann's "Des Vetters Eckfenster," both of which presented their respective cities in mechanic and organic terms. Studies such as Bücher's may have influenced the composition of city symphonies in the twentieth century more directly. Avraamov, for instance, attempted to combine patterns of regimented labour with periodic expressions of ludic festivity into a larger rhythmic whole. His article on the *Symphony of Sirens*, in which he traces the history of music back to Orpheus and the practice of communal singing as a means of social organization, bears the marks of Bücher's ideas. Similarly, Vertov, as MacKay argues, may have been directly influenced by Bücher, whose works he would have encountered as a student at the pioneering neuroscientist

Vladimir Bekhterev's Psychoneurological Institute in St Petersburg.[56] Such an encounter, along with Vertov's decades-long interest in music and sonic phenomena, casts his proclamations in "We. A Variant of a Manifesto" in a new light. Vertov's disdain for the clumsy movements of humans in comparison to the precise movements of machines should be understood against a backdrop of a Bücher-inspired search for greater rhythmic unity and harmony, especially as a means of proletarian communal expression.[57]

At the same time, city symphony films were concerned with reconciling not the rhythms of labour and machinery, but rather the array of rhythms that characterized the city. Ivens's *Rain*, Kaufman's *Les Halles*, Leyda's *Bronx Morning*, Storck's *Images d'Ostende*, and Carné's *Nogent: Eldorado du Dimanche* all feature moments of stillness, rest, or otherwise inexact rhythms. Even Vertov's feverishly paced *Man with a Movie Camera* – though it is typically viewed as sensory training for the creation of "perfect electric men" – began, as noted earlier, as a vacation film.[58] Such rhythmic comparisons and contrasts cut across city symphonies as part of their attempt to strike a new balance between the changing patterns that constituted modern urban life. Their interest in rhythm cannot be understood in purely visual or sonic terms. Rather, like noise and vibration, rhythm in the city symphony is presented as an audiovisual phenomenon that not only provides insight into the fabric of urban life but also can be actively deployed to create new conceptions of the city.

In *Berlin*, for instance, abstract forms do not simply marshal visual impressions according to linear and circular patterns; rather, as in the experiments of Fischinger and Pfenninger, they are a manifestation of sound, albeit one that is not heard through the ears. The interaction between these patterns composes the metropolis as a classical symphony. Circular figures build tension through disorienting perspectives that generate feelings of chaos; linear figures provide resolution through stable perspectives that reimpose control. This happens at various moments throughout the film. The opening train sequence disorients the viewer with a chaotic alteration of shapes and subjective perspectives, only to have order re-established in the next shot depicting a straight line to Berlin. The rollercoaster scene's jumble of circular and wavelike movements builds to a chaotic climax that culminates in a woman jumping from a bridge. It is followed by a sequence that reimposes order through depictions of police officers directing traffic. Spinning doors and roto-reliefs give way to train tracks and traffic signals. Their alteration drives toward the film's concluding shot – a spinning spotlight atop a radio tower – a metaphor for the vertical and circular striving of the modern city as well as the film that illuminates it.

The dynamics of Ruttmann's film may be related to the musical philosophy of Jacques Attali (outlined in chapter 1). For Attali, noise's threat to borders presents itself as a threat of violence that music, in turn, seeks to harness in order to generate reassurance. This dialectic embodies the dynamics of power, violence, and legitimacy that serve as the foundation for political communities. Ruttmann's city symphony manages noise in accordance with a similar dialectic of chaos and control. The film generates tension through a combination of fast editing, motion blur, and circular movement and provides resolution through steady editing, oriented perspectives, and linear motion. Cowan traces the origins of this dynamic to Ruttmann's career in advertising. The line, the circle, and the square, as Cowan argues, were more than just aesthetically engaging patterns; instead, they were a means of managing information flows, economies of attention, and democratic complexity. The abstract forms of Ruttmann's symphony sought to legitimate cinema "as a means of managing the multiplicity of mass society: of training and guiding perception, conceptualizing the city, winning audiences over for products, influencing public health, and – after 1933 – commanding audience allegiance to the new regime."[59] In *Berlin*, these forms of management sought to create a moving image of consistency. Circular and linear forms strove ultimately toward a uniform representation of various urban phenomena, hence "underscoring the similarities and regularities between, people, animals, technologies and objects from different spheres."[60]

The same scientific and technological developments that gave rise to Pfenninger's and Fischinger's experiments in visual sound supported Ruttmann's work in advertising. As Cowan notes, Ruttmann's understanding of the powers of the abstract trace developed out of the study of psychophysics.[61] An offshoot of vibratory modernism, psychophysics held that, since both consist of movements, mental and physical states could influence each other.[62] Popular with advertisers and avant-garde artists – not to mention corporate executives and labour managers – this idea emerged from the same kinds of studies that advanced the fields of photography and acoustics. Like audio and video, psychophysics followed the rhythmic pulsations of the line. The use of abstract forms in Ruttmann's film is thus not merely analogous to music; rather, it is a means of managing a political economy in accordance with scientific principles that govern visual, aural, and even mental phenomena. Like Fischinger's ornaments, these phenomena share a common structural logic based on physical laws of motion.

A similar lineage may be traced for Vertov and composers such as Avraamov, both of whom were influenced by the Soviet-Taylorist poet Alexei Gastev's time-motion studies of labour.[63] However, unlike Ruttmann, whose film created a dynamic of tension and release, Vertov's film drives toward a resolution of a different kind – one not of harmony and balance but of ecstasy and electricity. The movement interval's "kinetic resolution" is related to both aesthetics and engineering. The Russian word for resolution (*razreshenie*) may be used in both senses: as either the resolution to the dominant tone or the solution to a technical problem. For Vertov, this problem is bluntly stated from the outset: "our path – from the bumbling citizen through the poetry of the machine to the perfect electric man."[64] As a solution to this problem, the movement interval creates a counterpoint between humans and machines that culminates in the acceleration of time itself. For Vertov, machines do not beat with steady regularity. In fact, they are far more flexible than humans; their movements "curve, straighten out, divide, split, multiply again and again," all with a grace of control that makes Vertov "ashamed of humanity's inability to control itself." By composing these movements, the movement interval creates the sense that time itself is malleable material: "Drawing in motion," Vertov writes, "blueprints in motion." These manifest "the theory of relativity on the screen."[65]

Such a conception of time is evident throughout ммс in segments that make use of reverse, frozen, and sped-up motion. Indeed, one way to view the film is as an increasing progression of such temporal breaks. In this respect, the film begins subtly with a shot of pigeons flying in reverse and slow motion – the graphic equivalent of a crab canon (a musical palindrome) in which the same melody is played forward and backward simultaneously. This figure announces a break with the temporality of "nature," which the film exposes as an artificially imposed linear time. The next major segment is that of a running horse whose movements are decomposed into individual frames recalling Muybridge's photographs. Last, in the final segment of the film, these techniques return in a symphonic restatement of the film's main themes at greater amplitude and intensity. Two counter-rotating shots of the Bolshoi Theatre in Moscow cause the building to implode, signalling a break with the cultural past. Next, a shot of a pendulum swinging in fast motion announces the speeding-up of time that follows. The speed of the montage rips us out of the linear temporality of the everyday, yet at the end of the film, the original temporality is not restored – disorder is not provoked so that the order may be reimposed. Instead, the new, chaotic temporality takes the place of the old, ushering in an era of accelerated progress, in which the pace of human and mechanical production will overtake time itself.

To some, such a conception of time may recall the logic of Stalin's Five-Year Plan. Announced during the production of ммс, the plan combined utopian aspirations with a wartime economic mentality. In attempting a radical break with the past, it sought not to modernize in time, but to modernize time itself through scientific planning.[66] There is thus a fundamental ambiguity in Vertov's presentation of time. To be sure, time is a material whose manipulations are subject to regimes of observation and scientific planning, particularly in the interest of coordinating efforts for the sudden advancement of society. At the same time, as Devin Fore has pointed out, these various spatiotemporal "flections" create an image of urban life that is anything but linear, thus undermining the Five-Year Plan's narrative of progress. Indeed, in subverting linear temporality, as well as its three-dimensional analogue, Euclidean space, the film undermines the very temporal and spatial foundations on which the Five-Year Plan is built. As instances of the movement interval, the above segments stop, reverse, repeat, slow down, and speed up motion to demonstrate that time as well as space is a "heterogeneous and fundamentally plastic field of investigation."[67] In Ruttmann's terms, this tension between linear and non-linear time – as well as Euclidean and non-Euclidean space – might be restated as one between order and chaos – linearity and circularity. Ruttmann attempts to resolve this problem in the idea of the repetitive society – society as an automaton of controlled growth. Vertov, on the other hand, exacerbates it, stretching it to the point of annihilation. The film's concluding scene accelerates montage – the pace of progress – but only to recapitulate the entire film; the film masters time, only to send it streaming in the opposite direction. In this sense, the film does not resolve this tension, but rather, in a manner similar to Rabelaisian laughter, connects those sides – future and past, progress and regress – that totalitarian powers would rather keep separate.

2

Rhythm as, in Benveniste's words, "form in the instant that it is assumed by what is moving, mobile and fluid," is at the heart of the city symphony film's audiovisual conception. In this respect, the city symphony film performs in both sonic and visual terms what Henri Lefebvre, borrowing a term from Gaston Bachelard, calls *rhythmanalysis*, a method of investigating the phenomena of everyday life in terms of their biological, psychological, and social rhythms. As Stuart Elden notes, Lefebvre "uses rhythm as a mode of analysis – a *tool* of analysis rather than just an object of it – to examine and re-examine a range of topics."[68] These include Lefebvre's main preoccupations, the production of space and time, but also the city, the media, commodification, gesture, music, and many others. Lefebvre's analysis centres on the body as a unity of diverse rhythms, one that can be influenced in various ways by the rhythms of natural, mechanical, and social phenomena. Like Klages, he divides the world into natural and mechanic rhythms, what Lefebvre calls cyclical rhythms (waves, sleeping and waking states, the phases of the moon, etc.) and linear rhythms (machinery, the clock). As such, it is no surprise that Lefebvre thinks the camera incapable of rhythmanalysis: "No camera, no image or series of images can show these rhythms" – that is, the rhythms of the city. "It requires equally attentive eyes and ears, a head and a memory and a heart."[69]

The city symphony film as an audiovisual phenomenon makes a good case for the opposite conclusion – one that, moreover, accords with a broader Lefebvreian project of critiquing a Bergsonian conception of duration that, as Lefebvre sees it, stresses the unitary, cohesive, and continuous nature of time over the fragmentary and discontinuous. As Elden points out, a precursor to Lefebvre's late notion of rhythmanalysis is his "theory of moments," which he articulated in the 1920s. "For Lefebvre, moments are significant times when existing orthodoxies are open to challenge, when things have the potential to be overturned or radically altered ... Rather than the Bergsonian notion of *durée*, duration, Lefebvre [privileges] the importance of the instant."[70] Such a conception of the instant has its roots in Nietzsche's notion of the *Augenblick*, the moment, "the blink of an eye," and the "image of eternal recurrence."[71] To illustrate this idea in terms of rhythm, Elden, following Elizabeth Deeds Ermarth, cites a passage from Vladimir Nabokov's *Ada or Ardor*: "Maybe the only thing that hints at a sense of Time is rhythm; not the recurrent beats of the rhythm but the gap between two such beats, the grey gap between black beats: the Tender interval. The regular throb itself merely brings back the miserable idea of measurement, but in between, something like true Time lurks."[72] As an illustration of Lefebvre's ideas, Nabokov's description of time brings us back to the city symphony by way of Vertov's conception of the movement interval, of *Kinochestvo* as "the art of organizing the necessary movements of objects in space as a rhythmical artistic whole, in harmony with the properties of the material and the internal rhythm of each object."[73] Of course, not all city symphonies embody Vertov's idea. Nevertheless, this quotation suggests that the city symphony film as an exploration of the audiovisual rhythms of the city is far from imposing a regimented mechanical schema onto temporality, whether conceived as duration or as rhythmic moments. Rather, the city symphony is capable of exploring the discontinuous-yet-repetitive temporality of everyday urban life. Instead of starting with duration and then thinking of the cinema as cutting into time, why not start with rhythm, which is already a segmentation of time, and consider the cinema as further exploring the gaps where time is rumoured to lurk – that is, as a form of rhythmanalysis?

The musical idea at the heart of the city symphony film suggests that such an analysis is certainly worthwhile. The "symphonic" is more than just an analogy for film form; rather, it invokes a robust conception of sound as a multi-sensory phenomenon. This conception concerns three specific developments: the rise of noise as a social, aesthetic, and technological issue; the increasing prevalence of inscription technologies as a means to both reproduce and analyse sound; and an interest in reconciling human and machine rhythms in modernity. All three developments are central to Ruttmann's and Vertov's techniques of inaudible sound – the visual amplification of noise; the treatment of motion as sound; and the analysis and reconciliation of audiovisual rhythms. With regard to the first, the visual dynamics of Ruttmann's and Vertov's films – as well as their representation of noise – perform noise's central paradox – its ability to define as well as distort boundaries. With regard to the second, their films manifest an understanding of the line as the meeting point of audio and video through a play of abstract forms that are indebted to experiments in the visual tracing of sound, as well as anticipate experiments in the sounding of the visual trace. Finally, with regard to third, both films aim to reconcile human and machine rhythms that can be perceived through the interplay of audio and video on screen. Far from a mere formal exercise, the musical conception behind these films engages sound as site of fluid exchange between sonic and visual phenomena. In sounding the inaudible, these films demonstrate that sound as sound is never separate from vision as vision; rather, the two are interwoven in the social and technological fabric of audiovisual modernity.

4

ON THE AIR
German Experimental Radio and the Radio City Symphony

The original dust jacket cover of Alfred Döblin's 1928 memoir, *Alfred Döblin: In the Book, at Home, on the Street*, features two images of the author. The first is that of Döblin writing at his desk, pen in hand; the second is that of the author auscultating a patient, his stethoscope gently placed on a body just outside the frame. Like Anton Chekhov, Döblin was a physician whose patients provided raw materials and inspiration for his work. Döblin drew on the argot of his working-class clientele to develop a distinct style that fused Berliner dialect, witticisms, and idioms – peppered with onomatopoeic rumblings, bumblings, and nonsense rhymes – with the language of newspapers, scientific journals, advertisements, radio broadcasts, and literature. Designed by the photographer Sasha Stone, the cover-designer for Walter Benjamin's *One-Way Street*, the dust jacket of Döblin's memoir is a collage composed of images of Döblin the writer and Döblin the physician set against the backdrop of a Berlin cityscape. Hovering over the author's desk, the famous clock tower of the Rotes Rathaus – a red-bricked townhall that looms over the action of the author's renowned city symphony novel, *Berlin, Alexanderplatz: The Story of Franz Biberkopf* – is a reminder of the book that would come to define the writer's career. The collage also serves as a roadmap for an analysis of the novel, one that provides an entry point into a further discussion of the city symphony phenomenon that goes beyond the silent city symphony films of the 1920s.

Berlin, Alexanderplatz draws attention to Germany as the site of novel forms of radio experimentation that develop in tandem with the city symphony phenomenon. While Soviet artists such as Dziga Vertov certainly experimented with the possibility of radiophonic works in films such as *Enthusiasm: Symphony of the Donbass* (see chapter 5), it was in Germany that the connection between radio, urban connectivity, and political community were put to the test in works designed specifically for the new medium. This was in part due to the further reach of radio in Germany at the time. As Stephen Lovell points out, while holding great promise for Bolshevik propaganda, Soviet radio was rather underdeveloped in contrast to its German counterpart. By the time the Nazis took power, there were 8.2 million radio receivers in Germany in comparison to 2.5 million in the USSR.[2] Although cautious and conservative, the political climate during the Weimar Republic was nonetheless conducive to the radio experiments of figures such as Hans Flesch and Walter Ruttmann, whose radio city symphony *Weekend* (1930) plays an important role in this chapter. Billed as a film without images, this work treats the city as a sonic medium in accordance with a networked conception of urban space. It demonstrates how the city is more than an object for sonic representation, but rather a sonic medium whose spatial dynamics pose distinct problems for technological re-mediation.

Returning to the dust jacket cover of Döblin's memoir, one finds a fruitful metaphor in the figure of the stethoscope-wielding doctor himself. According to Jonathan Sterne, auscultation – the art of listening to and diagnosing patients using a stethoscope – is at the center of a broader set of transformations in the "practical orientations toward listening" in the nineteenth and twentieth centuries. "Over the course of a century," Sterne writes, "this practical orientation would move from the specialized province of physicians diagnosing their patients to the much larger context of listening to technologically reproduced sound."[3] From the first treatise on the use and advantages of stethoscopes – a 700-page behemoth written by the French physician René-Théophile-Hyacinthe Laennec – to single-page advertisements for radio headsets, phonographs, and telephones, the practice of auscultation was popularized and conditioned through techniques of listening that were once the specialized province of nineteenth-century

Figure 4.1 / Sasha Stone, book jacket design for Alfred Döblin, *Alfred Döblin: Im Buch, zu Haus, auf der Strasse* (1928).

scientific rationality. The image of Döblin listening to a patient and Döblin writing a novel – presented against the backdrop of a city that is the basis for both his medical and literary practice – leads to the idea that Döblin's novel auscultates the city.[4] *Berlin, Alexanderplatz* treats Berlin as the body of a patient – that is, as a sonic medium to which one may listen and derive information regarding various ailments. In this regard, Döblin's Berlin is a resonant medium that produces and amplifies its own sounds – crowds, construction, conversations, sighs, and cries – particularly those of its protagonist, Franz Biberkopf, an ex-convict trying (and largely failing) to live a straight life in the city. In the novel, one hears how these sounds are mediated by a sonic network of technological media that began to dominate the urban soundscape of the early twentieth century. These media have the potential to reproduce the sounds of the city, to re-mediate them, as it were; but they are also part of the sonic-urban infrastructure itself. They generate a feedback loop in which the sounds of the city (of buildings, streets, and squares) and the sounds of media technology (radios, telephones, and phonographs) mutually condition each other to such an extent that they can only be arbitrarily and artificially distinguished.

The purpose of the *Berlin, Alexanderplatz's* auscultation of the city is not, strictly speaking, diagnostic; though the novel does an excellent job diagnosing the many cultural ailments – the cycles of resentment, information overload, paranoia, and violence – that would lead to the rise of German fascism. Instead, the novel teaches a technique of listening to and composing the sounds of the city, one that is paralleled by the truncated history of experimental radio works in the Weimar era such as Ruttmann's *Weekend*. *Berlin, Alexanderplatz* is, indeed, connected to the experimental tradition of Weimar radio. As Peter Jelavich documents, Döblin, himself a radio enthusiast, participated in the novel's adaptation into a *Hörspiel*, a radio play.[5] The adaptation went through several iterations, though it never made it on to the airwaves due to the acquiescent regime of self-censorship imposed by Germany's state-run radio stations – a harbinger of the Nazis' rise to power.

Despite this connection, the novel is largely interpreted in visual-cinematic terms; its status as a city symphony novel – alongside other modern epics such as James Joyce's *Ulysses* and Andrei Bely's *Petersburg* – hinges largely on its montage-like construction. Visual montage is an important factor in the composition of Döblin's novel, though it does not necessarily follow the juxtapositional style of Sergei Eisenstein's *Battleship Potemkin* or even the cross-sectional one of Ruttmann's *Berlin*.[6] Rather, as Jelavich points out, Döblin, in developing his own *Kinostil* in his 1927 novel, was largely inspired by the programs of an earlier era of Nickelodeon theatres from the 1900s and 1910s – one that Tom Gunning would define as operating according to an exhibitionist logic of "attractions."[7] In his 1913 "Berlin Program," Döblin advocates that writers should take up a Kinostil to combat psychologism in the novel. Like many members of the avant-garde (though he himself did not belong to any avant-garde movement), Döblin advocated replacing storytelling with construction, and likewise replacing the author with a more mechanical, depersonalized process. "The dawdling of story telling," he wrote, "has no place in the novel; one doesn't tell stories, one builds." Likewise, the "hegemony of the author must be smashed; the fanaticism of self-abnegation cannot be pursued far enough.

Nor the fanaticism of renunciation: I am not I, but the street, the lanterns, this and that event, nothing more."[8] At the same time, Döblin was somewhat skeptical of the powers of the cinema, viewing its ability to insinuate ideas into a docile population (of which the gullible Franz Biberkopf is an exemplary subject), as well as act as an instrument of crowd control, with suspicion.[9]

Despite the fact that Döblin's interest in the cinema was largely based in an already-bygone era of "attractions" – of a cinematic experience defined by programs of unrelated shorts (slapstick comedies, newsreels, short dramas, etc.) – the perception that *Berlin, Alexanderplatz's* montage style parallels that of films such as Ruttmann's *Berlin, Symphony of a Great City* has maintained its cultural currency – and with good reason. The kaleidoscope of rapidly changing impressions; the sudden, unannounced shifts in perspective; the at-times roving, dispassionate, and objective style of the narration (e.g., the description of a slaughterhouse); all suggest the dynamics of the city symphony film, as well as the urban experiences analyzed by theorists such as Georg Simmel.[10] When Franz arrives in Berlin, the buildings of the city appear to sway to and fro, highlighting the visual disorientation that a newcomer to the city (or one that has recently returned after a long absence) faces. Yet focusing on these overwhelmingly visual details tends to obscure the novel's equal fascination with sound. The swaying of the houses is triggered by the romping and ringing (*tobten* and *klingelten*) of street cars. Such sounds play an important, compositional role in Döblin's novel.

More than just a catalogue of city noises, the novel is an instructional manual in how to listen to the sounds of the city, as well as how a person orients themselves in the city via sound. *Berlin, Alexanderplatz* gets off to a noisy start with the whistling of an electric tram that takes Franz from Tegel prison to the heart of Berlin. Upon arriving in the city, Franz is practically mute, he is capable only of sighs, groans, and moans, which the novel describes as Franz's "music" and at times renders directly using onomatopoeia.[11] This device is also used to render the sounds of the city. Overwhelmed by the noises that surround him, the rush of street cars, and the swaying of houses, Franz takes refuge in a courtyard, where he is looked after by a red-haired Jewish character named Nachum. Here, in his struggle to right himself, Franz begins to sing an old war song – "Die Wacht am Rhein," which becomes a frequent refrain throughout the novel: "He was standing beside the garbage bins. And suddenly began ear-splittingly to sing. He pulled the hat off his head like a hurdy-gurdy man. The sound bounced off the walls."[12] With the gestures of an organ grinder, Franz sings to no one in particular, performing a kind of physical and spiritual echolocation within a hostile and alienating city. Franz literally makes a small portion of Berlin, a courtyard, vibrate sympathetically to the sounds of his voice, which returns to him in the form of an echo.

Franz's performance accords with others we have witnessed throughout this book, if on a miniature scale. Like Luigi Russolo and Arseny Avraamov, Franz is aware of the city's ability to function as a resonant medium – to register, amplify, and reproduce sounds in its materials – whether pavement, concrete, or overhead wires. His performance has the effect not only of affirming his existence but also of humanizing the city, of bringing it, however temporarily, into accordance with his own voice. But the singing only goes so far. Such spiritual echolocation is limited by the fact that the city merely repeats whatever Franz sings; it does not truly interact with him. It is only the power of storytelling – in particular Nachum's tale of the young Zannowich – that brings Franz back to life. Nachum's story of Zannowich, a Jewish-Albanian trickster who manages to swindle the bankers and royalty of Europe by convincing them he is of noble origin, literally places Franz back on his feet, taking him from the floor of Nachum's apartment, where he sits moaning and babbling nonsense, to the couch where he regains his power of speech. Yet Nachum never gets the chance to finish telling his story. He is interrupted by his brother-in-law, Eliser, who skips to the end and causes an argument by revealing Zannowich's downfall and suicide. The morbid topic – one that portends ominously for Biberkopf – miraculously gives Franz the urge to live, in no small part due to the liveliness and humour of the dispute between Nachum and Eliser.

Despite its experimental and polyphonic structure, the novel's opening suggests that narrative – active, lively, interrupted, incomplete, and oral narrative – has a role to play in orienting the city-dweller, in helping him manage the urban environment. The novel itself performs this function. It turns noise into narration, makes sense out of noise while auscultating the city, all without allowing noise to lose its fundamental character as noise.

Nachum's tale, of course, is not drawn from street sounds, despite taking Franz in from the street. *Berlin, Alexanderplatz*, by contrast, is composed of street sounds, which it weaves into a polyphonic narrative structure that incorporates all-manner of sound-making and listening practices. "In urban noise," writes Kurt W. Foster, "Döblin recognized a secret language full of meaning to a trained ear. He edits fragments of this noise track into his monologues and flips back and forth between them, as if he were fiddling with a radio dial."[13] The channels on Döblin's radio range from the sounds of electrical wires to the thoughts of human beings. In the novel, the sounds of tram cars ("Ruller ruller fahren die Elektrischen"),[14] marching bands, slaughterhouses ("Und das Kälbchen: prrr-prrr"),[15] horses ("Hopp hopp hopp, Pferdchen macht wider Galopp"), trumpet blasts, and piledrivers ("Rumm rumm wuchtet vor Aschinger auf dem Alex die Dampframme")[16] accompany Franz and his crew of Lumpenproletariat everywhere they go. These noises are more than just a background hum; they are placed on equal footing with the speech and thoughts of the novel's characters. The borders between the noises of Franz's inner voice and the external world are porous – as are the borders between the worlds of the living and the dead. When Franz rings the doorbell of Minna's apartment, for instance, the sounds of his anticipation meld with those of the opening door, behind which stands not Minna but her husband: Franz "zieht die Klingel, und wer öffnet, wer wird es sein, kille kille. Klapps. Ein – Mann! Ihr Mann!"[17] Likewise, when death blasts his trumpets and beats his drums, he makes the same sound as the piledriver: "dann nimmt [der Tod] die Posaune, wird er die Posaune blasen, wird er die Pauken schlagen, wird der schwarze furchtbare Sturmbock kommen, wumm, immer sachte, rumm."[18]

This ability to shift registers, change radio frequencies, is built into the novel's conception of words. "Words," Döblin writes in *Berlin, Alexanderplatz*, "are sound waves, swirls of noise, filled with content."[19] These noises have their origins in the spaces that Döblin sought out to write his novel. During his lunch hour, Döblin recalls, he would often visit "the Café Gumpert, a large, lively place where business people met. You could read newspapers from all over the world there, and drink coffee. Sometimes, I brought a manuscript with me, and soon I would be writing. I enjoyed all the noises around me as I wrote."[20] Such a method and the resulting novel, as Foster points out, bring to mind Futurist and Dadaist noise experiments such as Kurt Schwitters's "Ursonate" (1922), Marinetti's "Zang Tumb Tumb," and even Russollo's *Art of Noises*. The main difference between these works and Döblin's concerns the role of narration and storytelling. "I do not want only fifty times 'trumb-trumb, tatetereta,'" Döblin writes with respect to Marinetti's novel *Mafarka*, "but wish to see your Arabs, yet these you are not showing us."[21] Experiments such as Marinetti's, and by extension Russolo's, came across to Döblin as flat, lacking the crucial dimension of signification that the author believed all sounds and utterances share.

In *Berlin, Alexanderplatz*, words and noises are placed on equal footing, not as sounds devoid of content but as signifying in collaboration with one another. The story that marks the beginning of the world is placed on equal footing with a nonsense rhyme. In book 2, a retelling of Adam and Eve is followed by a brief, rhythmic summation: "So wollen wir fröhlich beginnen. Wir wollen singen und uns bewegen. Mit den Händchen klapp, klapp, klapp, mit den Füßchen trapp, trapp, trapp, einmal hin, einmal her, ringsherum, es ist nicht schwer."[22] The song and dance of onomatopoeic noises are channelled through the city as a sonic medium, reverberating in different characters, buildings, parks, and squares. It is the city that produces and resonates them, composing them into a network of noises.

Yet in an unaired radio adaptation of Döblin's novel, this noise network – the polyphonic experience of the city – is largely missing. As Jelavich points out, in the radio play, "Döblin chose to focus on the plot and the central character rather than the metropolis: hence the new work was entitled *The Story of Franz Biberkopf*."[23] "Berlin, Alexanderplatz" was dropped; the subheading became the title; and the noisy setting receded into the background. There were several reasons for this change. Length was certainly a factor – the five-hundred-page novel had to be condensed into a one-hour program; censorship was another – many of the most polyphonic episodes in Döblin's novel were sexually explicit. What is more, the radio adaptation was to be aired following the 14 September elections, which brought the Nazis to power as the second-largest party in the Reichstag. Political censors – whether from cowardice, anti-Semitism, or both – hesitated to broadcast "a work by a well-known leftist Jewish author."[24] It is for this reason that Döblin's radio rendition of his novel never made it on to the airwaves.

Paradoxically, the medium of radio itself also seemed to pose a challenge to composing the noisiest elements of *Berlin, Alexanderplatz* into a broadcastable work. By 1930, radio already seemed more suitable to narrative, as opposed to experimental sound art. Indeed, Döblin and his contemporaries subscribed to this notion, though they did not think that the adaptation of literary works for radio performance could be done in such a straightforward manner as simply reciting the work on air. At the 1929 Kassel "Literature and Radio" conference, Döblin suggested that radio was best suited to music and news, which did not have to be significantly altered to be broadcast. "Radio," he claimed, "is a medium that alters literature. Literature must or would have to change its form, in order to conform to radio."[25] This was not necessarily a bad thing. The reworking of literary works for the radio, Döblin noted, could help revitalize the oral tradition of literature, not to mention bring literary authors a larger audience. Radio would, in Jelavich's words, "compel writers to return to their pretextual roots: they would have to revert back to the times when story-*tellers* actually spoke (rather than wrote) their tales."[26] As such, when forced to chose between the *noises* of "Berlin, Alexanderplatz" and "The *Story* of Franz Biberkopf," Döblin settled for the latter.

This is not to say that the noises of Berlin are completely absent from the radio play. Both the script and, to a lesser extent, the recorded version that never aired, feature moments in which Biberkopf or the narrator's voice emerges from the crowd, as well as moments when the narrator and characters interact in a manner that recalls the structure of the novel. In particular, as Jelavich suggests, the novel's retelling of the story of Job parallels the disembodied voice of the radio itself, thus offering a critique of its acousmatic power. Likewise, Döblin struggled to maintain a certain degree of ambiguity in the radio play with respect to who is speaking a particular line because radio makes it far easier to recognize a specific character's voice. Putting these acoustic similarities aside, however, it is clear that sound has a much lesser role to play in the radio play than in the novel. The noises of the city function primarily as background; they are not placed on the same level as the story, but are a kind of wallpaper. Döblin's belief that this compromise between the setting and the plot would usher in a new era of oral storytelling is somewhat of a self-deception, not least because the type of epic storytelling to which Döblin is referring is characterized by a spontaneity born of repetition – of repeated tellings of the same tale. By contrast, by the time *The Story of Franz Biberkopf* was set to air, radio was already shifting to pre-recorded, as opposed to live, broadcasts – that is, toward a process of editing, mixing, and remixing. In fact, a dispute over the technical uses of sound recording was cited by Hans Flesch, then the artistic director of the Berlin Radio Hour, as the reason for delaying the broadcast of Döblin's radio play, though the excuse was largely a cover for censorship concerns.

Like narrative film, whose montage disruptions are masked by techniques such as eye-line matches and cross-dissolves, radio, too, can maintain an illusion of spontaneity and unity. But was a focus on the sounds of the metropolis – particularly one that highlights the montage disjunctions that characterize both the novel and technical mass media – possible for *Berlin, Alexanderplatz* as a radiophonic work? And what would it have sounded like? Döblin consciously avoided turning his novel into an experimental *Hörbild* – the genre to which works such as Flesch's *Zauberei auf dem Sender* (1924) and Ruttmann's *Weekend* belong. He preferred instead the more narrative-oriented *Hörspiel* – a genre made famous by works such as Bertolt Brecht's *Flight of the Lindberghs*. The problem with the Hörbilde, Jelavich writes, "was that they generally used only stereotypical sounds from offices, factories, shops, or places of entertainment; they were not conducive to psychological or thematic complexity."[27] That said, in keeping with the anti-psychologism that Döblin also espoused, one may rightly ask whether there are ways in which city Hörbilde – that is, radio city symphonies such as Ruttmann's – parallel Döblin's treatment of the city as a symphonic medium. Is there a sense in which this work also auscultates and re-mediate the city's sounds in a manner that points to a new kind of orality, one that does not look backward in an attempt to revive a lost oral, epic tradition of storytelling, but forward in order to exploit the networked potential of a new medium and urban environment? The radio city symphony rebels against the use of radio for retelling psychological narratives, not to mention playing music and news. At the same time, its creation of a "network of noises," to reframe Russolo's term, addresses one of *Berlin, Alexanderplatz's* fundamental questions – how to render and connect the spaces of the city through sound. This, as it turns out, is a fundamental question for early German radio itself, one that goes back to its establishment as an entertainment medium.

Deep Listening

Although not a city symphony in its own right, one of the earliest entertainment broadcasts on German radio – a 1923 recital of Heinrich Heine's "Sea Apparition" (1825–26)[28] – revolves around an episode of deep-sea, urban auscultation. The poem both echoes the city symphony tradition, as well as foreshadows later city symphony broadcasts, not to mention the technological, military, mythic, and political entanglements of German radio. As Daniel Gilfilan points out, "the remediation of Heine's poetic text into broadcast sound holds profound significance for the beginnings of artistic practice with sound-based media."[29] In particular, the broadcast "evokes the techno-historical origins of the radio in maritime communication, while still drawing on the ritual and myth production of the maritime culture."[30] One of these myths is an urban one – the legend of Atlantis, a civilization on the ocean floor. After a tumultuous and noisy storm, the narrator of Heine's poem perceives this city through the crystalline calm of the sea.

> But I lay at the edge of the ship
> With eyelids dreamy, and gazing
> Below in the crystal water-mirror,
> And piercing deeper and deeper
> I saw the ocean bottom,
> First like a glimmering shadow,
> Then growing sharp and clear-cut in color;
> Spires of churches and towers were visible,
> And then a city, sharp as the light of day,

> Medieval, netherlandish,
> And teeming with life.
> Deliberate burghers clad in black capes,
> With neck ruffs snow-white and with chains of
>   honor.[31]

Heine's poem initially emphasizes sight, clarity, and light in the perception of this Dutch village. Over the course of a stanza, the narrator's vision becomes more and more defined, to the point of describing glistening "mirrored windows"; "pyramid lindens"; "gay cavalieros in Spanish attire"; golden-haired, slender-waisted maidens with "flower-like faces"; and so on. These visions, however, are cut short by the "chiming" of church bells and the "rush of organ tones," which turns the narrator's gaze inward, pulling him into a deeper, darker world.

> Me, too, that distant clang hath gripped,
> Mysterious shudders seize me.
> And endless regret, a depthless sorrow
> Surprise my heart,
> My scarcely healed heart,
> Meseems as though its wounds again
> Were kissed by my beloved's lips,
> And kissed anew to bleeding –
> Hot, encrimsoned blood-drops
> Drip slowly down and strike upon
> An ancient house thereunder
> In the deep sea-city,
> An old house with pointed gables, a house
> Deserted, melancholy, deathlike,
> Except that by a window
> A maiden sits,
> Her head on her arm is laid,
> As a poor, neglected child's might be, –
> And I know thee, thou lonely, neglected child![32]

While the first half of the poem evokes surface fascination, the second half plunges the reader down into sounds of longing, nostalgia, myth, melancholy, and unrequited love. Sound plays the role of a deeper, more profound sense. But the poem also underscores sound's ability to seduce and deceive, to act as a siren call of mythic wholeness. Fortunately, in the nick of time, the narrator is rescued from drowning in this myth by the captain of the ship: "By the foot the captain seized me, / And pulled me to safety; / He called, angrily laughing: / 'Doctor, have you gone crazy?'"[33] The episode recalls the *Symphony of Sirens* (chapter 2). Like Avraamov, who composed music for an entire city that never heard it, the narrator listens to a siren song that ultimately only he can hear. This song is one that promises wholeness, completion, and reunification with a beloved. It is a song that emerges from the city, is produced and mediated by the city, but turns out to be just an echo of the composer's own imagination.

That Heine's song of longing was broadcast to cities across Germany raises questions about how radio networks and urban networks interact in the creation of radiophonic compositions: How do such compositions auscultate the city? And how does the city, in its own right, auscultate the radio? To answer these questions several points about the history of German radio need to be kept in mind. First, it is important to recall that, throughout the 1920s, most radio listeners were city-dwellers, largely as a result of the limits and economics of radio technology. While longer-range tube-based radio receivers would become cheaper with time, most listeners in the 1920s and early 1930s could only afford crystal-based detectors. These had to be placed within 15 miles of a radio tower – the majority of which were located in cities – to receive a signal.[34] Of a population of about 15 million city-dwellers living near radio towers, 2.1 million had radio receivers; while amid a population of 49 million country-dwellers, one could only count 1.2 million receivers. Not surprisingly, of these city-dwellers, Berliners accounted for the majority of radio sets. Indeed, in 1928, Berlin was the city with the highest density of radio sets in the world.[35]

In this respect, despite promising to collapse distances, in its early days, radio was largely an urban affair. The ability to hear farther was unevenly distributed, privileging the urban center, and most likely exacerbating the urban-rural divide. On the whole, listeners in these cities would be used to the sound effects of construction and traffic (for a time recorded live on the street) that accompanied their *Hörspiele*.[36] What is more, listening to the radio was not a passive activity, as it is often made out to be. Isolated by their headphones, a requirement for most early radios, listeners had to regularly tune their crystal detector sets during a program to receive a clean signal.[37] As a result, they were often prevented from just kicking back and enjoying the evening's programming, let alone concentrating exclusively on a difficult musical work. An average listener – adjusting his set, tuning his headphones – was instead closer in terms of activity to the pilots and adventurers lionized by early radio plays such as Friedrich Wolf's sos ... *rao rao ... Foyn: "Krassin" saves* (rettet) *"Italia"* (1929) and Bertolt Brecht's *Flight of the Lindberghs* (1929). At the very least, audiences understood their sets not just as means of receiving entertainment but as instruments for military expeditions.

In Germany, the activity of the radio listener was in fact something to be feared. Most readers are familiar with Brecht's idea of a bi-directional radio – of transforming the radio from "a distribution apparatus into a communications apparatus."[38] Such an apparatus could both send and receive signals, thus allowing audience members to actively participate in radiophonic works. Brecht attempted to realize this idea, with limited success, in his radio play *The Flight of the Lindberghs*, which premiered at the 1929 Baden-Baden music festival alongside Ruttmann's *Weekend*. Less well known is that Brecht's idea was not simply a Marxist vision of turning the means of production over to the producer/consumer; rather, it drew on radio's earlier bi-directional and military history – something that Brecht, as Friedrich Kittler points out, curiously overlooks in his famous essay, "The Radio as Communications Apparatus."[39] In this essay, Brecht personifies the radio as going through a kind of mid-life crisis. In its infancy, its "gilded youth," radio "imitated practically every existing institution that had anything at all to do with the distribution of speech or song." It was a substitute – "a substitute for theatre, opera, concerts, lectures, coffeehouse music, the local pages of the newspaper, etc."[40] But now – i.e., in the late 1920s and early 1930s – it was time for radio to find its purpose in life. This purpose was to facilitate a network in which the listener could hear as well as speak, in which she was no longer isolated.

Brecht's essay, however, seems to have confused radio's youth with its middle age. The history of German radio was in fact one of a central authority trying to maintain control over a network in which an increasing number of listeners could both send and receive signals due to rapid advancements in radio technology. These included bi-directional devices that amateurs and enthusiasts – many of whom received training during World War I – deployed in various ways. As Gilfilan and others have documented, the origins of the regulatory mechanisms that oversaw German radio go back to the April 1892 Reich Telegraphy Act (Gesetz über das Telegraphenwesen des Deutschen Reiches), which gave the state sovereignty over telegraph operations as well as the transmission of all "news, signals, images or sounds, either through means of electric wireless devices or by means of the conducting of electric waves along a conductor."[41] The law held up through World War I, the conclusion of which both accelerated the adoption of wireless transmission, as well as created the need for further regulations and technologies. Indeed, it was not until after the war, in 1919, when the law needed to be expanded to actually "include governmental control over systems of broadcasting and transmission."[42]

The incident that prompted this expansion was the "takeover of the news agency Wolff'sche Telegraphenbüro (Wolff Telegraph Office) in Berlin by former members of the military signal corps on 9 November 1918."[43] The takeover, which followed on the heals of the Kiel mutiny (3 November), was instrumental in providing a voice to the soldiers and workers of the November Revolution. It legitimized the overthrow of the monarchy and the proclamation of a republic. In this respect, Erich Kuttner, editor of the Social Democratic Party newspaper *Forwards* (*Vorwärts*), drew explicit parallels with Revolutionary events in St Petersburg.

> At that time I was of the opinion that it was probably good to send a dispatch through the Wolff'sche Telegraphenbureau. I arrived at these thoughts through my own experience, because I knew that in March 1917, when the reports about the victories in the Russian revolution were made known, that nothing had as much of an impact as the fact that the news was broadcast through the Petersburger Telegraphenbureau. [Petersburg Telegraph Bureau] ... I also told

myself: if one issued a dispatch about the victories of the [November] revolution through the Wolff'sche Telegraphenbureau, then it would be believed throughout the world.[44]

Kuttner's comments echo those of Arseny Avraamov, who believed that a recital of the *Symphony of Sirens* in Berlin would bring about a revolution in Germany. Such a recital would in fact be "broadcast," since the symphony was conducted from a radio tower. Yet the takeover of the Wolff'sche Telegraphenbüro did not lead to the establishment of worker's councils and Soviets. On the contrary, despite aiding in the establishment of the Weimar Republic, the event was viewed with suspicion by radio authorities. While the takeover temporarily led to the establishment of an independent Zentralfunkleitung, which also happened to promise employment for the 190,000 members of Army Signal Corps, it was ultimately neutralized when the Zentralfunkleitung was brought under the authority of the Postal Ministry.

The events of 9 November 1918 would come to be known as the *Funkerspuk*, a term that combines the words for radio operator (*Funker*) and ghost (*Spuk*). The term captured the fear radio authorities had of uncontrolled airwaves – of a haunted radio space in which any political group or persuasion could have their say. In this regard, the establishment of an entertainment-oriented radio was not a result of the medium's infant-like miming of other sonic art forms, nor even the result of radio succumbing to market forces that pushed it toward the lowest common denominator; rather, it was the result of an attempt to control the airwaves. The first entertainment broadcasts in 1923 followed on the heels of an outright ban on private radio receivers in 1922. This largely ineffective ban sought to limit the proliferation of bi-directional radio sets. As Gilfilan notes, up until the early 1920s, consumer radios could in fact receive as well as send signals through a process of regenerative feedback known as back-coupling waves (*Rückkopplungsschwingungen*). In part because of this ability, the ban on private radio receivers was lifted only shortly before the first entertainment broadcasts commenced.

One of the factors that contributed to the lifting of the ban was a prohibition on the sale of bi-directional radio sets. As Hans Bredow, the first chair of Weimar Germany's National Broadcasting Service notes in his memoirs, this prohibition was a way to appease the German military.

> The military was prepared to shelve its opposition if its interests were protected. One consideration was that any request for a receiver should be accompanied by the issuance of a reception licence, but that to protect radio communications certain technical constraints also had to be imposed on listeners and the radio equipment industry. The licensed receivers should be designed in such a way that reception of military and postal radio signals could not be disrupted by the transmission of regenerative feedback or back-coupling waves [Rückkopplungsschwingungen]. Additionally, the wiretapping of military radio transmissions was to be made technically impossible through the institution of a wave frequency range reserved for military communications.[45]

The imposition of "certain technical constraints" – namely, the ban on bi-directional radio sets – was coupled with the rise of German entertainment broadcasting. This programming was not, as Brecht's essay might lead one to believe, radio in its "youth," but rather its early middle age. It was a conscious decision on the part of regulators and programmers.

As a mode of entertainment, the radio in Germany did not resemble the cinema or print journalism. As Jelavich points out, unlike cinema and publishing, which were dominated by private interests, the radio was a state-supported and -regulated medium. Regulators, both conservative and liberal, sought to avoid the commercial model of the United States, where, as one ultraconservative radio bureaucrat put it, "hundreds of private stations" were supported "by factories, department stores, newspapers, and religious sects ... touting their own interests."[46] The something-for-nothing approach of the United States – in which the "nothing" was filled in by advertisement dollars and corporate sponsors – was anathema to regulators and politicians, who thought that "radio ought to serve the interests of the whole community, rather than particular interest groups." In "true Hegelian fashion, they contended that the only entity representing the interests of the nation was the State."[47] Coming to the same idea from the left, members of the Social Democrats felt that the only way to prevent a right-wing takeover of mass media by wealthy capitalists was to ensure a robust system of public broadcasting. As such, a public system emerged in which listeners supported the radio through a tax and programming decisions were made through entities that sought to balance the interests of the Reich, individual states, political parties (excluding Nazis and communists), and religious organizations. By 1926, all news was delivered by a central "Wireless Service" (Drahtloser Dienst), while cultural and educational programming was left up to state radio stations. These were regulated by political oversight boards (*politische Überwachungsausschüsse*), each of which were made up of three members, one from the Reich and two from the state.[48]

Of course, difficulties soon emerged in this system. Even if one excluded the viewpoints of Nazis and communists, it was difficult to balance the range of interests, ideological persuasions, and tastes in Weimar Germany through a single regulatory body and dissemination apparatus. Neutrality was impossible while pluralism remained elusive. How could a single station in a given state create programming that satisfied even a plurality of its audience? Even entertainment, which at first seemed like a solution to the problem of unduly ideological content (e.g., news), proved too divisive. "Highbrow listeners complained about popular music; the lowbrow audience found opera boring; traditionalists carped about everything new; innovators deplored the prevalence of well-known works on the airwaves."[49] What emerged from this context was the radio department store that Brecht criticized – a situation in which stations struggled to fill airtime, giving the appearance that the new medium had nothing to say. Brecht's proposed solution to this problem was a return, as it were, to radio's earlier, bi-directional era. Better put, he proposed developing the lost potential of this era into the programming of a bi-directional *Hörspiel*, *The Flight of the Lindberghs*.

The Hörspiel – a genre that also includes the radio adaptation of Döblin's novel – was one of two directions that the development of a truly radiophonic (or *Funkisch*) art would take in Germany. While the Hörspiel, like narrative cinema, emphasized the fusion of various art forms into a *Gesamtkunstwerk* suited for the new acoustic medium, the *Hörbild* (or sound-image), like *Cinéma Pur*, stressed the composition of an acoustic work using elements unique to radio itself. Greatly aided by the advent of sound film, which allowed for more precise editing, radiophonic *Hörbilder*, like Ruttmann's *Weekend* and Max Ophüls *Typewriters* (1929), took the principle of montage in an acoustic direction, splicing together sounds from across the city and countryside into a single composition. *Weekend* was billed as a film without images, a *Hörfilm-Symphonie*. As Jelavich notes, the Hörbild, which aired on the Berlin Radio Hour on 30 June 1930, "consisted of 240 soundbites, averaging less than three seconds each, spliced together to form an eleven-minute work."[50] Like *Berlin, Symphony of a Great City*, the Hörbild took one through a day in the life of a metropolis, starting on Saturday afternoon and ending with the resumption of work on Monday. Six sections described this period, starting and ending with the famous *"Jazz der Arbeit"* ("Jazz of Work"), a "contrapuntal montage" of typewriters, telephones, cash registers, saws, files, and various other machines.[51] In between, one hears the farewells of departing workers ("Feierabend"); cars and trains leaving the city ("Fahrt ins Freie"); a pastorale of birds, cows, and church bells ("Pastorale"); and the ringing of bells and telephones signalling the return to work ("Wiederbeginn der Arbeit"). Each passage blends into the other, creating dense and at times disorienting layers of sound. Indeed, this montage of sounds was so difficult to parse that, as Jelavich notes, the program director Hans Flesch decided to play it twice in succession, along with a lengthy introduction.[52]

One of the reasons that Döblin eschewed modelling his adaptation of *Berlin, Alexanderplatz* on the *Hörblid* was its reliance on what Jelavich calls an "additive principle," the idea of composing a radiophonic work by layering sounds on top of one another. While this may be an excellent technique for building a city soundscape, it is not suited to crossing the boundaries between cityscape and character psychology. As noted earlier, faced with a decision between "Berlin, Alexanderplatz" and "The Story of Franz Biberkopf," Döblin settled on the latter as the focus of his adaptation. This decision does not mean, however, that both the novel and the Hörbild do not have things in common when it comes to auscultating the city. Both, as it turns out, honour the legacy of Heine's poem by exploring how the city functions as a medium for sound. As with Heine's poem and the "Symphony of Sirens," the "danger" of hearing what one wants to hear emerging from the city is ever present, but so is the possibility of composing the city into a symphonic image – one with both aesthetic and political consequences.

Radio Sound and City Space

The Hörspiel and Hörbild are frequently placed in opposition to each other; yet it is also possible to consider these seemingly opposed formats as complimentary. In a 1984 essay for West German radio, the writer Helmut Heißenbüttel argued that, viewed from a contemporary perspective, the two kinds of radio works supplemented each other. Together, they made the metropolis audible (*hörbar*). This making audible concerned the re-mediation of different sounds that characterize the city. For Heißenbüttel, who was nine years old in 1930 (the year, according to his essay, that he began listening to radio), Döblin's radio play (Hörspiel) sounds nostalgic in comparison to the documentary qualities of Ruttmann's Hörbild. It may only be the effects of time, but *Weekend* seems like an "acoustic supplement and background music" (*akustische Ergänzung und Untermalung*) of *The Story of Franz Biberkopf*: "I recognize sounds and noises from my own childhood. This is the city for me. The character of the Berlin metropole is best characterized by the dialect-colors of parts of speech. At the same time, I hear elements of an acoustic collage here for the first time. Much that is formally familiar to us today becomes audible here [*Weekend*] as a discovery, as something that seems simultaneously naïve and bold." [53] Different colours of dialect (*Dialektfärbung*) come through Döblin's radio play, but they are augmented by the city sounds of Ruttmann's Hörbild. For Heißenbüttel, these sounds compose a metropolis that has lost contact with its etymological roots as the "mother" of all cities. Instead, they paint a portrait of an urban center whose fragmentary composition and cancerous growth threatens to overwhelm the very concept of the mother-city idea.[54]

Heißenbüttel recognizes that these once threatening sounds now appear common (*geläufig*), a part of the typical experience of any city-dweller. It is important to note, however, that this appearance of commonness, which Heißenbüttel attributes to the passage of time, is in fact the product of a radiophonic sensory education in the sounds of the city. What seems like a natural, if somewhat quaint, layering of city sounds is actually the result of sound-editing techniques to which the listener would have to have been accustomed. Indeed, as noted above, beyond simply introducing the piece, the director of the *Berlin Radio Hour*, Hans Flesch, opted to play Ruttmann's *Weekend* twice so that audiences could get a better listen.

In his aptly titled *Radio*, the film and radio theorist Rudolf Arnheim outlines a program of radio sensory education that is worth keeping in mind when considering how Ruttmann's *Weekend* functions as a city symphony. For Arnheim, the function of the radio – what he calls the "wireless" – "is to present the world to the ear."[55] In a rather Russoloesque passage, Arnheim writes that the "rediscovery of the musical note in sound and speech, the welding of music, sound and speech into a single material, is one of the greatest artistic tasks of the wireless."[56] Natural and mechanical phenomena, in other words, all have musical properties. They exist along a continuum.

> The howling of a wind, a siren, a dog, a propeller and the noise of a car reversing have a common and very characteristic sound-character, even though they are all such different things. Common to all such sounds is the chromatic rise in intensity and pitch, the swelling and increase of strength, and just this is the special expression that such a sound transmits to us. On the other hand, a sigh, a sob, or the slowing down of a machine have the effect of a decrescendo, an ebbing of strength, mostly characterized by a fall in intensity and pitch. The direct expressive power of a hammered-out rhythm and a soft blurred sound, a major and a minor chord, a fast and a slow pace, a sudden or a gradual rise and fall in pitch, a loud or a soft tone – these are the most elemental and the most important creative means for every form of acoustic art, for music just as much as for the arts of speech and sound![57]

As we have seen, mastering and re-mediating the sonic properties of such materials was the aim of Russolo's intonarumori and Avraamov's experiments in sound synthesis. The radio, for Arnheim, was a means of augmenting both the capacity and reach of this process. With the advantages of sound recording, editing, and broadcast transmission, any sound whatsoever could be recorded, manipulated, composed, juxtaposed, and sent to thousands of receivers across the country.

This fact promised an entirely new kind of musical work – one that suggested itself in the archive of "sound effects" that the burgeoning art of radio had quickly amassed. "Only when one has sat at the 'effects table' oneself," Arnheim writes, "fantastically mixing all sort of record at will and blending them together, does one know the fascination"[58] of combining and recombining studio-made and documentary-based sounds. To illustrate this game, Arnheim quotes from an article by the journalist Curt Corrinth, in which he describes a hypothetical composition that is very similar to Ruttmann's city symphony. Corrinth's city symphony "composer" is in fact a radio librarian.

> And now the smiling librarian, a new record in her hand, goes up to the gramophone: the little room is filled with the deep breathing of a man, as aloud as if a giant were snoring! ... Then the narrow walls seem to fade away, a landscape appears, enlivened by the prattling and plashing of rushing streams. Then cars go racing through the tiny room, rumbling omnibuses and little rattling tin lizzies; a storm crackles and thunders by; noises of the stock-exchange emerge and turn into children's voices; we hear the wheezy organ on the merry-go-round and the subdued roar of the fair ... Again space dwindles to the size of the room, and suddenly invisible hands begin brushing clothes, crumpling paper, blowing noses, and then, in bewildering contrast, the walls extend into a factory with machines stamping and engines humming, harbour-noises surge up and mills creak, and so it goes on almost indefinitely: laughter of girls and growls of rage, battle-cries, drumrolls and trains puffing ... The young lady smiles again, conscious of the astonishment in store for the listener: an entire zoo with its thousands of voices appear! Monkeys scream and chatter, the walrus snorts, the polar-bear yawns, deer bell, dogs of all sizes and breeds bark, the tiger growls,

the lion "speaks his mind," a pig grunts, bees hum – and birds trill and whistle and sing, from the canary and nightingale to the kestrel.[59]

Such a composition does a lot more than merely represent the city; it actively re-mediates it, channelling and augmenting its resonant qualities through the radio. The ability to create novel compositions from a library of sounds gives rise to a city symphony. The urban is, in this sense, wired into the radio; the types of sounds the city produces – the sharp and aggressive sounds of modernity – are remixed through this modern medium.

The broadcast of a city symphony such as Ruttmann's, however, involves a lot more than merely recording and replaying specific sounds. "It is neither technically necessary nor artistically advisable," Arnheim writes, "to cling slavishly to the idea of transmitting 'the sound-in-itself' at its clearest and best."[60] One must rather freely adapt the sonic composition of a scene to achieve the desired effect – for example, portraying an intimate conversation between two people in a crowded restaurant. Doing so requires a nuanced understanding of how sounds and spaces interact. Arnheim dedicates a large portion of his study to analyzing this interaction, particularly with respect to how to emulate and re-create the real-world resonances of sounds and spaces in the studio. In this respect, he considers how to re-mediate the resonant properties of the city.

> Can we hear space? Yes; our ear is certainly indirectly aware of space by the way sounds behave in it. Sounds can inform our ear in two ways about the extension of space. First by the kind of reverberation that the sound finds in the walls, or by the lack of echo (in open spaces or in artificially deadened rooms). Secondly, by the distance between the places where the sounds occur in a scene; if all the sounds in a scene are crowded together into an inconsiderable space, it gives a spatially narrow effect, but if one hears perhaps bells ringing at a great distance while near at hand a conversation is in progress, such widely separated sounds will denote great space.[61]

What Arnheim says here about the sonorous quality of walls can be extended to other materials of spatial construction – to steel beams, cement, telegraph wires, plumbing, and so on. Any of these can function as resonant channels, thus underscoring that the city is a medium for sound. Likewise, how these materials are placed in relation to one another, not to mention how they are "filled," affects how the spaces they construct resonate. This sound is one that radio must re-mediate through a process that involves more than mere recording and transmitting. As such, Arnheim goes on to consider the ways in which the radio can generate spatial effects including distance, reverberation, perspective (e.g., whether a sound is coming from the left or right), superimposition, and transition (e.g., from one space to another). Certain methods are simple, such as standing farther away from the microphone;[62] others are complicated, including amplifying and rerecording a sound in different rooms, thus giving the same sound different properties (e.g., echo).[63] In describing such techniques, Arnheim shows how to re-mediate real-world sounds for a radio audience.

Arnheim's ultimate purpose is to create a sense of spatial unity – one that does not disturb the audience member's illusion that she is at the center of a sonic world. Spaces should be felt but not heard; they should not announce their presence along with the sound, but rather facilitate the transmission of the sound.[64] In recording a speech made in a large auditorium, for instance, one should hear the speech, not the auditorium. In other words, one ought to make use of the resonant qualities of different materials and spaces without seeking to literally reproduce the sounds *of* these spaces. In this regard, Arnheim's ideas echo those of the Soviet film director Vsevolod Pudovkin, whose theory of film editing stressed the perspective of an ideal observer.[65] Likewise, Arnheim stresses an ideal listener – one who can shift between sonic distances and perspectives (near and far, and inside and outside) without rupturing the illusion of a single point of listening.

Arnheim's considerations went beyond those of Avraamov, whose *Symphony of Sirens* did not articulate a position from which the listener could hear the work, only one from which she could participate. This oversight, as we saw in chapter 2, contributed to the failure of the work on a city-wide scale. Yet it raises an important question with respect to city symphony in general. Namely, does the sonic city symphony seek to maintain some sense of spatial coherence – an imaginary site from which all listeners can hear more or less the same sounds?

Ruttmann's *Weekend* appears to undermine Arnheim's ideas on spatial unity. Where Arnheim stresses fluidity and continuity – a "loose hazy texture ... which conveniently hides the seams of montage"[66] – Ruttmann suggests stark juxtapositions and discontinuity – a texture that emphasizes the very seams that Arnheim is at pains to cover. That said, the presentation of a more-or-less uniform, audible space is also important for Ruttmann's Hörbild. *Weekend* is edited in a manner that emphasizes a structured relationship between country and city, between zones of leisure and zones of labor. It presents the city and its environs in terms of an easy-to-grasp dichotomy of work and play. As in film, montage is the principle means of making this connection. *Weekend* was not made on the street (where Ruttmann secretly recorded sounds and conversations from a van), but on the editing table, where he sought to create coherent audio-spatial transitions between city and country. In her review of *Weekend*, the famed film critic Lotte Eisner stresses this point: "And now the main work begins for him: the cutting – the montage. A much different cutting than with the optical filmstrip, where the image is already there as a visible moment. After some practice, the sound-image-strip reveals which sound it is, depending on how it's edited. But a bringing together of the individual sounds must happen far more precisely than with the optical image. "Sound montage," Ruttmann writes, "depends on 1/5th of a second."[67] Eisner used Ruttmann's quotation to title the subsection of the article in which this passage appears, thus stressing the importance of precision in sound editing. This process is "essentially different" from editing images. Unlike the image, there is no precise and recognizable moment of sonic sample. By listening to a single sample, one can rarely tell what the sound is about. By contrast, by viewing a single frame of film, one can usually tell what the image is referencing. This difference, according to Eisner, means that a much greater amount of care must go into choosing where and when to make a cut; how and with what to stitch together a particular sonic image.

To realize this level of precision, Ruttmann took full advantage of the recently invented Tri-Ergon optical-sound system. Unlike sound recorded on disc, optical sound made use of the film strip, thus allowing Ruttmann to apply his montage editing techniques to a radiophonic and electro-acoustic context. Such an application, as Andy Birtwistle points out, made Ruttmann a forerunner of musique concrète as it would later be practised by Pierre Schaeffer, John Cage, and Jack Ellit.[68] In its handling of sound and space, Birtwistle argues, *Weekend* is a fundamentally intermedial work of art – one that combines aspects of film, music, and radio to re-mediate the city. This makes *Weekend* a radical work in that it goes against one of the main trends of the modernist avant-garde – namely, that of medium specificity, the notion that an artwork should be unique to the specifications of a given medium.[69] "For Ruttmann," writes Birtwistle, "the path to creating 'a wholly new type of art' lies not in differentiation and autonomy, but rather in combining forms of expression, in order to engage with the changing modes of experience that define modernity."[70] He then quotes Ruttmann to the effect that "it is not a question of a new style or anything like that, but rather of producing a variety of possibilities of expression for all the known arts, a totally new feeling of life in artistic form."[71]

Birtwistle's main examples of medium specificity come by way of film – in particular the theories and works of Dziga Vertov and Sergei Eisenstein. Proclamations such as Vertov's "We are cleaning *Kinochestvo* of foreign matter – of music, literature, and theatre; we seek our own rhythm, one lifted from nowhere else" are taken at face value to set up a contrast with Ruttmann's work. In reality, as Vertov's reference to seeking one's own "rhythm" would attest, both Ruttmann and Vertov (not to mention Eisenstein) relied on intermedial ideas, methods, and processes to define the art forms distinct to their specific medium, whether filmic or radiophonic. This is not to say that Ruttmann pushes against the modernist avant-garde trend of medium specificity, but rather that the way in which the question of medium specificity is framed and addressed involves a certain degree of intermediality. At stake was a specific medium's ability to combine different media – and explore different medial possibilities – in specific ways. Artists could therefore speak in terms of both intermediality and medium specificity without sensing a contradiction, in part because this opposition would come to be defined in a later, post–World War II context.[72] Intermediality in Ruttmann's *Weekend* is interesting, not insofar as it demonstrates a unique mixing of media that other artists eschewed, but insofar as it underscores a mixing of media that is evident across city symphonic works. Such works recognize that the city is itself already a sonic medium – a means of conducting and conveying sound. The city symphony auscultates the city, listening to it at a deeper level than can be heard by the common ear. Yet, at the same time, it re-mediates the sounds that flow through the city's networks, transforming and recombining them through whatever means are available.

One such means, as Birtwistle points out, is the playing of sounds in reverse. *Weekend* opens with a passage in which the sounds of a drum roll and gong are played forward and backward through a process known as retrograding.[73] This opening demonstrates the power of optical-film sound – its ability to play sounds forward and backward at variable speeds. More importantly, it places the creation of novel sonic materials on par with the sounds of pounding hammers, screeching saws, and clacking typewriters. It establishes an exchange between the sounds of technology, the city, and those of traditional instruments, thus creating a sonic spectrum. This transformation extends to the relationship between the sounds and spaces of the city and those of the country as articulated through the *Hörbild's* structure. *Weekend* takes the listener from busy Berlin offices and factories to the idyllic countryside and back again. This circular structure essentially reverses that of *Berlin, Symphony of a Great City*, which takes an unsuspecting passenger from the countryside into the city, where she is bombarded by kaleidoscopic visual impressions. In *Weekend*, the listener escapes into the "freedom" of the country, which offers a brief respite from the daily urban grind.

In this regard, Ruttmann sought to capture space through sound. As Eisner points out, the "most important thing for him was the ability to photograph space through sound, that is, to bring out spatial structure in its diversity."[74] Here, re-mediation occurs on two interrelated levels: 1) re-mediating the visual as audible (photographing sound); 2) re-mediating the spatial as audible (creating a spatial structure in sound). A similar set of concerns motivate Vertov's filmmaking practice as well (see the diary entry discussed in chapter 3). Yet unlike as with Vertov, the spatial configuration that Ruttmann articulates in *Weekend* is essentially conservative and circular. Rather than connect city and country in novel ways, it reinforces a stereotypical opposition between the oppressive, capitalist city and the free, open countryside.

At the same time, *Weekend* suggests another way of conceiving city space – one that is more radical than its presentation of the city-country dichotomy. The Hörbild models the city as a radio network, one in which the instantaneous connections of the radio manifest themselves through the coupling of sounds from different spaces. *Weekend* emulates the tuning of a radio dial that brings heterogeneous spaces together. It encourages a kind of "reduced listening," to use a term that Michel Chion borrows from Pierre Schaeffer – one that brings attention to the sonic properties of different spaces *as* re-mediated through the radio. For Chion, reduced listening "focuses on the traits of the sound itself, independent of its cause and of its meaning. Reduced listening takes the sound – verbal, played on an instrument, noises, or whatever – as itself the object to be observed instead of as a vehicle for something else."[75] Chion's use of the modifier "reduced" is a nod to Edmund Husserl's notion of a phenomenological reduction – the description of an item as it is experienced from a first-person point of view.[76] *Weekend* gets listeners to pay attention to "sounds in themselves" by decontextualizing them, forcing listeners to abstract sounds from their time, place, and material cause. Much of the "difficulty" of listening to the Hörbild is in fact a manifestation of resistance to the activity of reduced listening. As Chion points out, "When faced with this difficulty of paying attention to sounds in themselves, people have certain reactions – 'laughing off' the project, or identifying trivial or harebrained causes – which are in fact so many defenses."[77] Such a defensive posture is clearly present in the reactions to *Weekend*, which was generally received as a clever experiment in sonic portraiture, but little else.

Reduced listening, according to Chion, "requires the fixing of sounds, which thereby acquire the status of veritable objects."[78] In other words, reduced listening necessitates mechanical means of reproduction. "One has to listen many times over, and because of this the sound must be fixed, recorded."[79] Yet, in the same moment that *Weekend* decontextualizes the sounds of the city, giving listeners the opportunity to better focus on the sounds themselves, it also recontextualizes these sounds, offering new semantic and causal interpretations. Listening for the material cause of a sound (causal listening) and for the meaning of a sound (semantic listening) are the other two modes of listening that Chion analyzes in *Audio-Vision*. (The three activities rarely occur independently.) Causal listening stresses the object that produces a particular sound – for example, clapping hands; semantic listening stresses the significance of the sound – for example, approval. Aside from encouraging audiences to listen to sounds "in themselves," *Weekend* gets listeners to think causally and semantically about city sounds along the lines of a radio network. It highlights the networked quality of different sounds, not to mention how a radio network can affect their perception. Such perception, writes Chion, taking his cue again from Schaeffer, "is not a purely individual phenomenon, since it partakes in a particular kind of objectivity, that of shared perceptions. And it is in this objectivity-born-of-intersubjectivity that reduced listening ... should be situated."[80] In the case of *Weekend*, this intersubjectivity is embedded in the city as radio network – a fact that harmonizes nicely with the concluding shot of a radio tower in *Berlin, Symphony of a Great City*. The capacity of the radio to isolate, combine, transfer, and connect sounds heightens the listeners' awareness of the causes, meaning, and phenomenological appearance of sounds in the city.

The City as Radio Network

For Kittler, both the establishment of the radio as a uni-directional entertainment apparatus, as well as Brecht's attempt to repurpose the radio as a bi-directional communications apparatus, were based in the military's development of radio technology. To ignore this history is to miss the fact that, as Kittler eloquently puts it, "the trench is the father of mass radio."[81] In this regard, Kittler concludes his short essay on the radio with a quotation from Wilhelm Hoffmann, a *Hörpsiel* theorist and student of Martin Heidegger's: "The radioplay [is] feedback from a World War."[82] Hörspiele such as Brecht's *Flight of the Lindberghs* or Friedrich Wolf's *sos ... rao rao ... Foyn: "Krassin" saves "Italia"* deal with the thematic of death, not simply because the topic attracts listeners, but because the military design and use of the radio, in a way, necessitates it.

While there is some truth to this idea – one cannot deny that the radio's military history plays an important role in its function – it overlooks a more interesting point Kittler could have made given his own media theory. Namely, that the city as a networked medium for sound may be re-mediated on to the airwaves; its connections can be doubled or reconfigured in novel ways to engage the causes, meaning, and appearance of sounds. The connections that characterize the city as a network and those that characterize the radio are not easy to disentangle. They can be organized top-down or bottom-up, centralized or decentralized. Touching on this point, the media theorist Dieter Daniels characterized early German radio (that is, pre-1923 German radio) as a "frequency jungle," one in which amateur broadcasters sent and received signals (including music and other forms of entertainment) to/from one another. Daniel's describes this network in Deleuzian terms: "Before World War I, there were already approximately 100,000 such wireless enthusiasts. They formed a communication structure outside of government or commercial control – a kind of rhizomatic collective of initiates. With Morse code, they developed their own language style and collective ideals. A few expanded their transmissions to include talk and music and produced small but periodic 'broadcasts' for their colleagues."[83] Such a narrative of amateur tinkerers creating a more-or-less utopian, decentralized network would replay itself throughout the twentieth century, most notable with the stories of amateur hackers creating the internet (another military technology).[84] That said, one does not have to fully embrace Daniel's optimistic assessment to understand its significance for Ruttmann's *Weekend*. The early, bi-directional history of German radio – of a radio network constructed for and by amateur enthusiasts – echoes through (and is amplified by) *Weekend*. The Hörbild creates space by connecting sounds in a manner that resembles the communication between different radio receivers. Of course, such a network is depersonalized. It is taken to the extreme point where it is not radio enthusiasts but spaces themselves that are connecting with one another. In this manner, the composition gives both sounds and spaces renewed significance.

Weekend constructs the city as a radio network. But how should one understand this network? Rather than thinking in strictly computational or technical terms, it is better to take our cue from Bruno Latour, who locates the significance of the term in Diderot's sense of *réseau*. According to Latour, the "word réseau was used from the beginning by Diderot to describe matter and bodies in order to avoid the Cartesian divide between matter and spirit."[85] In Latour's adoption of the term, it is used to describe not a hard-wired technical network, nor a loose social network, but one in which human and non-human elements – social and technical elements – are placed on equal footing. For Latour, a network is not "a piece of inert matter in the hands of others, especially of human planners and designers."[86] Rather, it is something that is in a constant state of evolution, in which, for example, things are elevated "to the dignity of texts" and texts are elevated "to the ontological status of things."[87] Such a flattening occurs in *Weekend* as well. Unlike Döblin's *The Story of Franz Biberkopf*, its composition of the city as a radio network decentres the human voice, allowing it to appear (for the purposes of reduced listening) as one of many interconnected sounds. Through this interconnection of sounds it constructs the spaces of a city and its environs. Although it does not reimagine this relationship – indeed, as we have seen, the composition is built on rather hackneyed notion of work/leisure – it nevertheless reconstructs it in a novel way. Namely, it reconstructs the city and the country piecemeal out of their sonic elements – from the bottom up instead of from the top down. The following chapter focuses on how this networked composition of the city expands to encompass the globe in both audial and visual terms.

5

AROUND THE WORLD
Sight and Sound in the Global Symphonies of Vertov and Ruttmann

In re-mediating the city, city symphonies use the material networks of existing urban spaces to sonically build new ones, yet this process need not be constrained to a single city. Often, the networked relations that compose the city symphony imply a larger constellation – the globe. In *Universe of the Mind: A Semiotic Theory of Culture*, the theorist Yuri Lotman provides a useful framework for thinking about this relationship. The city, he writes, "may be isomorphous with the state, and indeed personify it, *be it* in some ideal sense (Rome the city is also Rome the world); but the city can also be an antithesis to the surrounding world. *Urbs et orbis terranum* can be perceived as antagonistic to each other."[1] With regard to the former, the city "is like a church in relation to the city at whose centre it is situated, ... Jerusalem, Rome, Moscow have all been treated as centres of their worlds." Such cities are the ideal embodiments of their respective empires and, at the same time, images of "the heavenly city and a sacred place." With regard to the latter, the city is "placed eccentrically to its earth, beyond its boundaries," as when a ruler asserts his control over a new domain or cultural order through the construction of a new capital. In this sense, "what already exists is declared to be non-existent, and what has yet to appear is declared to be the only thing to exist."[2] Thus, when Peter the Great (1672–1725) began constructing St. Petersburg, he effectively declared Moscow and the cultural order it represented (Slavic, anti-Western) to be a non-entity, while the new capital itself was little more than a swamp.

Both these modes are helpful when considering the city symphony's relationship to the world. On the one hand, the city symphony presents itself as a kind of center – one that *is* the state not just "in some ideal sense," but in the very real sense of documenting modern metropolises that, even when they are not capitals of political states in the manner of Moscow, Berlin, and São Paolo, are nevertheless capitals of industrial modernity such as New York and Milan. On the other hand, the city symphony is antagonistic to the surrounding earth – a construction that is yet to be, a blueprint for a future capital. In this respect, the city symphony creates a new city out of the materials of the present. It fashions an imagined community through montage and sound links between disparate times and spaces. Russolo's *The Awakening of a City* sought to compose a city of the dead (chapter 1); Avraamov's *Symphony of Sirens* rearranged the actual spaces of Baku in the hopes of constructing a new capital for global communism (chapter 2); Vertov's MMC created a composite of four different cities to bring about the acceleration of communism through the rupture of space and time (chapter 3).

Most city symphonies are in fact global in some way, either by implying the world or by structuring global relations on the model of urban modernity through links of labor, production, and machinery (Vertov's *A Sixth Part of the World*, 1926). Curiously, despite portending the balkanization of cinema into separate language groups, the advent of sound film coincided with a broadening of this trend – one that manifests itself in global and regional symphony projects such as Ruttmann's *Melody of the World* (1930), Vertov's *Enthusiasm: Symphony of the Donbass* (1931), Joris Ivens's *Komsomol: Youth Speaks* (1931), and Esfir Shub's *KShE* (1931). How these films – specifically Ruttmann's and Vertov's – incorporated the ability to link sound and image into the symphony film as a global or globe-implying phenomenon is the subject of this chapter. The radical ability to record sonic phenomena as diverse as noise, music, and speech created new ways for these films to link spaces of production and consumption. While both films left the frame of the terrestrial city behind, they nevertheless constructed new, global cities through the bonds of sound and image.

It is not the case that the advent of sound led to the globalization of the city symphony. The city symphony was already global; its responses to the advent of sound were part of an attempt to preserve and further cinema's capacity to foster connections on a worldwide scale. These responses were not always coherent or successful, and it is not my intention to present them as such. Rather, I want to explore how two of the most important city symphony filmmakers responded to the challenge of sound and how they sought to incorporate it into their respective avant-garde programs. As such, it is necessary to take a closer look at one of the fundamental debates regarding the relationship between sound and image in the 1920s and '30s.

Counterpoint

The advent of sound seemed to threaten two of avant-garde film's pillars: the universality of film language and cinema's ability to structure montage links. To overcome this threat filmmakers doubled-down on the musical analogy by articulating various conceptions of cinematic "counterpoint" between sound and image – the treatment of sound and image tracks as if they were independent lines in a musical composition. Beginning in the late 1920s, this metaphor was routinely invoked by filmmakers, composers, and theorists including Walter Ruttmann, Alberto Cavalcanti, Bertolt Brecht, Rudolf Arnheim, Siegfried Kracauer, Béla Balázs, Hans Eisler, and Theodor Adorno as a way of extending and adapting the principles of montage to sound-filmmaking.[3] Its most famous articulation comes by way of Sergei Eisenstein, Vsevolod Pudovkin, and Grigori Alexandrov's famous "Statement on Sound," in which the filmmakers assert that "the contrapuntal use of sound vis-à-vis the visual fragment of montage will open up new possibilities for the development and perfection of montage." For this reason, "the first experiments in sound must aim at a sharp discord with the visual images. Only such a 'hammer and tongs' approach will produce the necessary sensation that will result consequently in the creation of a new orchestral counterpoint of visual and sound images."[4] Contrapuntal sound, these filmmakers contended, rejected the synchronized sound-editing techniques of narrative films – of "highly cultured dramas" – in favour of a conflict between sound and image. Rather than use sound to mask the disjunctive qualities of editing, they sought to heighten this disjunction.[5]

In thus emphasizing conflict, counterpoint disrupts the illusion of cinematic continuity in the service of such avant-garde ideas as Bertolt Brecht's *Verfremdungseffekt* (alienation effect) and Viktor Shklovsky's *Ostranenie* (defamiliarization), both of which force the viewer to slow down and contemplate an otherwise familiar occurrence. With this idea in mind, Kristin Thompson, in her survey of Soviet counterpoint, suggests that one of counterpoint's main functions is to "roughen" perception. "Perceptual 'roughening,'"[6] Thompson writes, "implies that the film confronts the spectator with an unusual device which is difficult to perceive smoothly; the purpose ... is to stimulate the spectator to a more intense, active perception."[7] From here, Thompson proceeds to examine how manipulations and disjunctions of the sound and image track facilitate the "chain reaction"[8] of Eisenstein's montage theory – from the lower levels of perception (metric, rhythmic) to the higher levels of cognition (overtonal, intellectual). Similarly, though he rejects Thompson's "formalist" approach, Ian Christie locates contrapuntal sound in the transition between two "higher-order" (i.e., mental) discursive regimes – the first based on montage's relationship to inner speech as theorized by Boris Eichenbaum; the second based on sound's relationship to outer speech and public discourse. In this regard, "the overall strategy of" Eisenstein, Pudovkin, and Alexandrov's "Statement on Sound" was to "mount a tactical defense of montage by conceding certain criticism, while seeking to relocate the inner speech/montage relationship within the new ensemble of sound cinema."[9] In other words, contrapuntal sound cinema was about preventing the overt vocalization of a film's main ideas. These ideas should not rain down on the spectator from a microphone; rather, they had to emerge through an inner dialogue between the spectator and the film.

Interestingly, the idea of renewal that is so important for cinematic counterpoint was also an issue for the original use of the term. The musical idea of counterpoint has its roots in the polyphonic style of the fourteenth century known as *ars nova*. Centred in Avignon during the time of the papal schism, this style is noted for utilizing increasingly complex rhythmic and polyphonic structures that broke with the monophonic tradition of Gregorian chant. As in Guillaume de Machaut's "Quant en moy," two singers could sing two different poems to two different melodies and rhythmic structures at the same time. From the perspective of the twentieth century, this polyphonic complexity appeared to reflect the upheavals of the fourteenth, a period which saw the schism of the church (1378–1417), the Hundred Years' War (1337–1453), and the Black Death (1347–50),[10] as well as the invention of the magnetic compass and the mechanical clock. Accompanying these disruptions, as music historians J. Peter Burkholder, Donald Jay Grout, and Claude V. Palisca note, we also see the emergence of arguments over the aesthetic value of the new. The very name, *ars nova*, first coined c. 1320 by Johannes de Muris in his treatise *Ars Novae Musicae*, appears in opposition to *ars antiqua*. Defenders of ars antiqua, such as Jacques De Liège, charged the new art with consisting of mere novelties that would soon grow stale: "Wherein does this lasciviousness in singing so greatly please," de Liège wonders, "this excessive refinement, by which as some think, the words are lost, the harmony of consonance is diminished, the value of the notes is changed, perfection is brought low, imperfection is exalted, and measure is confused." As with the church, a schism opened between the enthusiasts of the new and defenders of the old. Likewise, the acceleration of technological innovation began increasingly to manifest itself as a force to which music must respond.

Six centuries after ars nova, the practitioners of another new art, the cinema, invoked the ideas of polyphony and counterpoint as a way of renewing their tradition. In contrast to ars nova, however, contrapuntal cinema in the 1930s had a more ambiguous relationship to the new. Instead of simply breaking with tradition, it seemed to defend the New (the avant-garde) as a tradition unto itself in the face of what Boris Groys considers its technological and ideological obsolescence. The avant-garde, as Groys argues, sought to outstrip the dialectic of tradition and change inaugurated, in part, by ars nova.[11] By the end of the 1920s, however, this attempt to surpass progress was under threat. In capitalist countries, the techniques of the avant-garde were being co-opted by a popular culture that promised endless novelties and technological innovations. In socialist countries, its aim of establishing a universal art was being absorbed by the monolithic style of socialist realism.

Coinciding with both tendencies, contrapuntal cinema reveals a dynamic attempt to renew the new – to engage recorded sound in the hopes of expanding the possibilities of the cinematic medium as a whole. One site of this expansion is the city symphony as *world* symphony. Of course, not all city symphony filmmakers bought into the idea of counterpoint. Dziga Vertov, for instance, rejected the notion, though he did at times characterize his earlier silent films, for instance, *A Sixth Part of the World*, as a "word-radio-theme in contrapuntal construction."[12] That said, in an article for *Kino i Zhizn*, the filmmaker wrote "that neither correspondence nor non-correspondence between what is seen and what is heard is by any means necessary for either documentary or played films."[13] What is more, since the publication of Michel Chion's *Audio-Vision*, the idea of counterpoint as a tool of cinematic analysis has fallen out of favour. Echoing Vertov's dismissal of counterpoint, Chion argues that this analogy forces a linear interpretation of the *meaning* of certain sounds – of their "*codedness* (seagulls = seashore) rather than their own sonic substance, their specific characteristics in the passage in question." This type of interpretation "reduces the audio and visual elements to abstractions at the expense of their multiple concrete particularities, which are much richer and full of ambiguity."[14] Chion, in turn, advocates investigating the particularities – the coupling and decoupling, continuity and discontinuity – of specific sounds and images largely in terms of their vertical relationships. Strictly speaking, Chion points out, there is "no image track and no soundtrack in the cinema, but a place of images, plus sounds."[15] In other words, the metaphor of a linear track – along with the corresponding notion of "inner speech" – must be supplanted by a holistic approach that pays attention to more than just the "meaning" of certain sounds in relation to the image.

That said, counterpoint is still useful for thinking about the city symphony, especially when considering historically concrete examples such as Ruttmann's and Vertov's. Although Vertov may have dismissed the idea as unnecessarily restrictive, his films nevertheless reveal a great deal of engagement with the idea through their reliance on conflict between sound and image. By contrast, despite relying far less on an aesthetics of discontinuity in his filmmaking, Ruttmann discussed his early sound films in largely contrapuntal terms. In both cases, counterpoint reveals how sound and music in the city symphony film are more than just analogies for film form; they connect to a history of sonic experimentation that resonates through the soundtracks (or sonic spaces) of city symphony films. Counterpoint highlights the avant-garde idea that conflict is the engine of the New, not just in the sense of a renewed relation to the cinematic medium, but in that of a renewed, audiospatial visual connection between disparate people, places, and things – a new conception of the global city. This novelty is at the heart of the sound in the city symphony film.

Melody of the World

One month after the appearance of Eisenstein's "Statement on Sound," Walter Ruttmann penned his own article on the emerging art of sound cinema, a topic both directors would soon get a chance to discuss in September 1929 at the first International Congress of Independent Cinema in La Sarraz, Switzerland.[16] Like Eisenstein, Ruttmann forcefully advocated for a relationship of conflict between sound and image.

> Sound film, whose technological and constructive challenges have now been solved, is beginning its artistic development. It would be utterly wrong to see it as a simple augmentation of silent film. It is not sound film's task to give voice to silent film. It must be clear from the outset that its laws have almost nothing to do with those of soundless film. A completely new situation is evolving here. Moving-image photography is being coupled with photographed sound. The whole artistic secret of sound film consists in the coupling of these two photographed elements in such a way as to create something new: namely, the activity that grows from the opposition between image and sound. Counterpoint, optical-acoustic counterpoint, must be the basis of all sound film design. The battle between image and sound, their play with each other, their temporary fusion, which dissolves again to enable further oppositional relations – these are the possibilities. In conclusion, let it be said: the sound film problem can never imply and enhancement or degradation of silent film, nor can it solve the problems of silent film or replace it.
>
> Sound film points in a new direction, and it will prove its merit.[17]

Here, one finds many of the essential components that make up the argument for a counterpoint of sound and image: a defence of (sound) film as art, as having "merit"; an emphasis on the new as a value in itself; an understanding of the new as emerging from a process of conflict, a "battle between image and sound"; and finally, the notion that silent film must be defended from either enhancement or degradation by the appearance of a new medium, that sound film and soundless film follow different "laws."

To what extent do these ideas manifest themselves in Ruttmann's first sound film is an open question. A co-production of the Hamburg-America Line (HAPAG) – one of the world's largest shipping concerns – and the Tonbild-Syndikat (Sound-Image Syndicate) – an optical-film technology producer and distributor – *Melody of the World* joins the advent of sound film to the acceleration of global trade. It deploys the cross-sectional method of *Berlin, Symphony of a Great City* to compose the world as a network of material and cultural exchanges. The relations that structure *Berlin*, in this sense, come to form a sound-image of the world. The film follows a sailor aboard a HAPAG ship as he makes his way around the globe. Rather than trace the linear route of the ship from port to port, however, the film opts for a three-act structure that renders the world through a compare and contrast of diverse sounds and images. The result is a catalogue or a database, to use the language of new media, of parallel cultural and economic practices.[18] Act 1 compares the world's architecture, city streets, and religious practices, situating these in the context of the trauma of World War I by a concluding sequence that compares the sounds of war. Act 2 compares the worlds of children, sailors, fishermen, and peasants. It concludes with a tour of the sporting world (calisthenics, archery, bowling, martial arts, etc.). Finally, act 3 traverses women's morning routines, the languages of the world, mealtimes, music, dance, and theatre. Much as in *Berlin* and *Weekend*, the film concludes with a resumption of the workday and the return of the HAPAG ship to its home port. These diverse sights and sounds are taken in by the HAPAG sailor, who appears occasionally throughout the film, maintaining a benevolent Western male gaze (figure 5.1). We see him, for instance, smiling bashfully as foreign and exotic women dress and do their hair; or laughing generously while buying bananas from half-clothed children. His parochial perspective is supplemented by the outer

Figure 5.1 / HAPAG sailor purchasing bananas.

edges of the film's narrative frame: an animated image of interplanetary space opens and closes the film, thus suggesting not only the smallness and fragility of the earth but also cinema's next frontier – a symphony of the universe.

Melody of the World sought to propagate a message of peace and universal understanding through monopoly-regulated trade. The opening title of the film is worth quoting in its entirety.

> The Hamburg-America Line has put its network of ships [*Schiffartsnetz*] at the service of the unity among peoples and has sent a film expedition around the world to increase understanding of the manifold forms [*formen*] of human life and to show what unites people. Its work was supported by the governments of Germany, Great Britain, France, Italy, the United States of North America, Holland, Greece, India, Siam, China, Japan, Panama and Cuba, whose territories the expedition explored on its journey. The Hamburg-America Line thanks the representatives of these governments and all those who have contributed to this work for their assistance on this project of representing humanity in its life and work.[19]

This statement presents *Melody of the World* as the obverse of Avraamov's *Symphony of Sirens*, a statement of capitalist (as opposed to communist) internationalism. Whereas Avraamov's symphony sought to compose the unity of oppressed toilers, be they from colonized or colonizing countries, through the sounds of a single industrial project (the construction of the October Revolution), Ruttmann's symphony seeks to compose the unity of workers and peasants through a composition based on the formal similarities of their daily habits and cultural practices. Through the same types of comparisons, the film further aligns these practices with those of the bourgeoisie, thus creating an image of the world where similarity reigns over difference. The ideological message of the film is that there is more that brings us together than sets us apart.

The film's emphasis on formal similarities is interesting as well. *Melody of the World* begins with an Oscar Wilde quotation from *The Picture of Dorian Gray*: "The real secret of the world is what we see, not what is hidden." The German translation of this quotation – "Das wahre Geheimnis der Welt liegt im Sichtbaren, nicht im Unsichtbaren" – reads somewhat more abstractly: "The real secret of the world lies in the seen, not in the unseen." It is an interesting quotation to begin a sound film, despite the fact that "Sichtbaren" may also be rendered as "appearance," which applies equally to both sound and image. On the one hand, the quotation suggests a shift to a phenomenological analysis of the world, one augmented by the power of technological apparatuses such as the camera that have the potential to reveal what Benjamin calls the "optical unconscious."[20] In the case of sound experiments and films such as *Weekend* and *Melody of the World*, one could perhaps speak of an aural unconscious – acute eruptions of otherwise unnoticed sonic phenomena. On the other hand, the film's approach to the world's audiovisual phenomena is far from revealing an unconscious structure, let alone the secrets they so playfully mask and reveal. Rather, the emphasis on the "manifold forms of human life" stresses the unity of seeming difference in formal similarity – a characteristic of the cross-sectional (as opposed to dialectical) approach to montage for which Ruttmann was known.

Cross-sectional montage creates a database of similarities based on shape and sound, one that ranges over higher-order cultural and economic practices in a manner that elides the material, social, and political significance of these practices. It was a key stylistic feature of the New Objectivity (*die Neue Sachlichkeit*), a popular artistic movement in the Weimar Republic that centred on surface manifestations of modern life. Channelling the criticism of Carl Mayer – Ruttmann's one time collaborator who first conceived of the idea for a Berlin Symphony – Siegfried Kracauer argued that Ruttmann's reliance on such a "surface approach" emphasized "the formal qualities of the objects rather than their meanings."[21] It stressed "pure patterns of movement," rather than, say, a dialectical conflict of movement.[22] A similar criticism may be levelled against *Melody of the World*. The film places an equals sign between social and cultural phenomena that are in fact the result vastly different processes. In the logic of the film, a sound-image of eating, praying, speaking, or dancing is equivalent to any other sound-image of eating, praying, speaking, or dancing. The implication is that all these phenomena are manifestations of some universal human spirit. In this manner, sound cinema, in conjunction with the mobility of global shipping, reveals that "we" – the term elided in the German translation of Wilde's aphorism – are more similar than different.

At the same time, in a proto-McLuhanist way, Ruttmann's cross-sectional approach highlights a shift in twentieth-century thinking about causality, one marked by the renewed significance that the proliferation of mass media gave to Aristotle's notion of formal cause.[23] Aristotle famously outlined four types of causality – material, formal, efficient, and final. The material cause is "that out of which a thing comes to be and which persists"; the formal cause is "the form or the archetype, i.e. the statement of the essence, ... and the parts in the definition [logos]"; the efficient cause is "the primary source of the change or coming to rest"; and the final cause is "the end or 'that for the sake of which' a thing is done."[24] Of these four, formal causality is the most enigmatic – an enigma that Aristotle's examples help only partially clarify. The "relation of 2:1," for instance, is the formal cause of "the octave"; the "definition" [logos] of a house is the cause of its form [eidos]. Definition and relation, in other words, are two key components of Aristotle's notion of formal cause. As Eric McLuhan points out, this connection between eidos (form) and logos is one taken up by Marshall McLuhan through the idea that the medium is the message.[25] For the latter McLuhan, it is the form of the medium (as opposed to the content) that structures its message; the relations that determine a particular medium constitute its formal cause. New media in the twentieth century manifest this shift by structuring investigations in terms of relation. Chronophotography, time-motion studies, cross-sectional montage, and data analysis all place the emphasis on form, as describing not only the shape of a certain process but also its definition [logos]. What, proto-cinema asks, is the formal cause of a horse's gallop? Similarly, Ruttmann's *Melody of the World* inquires into the formal causes – i.e., the music-like relationships – of everything from city traffic to religious practices.

Of course, form – whether of a medium or of a specific work – always carries a message that goes beyond the mere structural definition of what it means to be a certain thing. Investigations into formal causes are easily inflected with ideology; one need only consider the formal comparisons between skull shapes or criminal "types."[26] Hence, to accuse Ruttmann's film of being purely formal – i.e., unconcerned with meaning – would seem to cover up that it is in fact interested in suggesting an ideological message through structural comparisons and relations. This message, of course, is that we are all fundamentally similar, part of a great scale of sound and movement that could be brought together through the agency of global shipping. Capitalism, in this sense, is the ultimate formal cause of the world; Ruttmann's film is merely its agent.

As a strategy for generating the new, contrapuntal sound figures into this process at relatively rare moments. The first extended use of the technique comes at the end of act 1 during the sounds-of-war sequence. Here, the non-diegetic sounds of an upbeat military march – accompanied by images of marching soldiers from various countries – simulate the lead-up to World War I. After the music (in conjunction with an image of bubbling lava) takes an ominous turn, battlefield sounds of yelling soldiers and cannon fire are blended into the score, coupling and decoupling with the image track. One hears, for instance, the overwhelming sound of a cannon blast as a cavalryman fires his rifle, then a similar sound as waves rock a ship and a column of fire and smoke burst in the air. This contrapuntal mix of synchronous and asynchronous war sounds is interrupted twice by the contorted face of a mother screaming. Rendered in synchronized sound, the abruptness of this scream has an ethical force; it brings the belligerent parties to their senses.[27] The scream arrests the flow of war-images, which give way to a field of crosses and the hollow sounds of wind. Everything, then, is washed in the calm waters of the ocean – a common Ruttmann motif (see, for instance, the opening sequence of *Berlin*) – in preparation for the second act.

At the conclusion of act 2, one finds the second extended use of counterpoint. Here, after a long sequence comparing the martial arts of the world (archery, javelin, judo, fencing, sumo, and boxing), we find ourselves at the races. The contrapuntal ringing of a starting bell initiates a sequence in which the noise of a crowd (cheering and whistling) overlays images of humans, horses, dogs, and automobiles racing around tracks from around the world. The act concludes with an abrupt return of non-diegetic music accompanying visuals from an air show. Finally, the last major contrapuntal sequence comes in the middle of act 3. It concerns the languages of the world. Here, the image of two Muslim men fighting is juxtaposed with the sounds of barking dogs, followed by contrapuntal coupling and decoupling of images of men and women speaking languages from Africa, Europe, and Asia. The image track also makes use of superimposition, overlaying, for instance, an image of two Asian men having a conversation over an image of a European city. This spectrum of speech – from human to animal – is presented with no particular hierarchy in mind. There is, in other words, no evolutionary message in the sequence, just a series of comparisons and contrasts. The scene concludes with a stilted dialogue, rendered in synchronized sound, between the playwright Bernard Shaw and the filmmaker Ivor Montagu.

In these sequences, contrapuntal sound underscores the formal similarities between different sonic practices from around the world. "Speech is speech," "sport is sport," and "war is war," the film seems to say. Likewise, it is during moments of conflict (argument, competition, and battle) that humanity reveals itself, through juxtapositions of sound and image, to be largely the same. Thus, in *Melody of the World*, counterpoint is not so much the engine of the new as its precursor. The moments that are most charged with the new are in fact those which are rendered in synchronized sound following a contrapuntal sequence. A sound-image such as that of the screaming mother is far more disruptive and evocative than the subtle layering of voices and bells during the sporting sequence. Such a sound-image reflects a more interesting use of synchronized sound throughout the film – one that disrupts the general flow of the film. The rattling of anchor chains to announce the departure of the ship; the use of steam whistles and engine sounds to punctuate the montage of the ship's departure; the sound-image of an Indian man playing a hand drum incorporated into a montage of traffic; the synchronized sound of a trumpet announcing the beginnings of World War I; a proto–musique concrète composition of world instruments featuring hand drum, xylophone, sitar, cymbal, violin, piano, and oboe. All these suggest that the main conflict at the heart of the film is not one between sound and image but between what Chion calls the internal and external logic of a film's "audiovisual flow."

For Chion, sound film's internal logic is "a mode of connecting images and sounds that appears to follow a flexible, organic process of development, variation, and growth, born out of the narrative situation itself and the feelings it inspires." In *Melody of the World*, contrapuntal moments oftentimes follow precisely this sort of logic, the sounds from different diegetic spaces in the film essentially function like an extra-diegetic musical score. By contrast, external logic is "that which rings out effects of discontinuity and rupture as interventions external to the represented content: editing that disrupts the continuity of image or a sound, breaks, interruptions, sudden changes of tempo, and so on."[28] In this regard, in *Melody of the World*, synchronized sound-images often break into the internal logic of the film at key moments: departure, war, argument, and armistice. More than a counterpoint of sound and image, it is this conflict between external and internal logic that sustains the feeling of the new – of "perceptual roughening" – throughout the film. Such eruptions of the new, however, are tightly controlled, circumscribed by similarities of sound and image and underwritten by the benevolence of commercial shipping in a manner that fosters the creation of a homogeneous and orderly global city. By contrast, in Vertov's first sound film, *Enthusiasm: Symphony of the Donbass* (1931), connection between disparate locales is maintained not by formal but rather by efficient causes – material relations of cause and effect. Vertov places not only equals signs between disparate phenomena (as in the formula religious belief = alcoholism), but also signs of addition, subtraction, multiplication, and division (as in the formula Soviet power + electrification of the countryside = communism). In this respect, the distinction between internal and external logic is difficult to apply to Vertov's film. External sounds of the real world (i.e., noises) structure the film's internal flow but also threaten to break up this flow at any moment. Structuring these relations between sound and image is a job for synchrony and counterpoint alike. The network they create is the focus of the discussion that follows.

"Cine-Ambulance" vs Power Station

In his 1930 speech to the First All-Union Conference on Soviet Sound, Dziga Vertov put forward two options for recording sound film on location: one could either use a mobile system in the form of "a specially adapted sound cinema vehicle (like an ambulance or fire engine)," or one could use stationary equipment consisting of a "far-flung network of microphones" and "silent film cameras."[29] Initially, one might suspect that Vertov overwhelmingly preferred the first option, which harkened back to his time as an organizer and head of cinema aboard agitprop trains that traversed the former Russian Empire following the October Revolution.[30] Playfully decorated and bearing names such as *Lenin*, *October Revolution*, and *Red East*, these trains were practically small cities on the move. According to David King, Leon Trotsky's famous fifteen-car train, aboard which the War Commissar spent an incredible two and a half years, was equipped with "a radio and telegraph station, print-shop, library, electricity generator, a mobile garage equipped with cars and trucks for visiting and supplying the fronts at close range and a kitchen and a bathroom."[31] Trains such as Trotsky's transported everything from political leaders and military supplies to gramophone records bearing Lenin's voice and film's bearing his image.[32] Administratively, they also resembled cities. As John MacKay notes, "trains were comprised of a number of divisions and subdivisions, including an office that accepted complaints and petitions; an information division that prepared propaganda and agitational materials"; a division of the Russian Telegraph Agency in charge of publishing and radio broadcasts; "staff involved in the supervision and inspection of local bureaucracies ... ; accounting, technical, and maintenance units ... ; and the cinema division," which served as both a mobile production and screening unit, shuttling camera crews to remote locations during the day while housing screenings in boxcars at night.

Vertov appears to have adapted this dual function to his conception of a cine-ambulance or fire engine. Indeed, early train agitators frequently invoked the metaphor of "emergency [*pozharnaia*] assistance" to describe their goal of getting "to places beyond the reach of the more sparsely distributed and stationary propaganda outlets (or *agitpunkty*: agitational points)."[33] Vertov believed that a "mobile sound cinema-unit" should also be outfitted for such a goal. In other words, it ought to equipped for the production *and* screening of sound film. Not only should it be possible to film images and record sounds, as well as develop, view, and listen to short sequences ("of around twenty metres") directly from the vehicle; it should also be possible, as Vertov pointed out, to convert the vehicle "for sound projection on a small outdoor screen." Such a vehicle could "conduct a great deal of cultural educational work in acquainting the inhabitants of the remotest parts of our Soviet Union with sound cinema."[34] Rushing about on four (or more) wheels, such a cine-ambulance would bring sound film to the masses, thus strengthening the connections of a new global city.

The first conception of documentary sound cinema was thus predicated on the mobility of wheels and rails – on road and railway networks connecting the disparate peoples of the Soviet Union. At the same time, it also sought to bring aspects of city life – the proletarian, urban experiences of cinema, mass rallies, and speeches by political leaders – to the largely peasant population of the USSR. Vertov realized that, in the short term, this was the direction that documentary sound film was headed, and it was certainly better than the artificial sound effects being recorded in studios, a process that the fact-obsessed Vertov abhorred. That said, despite having served as head of cinema aboard the agit-train *October Revolution* in 1920, Vertov preferred the second option for sound cinema. And with good reason: the weight of the equipment used to record his first sound film, *Enthusiasm: Symphony of the Donbass* (hence: *Enthusiasm*), weighed roughly 2,700 pounds.[35] A stationary "network of microphones," Vertov thought, "would be much more flexible than a mobile sound unit, just as a vast power station with a network of lines is more flexible than a mobile generator."[36] In somewhat vague and guarded terms, lest he be accused of utopianism, Vertov envisioned a kind of television – a "sound-recording and sound-reproducing radio station"[37] – that would cover in the blink of an eye the vast expanses that he had traversed in the 1920s: "Instead of a few dozen sound-recording cinema vehicles – the recording of images and sounds regardless of distance. Instead of several hundred sound-reproducing cinema vehicles – the long-distance transmission of sound films."[38] Ever the Futurist, Vertov believed that the answer to the question of how to make sound films did not lie in cinema's past – in agit-trains and railway cars – but in its future – in the wireless transmission of signals across vast distances, in radio and television. Only in this manner could Soviet cinema hope to fulfill the Five-Year Plan's goal of overtaking capitalist countries.

Vertov's wholesale embrace of a "network of microphones" might strike one as odd given the extent to which his last silent film, *Man with a Movie Camera* (MMC), stresses the mobility of the cameraman. In MMC, one sees the acrobatic cameraman performing feats of agility and strength – scaling a smokestack, being trampled beneath a train, filming from a moving car, and riding with a fire brigade. This final image brings to mind the very cine-ambulance method of sound recording that Vertov regarded as the proximally pragmatic yet ultimately deficient method of the two sound-film recording options he put forward in his speech. The cameraman, as Gilles Deleuze notes, stresses the importance of mobility in Vertov's famed theory of the movement interval – the idea that "the elements of the art of movement are composed of the intervals (the transitions from one movement to another) and by no means by the movements themselves."[39] This theory could not function in practice were it not for the movement of a specific agent. As Deleuze points out, "the cinema could not run in this way from one end of the universe to the other without having at its disposal an agent which was capable of making all the parts converge."[40] In MMC, this agent is the cameraman.[41] He reveals that cinema's ability to relate and relay images across the Soviet Union is predicated on its mobility. Focusing on him, one sees that distances are not magically connected together; rather, they are the result of the actions and labour of specific people and machines – of cameras, crews, editors, projectors, cars, and railways.

Figure 5.2
The Komsomolka.

By contrast, Vertov's next film – and his first sound film – *Enthusiasm: Symphony of the Donbass* (1931) places less stress on the mobility of a specific individual and apparatus and more on the agency of a network – an agency that is much more difficult to personify. The individual meant to reveal the process of sound-filmmaking – to bear the device and de-reify the process – plays a relatively limited role in comparison to the cameraman in ммс. Instead of a man with a movie camera, we have a woman with a pair of headphones. She is a *komsomolka*, a member of the Communist Youth League (figure 5.2). Instead of traversing the production sites of the Soviet Union with a microphone, she listens to them with her headphones. The komsomolka is primarily featured in *Enthusiasm's* prologue. We see her entering the frame from the left, sitting down at a radio receiver, and placing a pair of headphones over her ears. The first note of *Enthusiasm's* score causes her head to jerk up. Throughout the first third of the film, she is regularly referred to both visually (her face, eyes, headset, and ears) and aurally (the sound her radio set makes) as the listener of the film's score. This fact is made explicit when a voice announces into her headphones – "Attention! Attention! We're broadcasting the march, 'The Last Sunday,' from the film, *The Symphony of the Donbass*." This march takes the komsomolka on a journey from the desacralization of churches to the production of coal.

As Oksana Bulgakowa notes, the komsomolka "functions as the mediator of filmic hearing just as the man with the camera acted as the mediator of filmic vision."[42] However, though she does invite us to reflect on the nature of sound-images, the komsomolka does not act – that is, move – in the same way as the man with the movie camera. The former is active while the latter is receptive. As such, as Bulgakowa points out, "in the attribution of senses [Vertov] follows the traditional distribution of gender roles as suggested by Adorno: vision is male, and hearing is female. The eye demands analytical concentration, while the ear is undifferentiated, chaotic, emotional and passive."[43] This focus on passivity de-emphasizes the role of a specific agent (or group of agents) in bringing together sound-images and focuses instead on receptivity. The komsomolka is stationary beside her radio. She does not partake in the recording of events from the Donbass; rather she is their receiver. She interacts with the commotion from the Donbass from a distance. She is not so much an agent in the full sense of the cameraman, and more of a node in a network.

This network is figured throughout Vertov's film in the form of telegraph noises, conveyer belt wheels, and the subject of the film itself – the production of electricity. The film places an emphasis less on mobility and more on the logic of signal and receiver. In one scene, for instance, workers in a movie theatre are called on to address a coal shortage. A combination of canted high- and low-angled shots depicts Soviet citizens making their way to the theatre. These images are intercut with those of coal plants, conveyer belts, trains, and smokestacks. The audio that plays over this sequence is a heterogenous mixture of the culturally recognizable – a voice announcing a story ("It happened in the Donbass!" "A coal shortage") – and harsh noises – dissonant whistle tones and harsh buzzing sounds. The transitions between the announcer's voice and the sounds of the whistle are sudden, yet they retain a kind of fluidity due to the rhythmic similarity between the voice and the intonations of the whistle. It is as if the noises are mimicking human speech, or as if they are translating speech into machine noise. Similarly, the relationship between sound and image is characterized by a high degree of counterpoint, one that stresses the fluid barrier between humans and machines. Inside the theatre, for instance, movie-goers watch a worker on screen;

Figure 5.3
A coal worker speaking with the voice of a telegraph.

the sounds of his speech are rendered through the noises of a telegraph (figure 5.3). Images of stalled factories and empty coal bins proliferate. At the end of the scene, moved by the noises of coal-starved factories, the audience rises to sing the "Internationale," thus affirming their commitment to fill the shortage. Their singing, unlike the preceding shots, is rendered in synchronized sound.

This transition from asynchrony to synchrony is accompanied by an acceleration in the pace of montage. Production kicks into overdrive. The camera races along superimposed images of multiplying railroad tracks to an industrial site. After a motivational speech and some images of shock-worker training, the film presents another scene depicting this networked, call-and-response relationship between humans and machines. Here, two rotating flywheels beneath a red star are set in motion by workers pledging to fill and overfulfill their quota (figure 5.4). Their enthusiasm, which is synonymous with the production of electricity itself, literally sets the wheels in motion. Such scenes of call-and-response – of signal and receiver – embody what MacKay has called Vertov's "sensory agora." According to MacKay, this agora aims "to establish cinema as a kind of surrogate public space wherein the perceptual worlds of different segments of Soviet society – as registered by the camera and sound-recording apparatus

Figure 5.4 / Shock worker pledging to overfill her quota and the machine's approving response.

– could at once be experienced, contrasted, compared, and ultimately grasped as familiar elements of an expanding sensorium." Central to this idea is what MacKay terms an "education ... in the sensory environments of all the members of society" such that "the 'noise,' the misunderstood and dishonored perceptual worlds of 'others' – and particularly of working people – might gradually be understood and incorporated into the creative imaginations of Soviet citizens as a group."[44] This expanding sensorium accounts for the so-called noise in *Enthusiasm*. It is not really "noise" but a way in which Soviet citizens could inhabit a shared sensory environment across vast distances.[45]

The aim of *Enthusiasm* is thus quite similar to Avraamov's *Symphony of Sirens*, which sought to structure a symphony of labour through the spaces of Baku. As I pointed out in chapter 2, in its conception, this city symphony was already a world symphony insofar as it presented Baku as a new Jerusalem or Rome that would unify the proletarians of the industrialized West with the toilers of the colonized East. Similarly, Vertov's regional symphony implies a global set of relations between humans and machines. These connections are facilitated by a network of audiovisual recording and transmission (Vertov's power station), one that Vertov hoped would extend beyond the senses of sight and sound to those of smell and touch. In an article titled "On the Radio-Eye," Vertov set down the relationship between these senses as proceeding, ladderlike, to the unification of all sensory and conceptual activities: "From the montage of facts seen and recorded on film (Kino-Eye) to the montage of facts seen, heard and transmitted over the radio (Radio-Eye) to the simultaneous montage of seen, heard, tactile, and olfactory (etc.) facts, to the 'capturing of human thoughts unawares,' and finally, to great experiments in the immediate organization of all ... human thoughts – such technical perspectives of the Kino-Eye have been called into being by the October [Revolution]."[46] For Vertov, the Kino- and Radio-Eye sought to realize a society controlled by a set of mass-media mechanisms that expressed the will of a networked organism. The ladder recalls the theories of Vertov's teacher, Vladimir Bechterev, who argued that the human nervous system is constituted by reflexes, some of which are hard-wired, others of which may be rechannelled (conditioned reflexes). The guiding metaphor for this conception of the human brain was that of a network – specifically, a telephone switchboard.[47] The conditioning of these reflexes depends on external stimuli, specifically movements (gestures, facial expressions, sound patterns) that trigger complementary movements in the brain (thoughts). The idea was influential not only in neurological circles (Pavlov) but also in those of the avant-garde (Vertov, Eisenstein, and Brecht).

Before becoming a filmmaker, Vertov studied at Bechterev's Petrograd Neurological Institute.[48] Thus it is quite possible that his theories influenced Vertov's ideas on the Radio-Eye, which posits a media apparatus that may register sights, sounds, smells, and even thoughts in the organization of society as a vast network of "facts." This network resembles – and even functions like – an organism in the Bechterevian sense. Facts – sights, sounds, smells, and thoughts – resemble reflexes that may be connected and reconnected. The result is a neural network that spans the Soviet Union.

It is important to keep in mind, however, that one of the touchstones of this network continues to be the city. In *Enthusiasm*, for instance, this touchstone is figured in a model city, complete with buildings and a railway, that announces the beginning of Stalin's Five-Year Plan. As a train carrying goods, grain, and tractors circulates through this model city, the words "Toward socialism" flash on the screen. Images of the train are superimposed on one another, filling the screen. The message is clear: production and abundance. The city as a network of humans and machines producing the means to realize socialism is the model for the Soviet Union as a whole. This network gains its senses – and organizes its sensorium – through the apparatus of the Radio-Eye. In this regard, in the transition from silent to sound film, one can see that Vertov was working on a single project through a change in the cinematic medium: to foster an industrial society by depicting the connections between people and machines across distances in accordance with the movements and rhythms of their cultural and productive practices. The emphasis on the movement of the cameraman in MMC is displaced on to the energy (enthusiasm) of the network as a whole. This was not a rearguard operation to salvage the principle of Vertov's silent filmmaking, but an extension of them in the hopes of bringing about a mediated society in which not only sight and sound but rather all somatic and mental responses could be organized.

Conclusion

The "essential myth of modern life," writes T.J. Clark, is "that the city has become a free field of signs and exhibits, a marketable mass of images, an area in which the old separations have broken down for good."[49] Ruttmann's *Melody of the World* generalizes this myth to the globe in terms of not only images but sounds as well. In the film, the world has become a "free field of signs and exhibits," each one formally equivalent to any other. As in many *Gestamtkunstwerke*, these produce an image of the world as an ideal polis (a yet-to-be city) in which differences are a matter of degree. All differences, in this respect, can be reconciled through a comparison of forms. The greater the distance between two practices, the more similar they become. To a certain degree, the external logic of the film – moments of synchrony as opposed to those of counterpoint – interrupts this internal flow of sounds and images. While it does not undermine the capitalist-universalist ideals of the shipping concern that sponsored the film, it nevertheless rubs against these ideals at key points. A screaming mother, rattling shipping chains, the banging of a hand drum; these synchronized sound-images cannot be easily assimilated into the film's overarching message of similarity despite difference. They cause the viewer to pause, to search for strategies for incorporating these moments into the otherwise flowing narrative. These synchronized sound-images are the ones that are the most difficult to perceive smoothly. They are also the one's that keep Ruttmann's film from descending into mere propaganda for global shipping.

Dismissed as cacophony, Vertov's *Enthusiasm* was not well received by critics, who accused it of formalism, of pointless experimentation.[50] Beyond just the harsh noises of the film, conflicts between sound and image – as well as those between counterpoint and synchrony (as when synchronous singing of the "Internationale" spontaneously interrupts a contrapuntal sequence) – no doubt contributed to this impression. However, Vertov's "cacophony" had two distinct purposes. One was building connections between the sensory environments of workers; the other was demonstrating the material relations of cause and effect that structure production. In the regard, the global city that Vertov's film constructs is quite different from Ruttmann's. Its focus is regional, though it still implies an international worker's movements. More importantly, it structures a network in which humans and machines interact through visual and audible cues (as in the scene where workers' pledges cause a machine to spin). This network embodies Vertov's ideas on the Radio-Eye, notably the idea that sound cinema should apply the principles of an electric grid – a power station – to the recording and transmission of audiovisual phenomena. Such an idea was more than a means to overcome the difficulty of transporting heavy audio equipment; it was a statement of Vertov's overarching ambition, informed by Bechterev's ideas on neurological reflexes, to wire the Soviet Union like an electric organism.

While the differences between Vertov's and Ruttmann's films are vast, it is important to stress one of their key similarities. This is the application of montage principles – developed in conjunction with and in response to the types of urban phenomena catalogued by Georg Simmel – to global relations. To reiterate, such an expansion of the city symphony is not a consequence of the appearance of sound film. Vertov, as I noted earlier, was making world symphony films long before the advent of sound cinema and in many cases, such as *One Sixth of the World*, in anticipation of sound film's inevitable arrival. Rather, the advent of sound forced the already-global city symphony to address a new set of challenges while struggling to preserve a set of practices that it considered guarantors of the new itself. Counterpoint, but also inventive and disruptive uses of synchrony, aimed to fuel a dynamic engine (be it a commercial steamer or a power station) of sound and image.

CODA

LISTENING TO CITY SYMPHONIES

Early in Karen Tei Yamashita's city symphony novel, *Tropic of Orange* (1997), we encounter a homeless man, Manzanar Murakami, conducting a symphony of Los Angeles's highway system from a freeway overpass. Manzanar is the namesake of the Manzanar War Relocation Center, the first of ten US internment camps that held Japanese immigrants and Japanese American citizens during World War II. His homelessness is thus all at once existential, political, and physical. However, to call Manzanar homeless, the narrator informs us, would be a mistake. "No one was more at home in L.A. than this man."[1] This sense of home without a house – or of constructing a home out of an alienating urban environment – concerns the city symphony, specifically the ways in which the city functions as a resonance chamber and purveyor of sounds for composition. These sounds – regardless of whether they are being actively composed or listened to – offer the impression of an intentional musical structure that the conductor controls, in which he builds himself a home.

Yamashita's novel follows a week in the life of Los Angeles through the eyes of seven characters. Its seven sections – Monday through Sunday – are broken up (more or less) into seven chapters corresponding to the main characters' perspectives. The chapters featuring Manzanar bring home the main point of this book. The idea of music in the city symphony is not just an analogy for form; rather, it actively engages the sounds of the city and issues related to sound. In the Manzanar sections of Yamashita's novel, the city is treated as a medium for sound and a material for composition. The conductor senses "the time of day through his feet, through the vibration rumbling through the cement and steel passing beneath him";[2] he breaks the city up into "movements" corresponding to the heaviness of traffic.

He combines notes into passages in which he would like to lose himself were it not for his fear of loss of control. Instead, he builds these notes into "a community, a great society of sound."[3]

The composition of this community is not necessarily harmonious. The sounds being conducted are part of the environmental and political rhythms of Los Angeles in the 1990s. We meet Murakami in the middle of the "third movement" of the L.A. Symphony – a movement centred around a break in traffic, a "window of opportunity," just before rush hour, when "a traveler might cruise between the congested clumps of aggravated" automobiles.[4] This window is nestled within a larger moment of suspense, that of the first day of summer, when "education" – in the form of commuting teachers, students, and parents – has "left the freeways," but summer activities have not yet begun.[5] The moment, in turn, is part of a larger cycle of symphonies that encompass the political and environmental climate of L.A. – a climate tuned to the apocalyptic sounds of disaster (riots, fires, traffic accidents, earthquakes).[6]

At the same time, the narrator informs us that it is most likely the case that the conductor's audience – or, rather, those who were both the performers and audience members of his city symphony – "never noticed him."[7] In this respect, the conductor resembles the figure of Arseny Avraamov (chapter 2) insofar as he gives musical form to a cacophony whose structure only he can hear. Likewise, his symphony's "third movement" hovers over a moment of suspense – the "window of opportunity" – that corresponds to the moment of silence in Avraamov's mass spectacle. More generally, Murakami embodies the impulse to compose the city's sounds – or, similarly, to listen to them musically, which is a way of structuring them, making sense of them. This impulse, as I have argued in this book, runs through the city symphony whether it is expressed through film, radio, music, the novel, or mass spectacle. On the one hand, the above episode in Yamashita's novel reveals the power of the musical analogy as a structuring device for capturing the dynamism of city life. On the other hand, it shows how the sounds, vibrations, and rhythms of the city go beyond the analogy of structure, how they may be treated and received as sounds in themselves, or as actual notes, which may be physically felt, caressed, given their "tender due."[8]

In this respect, the city symphony is always coming back to itself in a manner best captured by Jean-Luc Nancy's conception of musical listening. Music, as Nancy points out, "never stops exposing the present to the imminence of a deferred presence, one that is more 'to come' [à venir] than any 'future' [avenir]. A presence that is not future, but merely promised, merely present because of its announcement, its prophecy of the instant."[9] Such a temporal relationship manifests itself in the pause of Avraamov's symphony, the "window of opportunity" in Murakami's, and the intervals between movements in Vertov's films. These moments are filled with a sense of anticipation ("to come") rather than a presentiment of the future. Attali's conception of music as prophetic may thus be read against this idea of deferred presence. He conflates the sense of anticipation with the possibility of prediction.

This sense of anticipation – the opening up of time and its unfolding in urban space – is what allows Russolo to conjure a city of the dead in *The Awakening of a City*. The city symphony holds open the moment, allowing it to be filled with another world structured by will, desire, and fantasy. In this regard, Nancy continues, music "is the art of making the outside of time return to every time, making return to every moment the beginning that listens to itself beginning and beginning again."[10] This art of eternal recurrence – of the rhythmic instant, to use Lefebvre's terminology (chapter 3) – is itself based in the structure of sound as a wave. Each time sound "repeats the same beginning: the opening, the attack of sound, the one by which modulated sound is already preceded and succeeded without its zero point ever being able to be fixed in place. That is what sound resounds in: it demands itself again in order to be what it is: sonorous."[11] This demand also makes it possible to listen to or conduct a symphony even where there isn't one – where what is heard exists somewhere between intentional musical composition and ambient sounds. Avraamov's city symphony, for instance, was a form of call-and-response that began and ended with the composer's own idealistic longing. In Baku and Moscow, he was, to a certain extent, the only one to hear the echo of his proletarian symphony. Similarly, Murakami has the impression of conducting the sounds that his baton could not control but only touch.

The city symphony is always coming back to itself. For Nancy, this open-ended repetition is not just at the heart of sense and meaning; nor is it simply a matter of a conductor such as Murakami building himself a home in the repetitive rhythms of L.A. Rather, it is the basis of ethical and political communities. The sonorous is "methexic" as opposed to mimetic – that is, it has to do with "participation, sharing, or contagion" as opposed to imitation.[12] Communication, in turn, "is not transmission, but sharing that becomes subject: sharing as subject of all 'subjects.' An unfolding, a dance, a resonance. Sound in general is first of all communication in this sense."[13] This idea explains the communitarian impulses of city symphonies, how they hope to build urban "notes" into great societies of sound; how the city symphony is often simultaneously a global symphony. Such a dynamic may take radically different political directions. As manifestation of will and desire, it may be given form through Nazi musical practices.[14] In the hopes of articulating a radical proletarian community, it may silence the very oppressed peoples it sought to give voice (Avraamov). But it also may be endlessly dynamic and open-ended, as in Vertov's *Man with a Movie Camera*, where the Soviet political community is shown in a process of continuous formation, or in Murakami's L.A. Symphony, in which a city whose divisions and geographical structure make it difficult to consider a community at all are nonetheless registered as a whole.

As such, there is no univocal way to interpret the political implications of city symphonies. Instead, the city symphony creates space by composing sound and, conversely, creates sound by composing space. It structures sound into political communities that track the changes music and sound underwent in the twentieth century: the rise of urban noise, the ability to record and transmit sound, and the ability to produce (write) never-before-heard sounds (sound synthesis). These developments concern the structure of city symphonies, to be sure; they are part of the musical analogy. More importantly, they are part of the fabric of city symphonies; their medium and materials. They allow city symphonies to transform urban environments, build new cities in sound, and sacralize everyday spaces. They create dense networks of sound that galvanize, politicize, and spiritualize urban populations. Most importantly, they are sonic phenomena in their own right; they deserve to be heard.

Notes

Introduction

1 László Moholy-Nagy, *Painting, Photography, Film*, trans. Jillian DeMair and Katrin Schamun (Zurich: Lars Müller, 2019), 127.
2 Edward Dimendberg, "Transfiguring the Urban Gray: László Moholy-Nagy's Film Scenario 'Dynamic of the Metropolis,'" in *Camera Obscura, Camera Lucida: Essays in Honor of Annette Michelson*, ed. Richard Allen and Malcolm Turvey (Amsterdam: Amsterdam University Press, 2003), 110.
3 Moholy-Nagy, *Painting, Photography, Film*, 31.
4 Ibid., 32.
5 Ibid., 30.
6 See Malte Hagener, "László Moholy-Nagy and the City (Symphony)," in *The City Symphony Phenomenon: Cinema, Art, and Urban Modernity between the Wars*, ed. Steven Jacobs, Anthony Kinik, and Eva Hielscher (New York: Routledge, 2019), 48.
7 Moholy-Nagy, *Painting, Photography, Film*, 114 (emphasis Moholy-Nagy's).
8 Dimendberg, "Transfiguring the Urban Gray," 117.
9 Quoted in ibid.
10 Moholy-Nagy, *Painting, Photography, Film*, 35.
11 Ibid., 23–4 (emphasis Moholy-Nagy's).
12 These include "Produktion-Reproduktion" (1922) and "Neue Gestaltung in der Musik. Möglichkeiten des Grammophons" (1923). The articles may be found in Krisztina Passuth, *Moholy-Nagy* (Wiengarten, Germany: Kunstverlag Weingarten, 1986): 305–6; 308–9.
13 Thomas Y. Levin, "'Tones from Out of Nowhere': Rudolf Pfenninger and the Archaeology of Synthetic Sound," *Grey Room* 12 (2003): 32–79.
14 Ibid., 39.
15 For a more complete list and a fuller discussion of these films, see *City Symphony Phenomenon*; *Eselsohren: Journal of History of Art, Architecture and Urbanism* 2, nos 1–2 (2014); and Chris Dähne, *Die Stadtsinfonien der 1920er Jahre: Architektur zwischen Film, Fotografie und Literatur* (Bielefeld, Germany: Transcript Verlag, 2013).
16 David Bordwell, "The Musical Analogy," *Yale French Studies* 60 (1980): 142.
17 Quoted in Danijela Kulezic-Wilson, *The Musicality of Narrative Film* (London: Palgrave Macmillan, 2015), 19.

18 Dziga Vertov, "Pis'mo v redaktsiu Berlinskoi Gazetyi," in *Iz naslediia*, ed. A.S. Deriabin and D.V. Kruzhkova, 2 vols (Moscow: Eizenshtein tsentr, 2008), 2:181. A portion of this letter is translated in Dziga Vertov, *Kino-Eye: The Writings of Dziga Vertov*, ed. Annette Michelson, trans. Kevin O'Brien (Berkeley: University of California Press, 1984), 101–2.
19 Floris Paalman, "The Theoretical Appearance of the City Symphony," *Eselsohren: Journal of History of Art, Architecture and Urbanism* 2, no. 2 (2014): 13–28.
20 Werner Wolf, "Towards a Functional Analysis of Intermediality: The Case of Twentieth-Century Musicalized Fiction," in *Selected Essays on Intermediality by Werner Wolf, 1992–2014* (Leiden, Netherlands: Koninklijke Brill, 2018), 38–62. See also Alex Aronson, *Music and the Novel: A Study in 20th Century Fiction* (Totowa, NJ: Rowman and Littlefield, 1980).
21 Michael Hofmann, "Afterword" to *Berlin, Alexanderplatz* (New York: New York Review of Books, 2008), 452.
22 On this discourse, see Charlotte Brunsdon, "The Attraction of the Cinematic City," *Screen* 53, no. 3 (2012): 209–27. Brudson accuses the cinematic city of getting mired in a "city discourse" that "functions, in a crossdisciplinary context, to obscure substantial intellectual lacunae and potential disagreement. City discourse can be used about most cities – and so paradoxically become a way both of bringing together different objects of study (different particular cities) and of making them all the same (the city in general)" (221; referenced in Paalman, "Theoretical Appearance," 15).
23 See Tom Gunning and Vanessa Schwartz, *Cinema and the Invention of Urban Modernity* (Berkeley: University of California Press, 1996); Mark Shiel and Tony Fitzmaurice, *Screening the City* (London: Verso, 2003).
24 Ben Singer, *Melodrama and Modernity: Early Sensational Cinema and Its Contexts* (New York: Columbia University Press, 2001), 102. In *On the History of Film Style*, Bordwell famously criticized this idea as proposing a vague causal connection between modern capitalist cities and human perception, and of inconsistently stressing the similarities between the features of early cinema (attractions, montage editing) and the city. Singer has defended the thesis by articulating different ways in which one can think of the causal connection between cities and film – e.g., how cities affect neural plasticity – without falling into the trap of a quasi-Lamarckian biological determinism. For Bordwell's argument, see David Bordwell, *On the History of Film Style* (Cambridge, MA: Harvard University Press, 1997), 139–49.
25 On "container" metaphors, see George Lakoff and Mark Johnson, *Metaphors We Live By* (Chicago: University of Chicago Press), 29–32.
26 Malcolm Turvey, *The Filming of Modern Life: European Avant-garde Film of the 1920s* (Cambridge, MA: MIT Press, 2011), 17–47.

27 Thomas Elsaesser, "City of Light, Gardens of Delight," in *Cities in Transition: The Moving Image and the Modern Metropolis*, ed. Andrew Webber and Emma Wilson (London: Wallflower Press, 2008), 90.
28 Sam Halliday, *Sonic Modernity: Representing Sound in Literature, Culture and the Arts* (Edinburgh: Edinburgh University Press, 2013), 3.
29 Friedrich Kittler, "The City Is a Medium," *New Literary History* 27 (Fall 1996): 719.
30 Ibid., 717.
31 Scott McQuire, *The Media City: Media, Architecture and Urban Space* (London: Sage Books, 2008), 161–80.
32 Shannon Mattern, "Ear to the Wire: Listening to Historic Urban Infrastructures," *Amodern* 2 (October 2013), available online at https://amodern.net/article/ear-to-the-wire/.
33 Ibid., 5.
34 Ibid., 2.
35 Devin Fore, "Metabiotic State: Dziga Vertov's *The Eleventh Year*," *October* 145 (2013): 7.
36 Quoted in Mattern, "Ear to the Wire," 4.
37 Lewis Mumford, *The Culture of Cities* (San Diego: Harvest/HBJ, 1938), 4.
38 Quoted in Mattern, "Ear to the Wire," 6.
39 Ibid.
40 Hillel Schwartz, *Making Noise: From Babel to the Big Bang and Beyond* (New York: Zone Books, 2011), 677.
41 Oskana Bulgakowa, "Moskva-Berlin, Berlin-Moskau, 1900–1950: Memory and Forgetting," *Russian Review* 80 (October 2021): 581–602.
42 Ibid.
43 Ibid., 582.
44 This fact is noted in Delia Duong Ba Wendel, "The 1922 'Symphony of Sirens' in Baku, Azerbaijan," in *Journal of Urban Design* 17, no. 4 (2012): 549–72.

Chapter One

1 Barbara Barthelmes, "Music and the City," in *Music and Technology in the Twentieth Century*, ed. Hans-Joachim Braun (Baltimore: Johns Hopkins University Press, 2002), 99–105.
2 Francesco Balilla Pratella, "Manifesto of Futurist Musicians," in *Futurism: An Anthology*, ed. Lawrence S. Rainey, Christine Poggi, and Laura Wittman (New Haven, CT: Yale University Press, 2009), 76.
3 Russolo's name is featured on the title page of Marinetti's 1927 *Arte Fascista*. See Luciano Chessa, *Luigi Russolo, Futurist: Noise, Visual Arts, and the Occult* (Berkeley: University of California Press, 2012), 9.

4 Slavoj Žižek, *The Fright of Real Tears: Krzysztof Kieślowski between Theory and Post-Theory* (London: British Film Institute, 2001), 25. Ernesto Laclau, *Ideology and Politics in Marxist Theory* (London: Verso, 1975).
5 Michel Chion, *Sound: An Acoulogical Treatise*, trans. James A. Steintrager (Durham, NC: Duke University Press, 2016), 61.
6 The definition is Claude Shannon and Warren Weaver's (1948); quoted in Greg Hainge, *Noise Matters: Towards an Ontology of Noise* (New York: Bloomsbury Academic, 2013), 4.
7 Paul Hegarty, *Noise/Music: A History* (New York: Continuum, 2007), 5.
8 Karin Bijsterveld, *Mechanical Sound: Technology, Culture, and Public Problems in the Twentieth Century* (Cambridge, MA: MIT Press, 2008), 4.
9 Jacques Attali, *Noise: The Political Economy of Music*, trans. Brian Massumi (Minneapolis: University of Minnesota Press, 1985), 28.
10 Attali, *Noise*, 5.
11 Christine Poggi, "The Futurist Noise Machine," *European Legacy* 14, no. 7 (November 2009): 824.
12 Ibid.
13 Luigi Russolo, *The Art of Noises*, intro. and trans. Barclay Brown (New York: Pendragon Press, 1987), 28.
14 The idea is a version of the "spontaneity-consciousness" paradigm, the idea that Bolshevik workers are, in the words of Anna Krylova, "conscious makers of history who have successfully overcome the spontaneous – that is, chaotic, misleading, and not fully comprehended – dissatisfaction with their condition under capitalism." Anna Krylova, "Beyond the Spontaneity-Consciousness Paradigm: 'Class Instinct' as a Promising Category of Historical Analysis," *Slavic Review* 62, no. 1 (Spring 2003): 1.
15 Russolo, *Art of Noises*, 24.
16 We do, however, have an idea of how they sounded from a single recording of the intonarumori accompanying two pieces by Russolo's brother, Antonio (Chessa, *Luigi Russolo*, 222).
17 Quoted in Brown, "Introduction," in Russolo, *Art of Noises*, 4–5.
18 Ibid., 5
19 Quoted in Poggi, "Futurist Noise Machine," 832.
20 Bijsterveld, *Mechanical Sound*, 139.
21 Poggi, "Futurist Noise Machine," 832.
22 Russolo, *Art of Noises*, 31–6.
23 Russolo, "Art of Noises," in *Futurism: An Anthology*, 135. I have opted for Rainey, Poggi, and Wittman's translation of this passage due to its superior sonority.
24 Russolo, *Art of Noises*, 44–5.
25 Ibid., 45.
26 See Hermann L.F. Helmholtz, *On the Sensation of Tone as a Physiological Basis for the Theory of Music* (New York: Dover, 1954), 41–2. Russolo, *Art of Noises*, 37–40.

27 Russolo, *Art of Noises*, 39.
28 Tram wires, e.g., have "many enharmonic variations of pitch" that feed into "an entire aerial network ... with a fantastic number of resonances" (Russolo, *Art of Noises*, 45).
29 Anthony Enns and Shelly Trower, "Introduction," in *Vibratory Modernism*, ed. Enns and Trower (Houndmills, UK: Palgrave Macmillan, 2013), 1.
30 Quoted in Matthew Wraith, "Throbbing Human Engines: Mechanical Vibration, Entropy, and Death in Marinetti, Joyce, Ehrenburg and Eliot," in *Vibratory Modernism*, 99.
31 See Chessa, *Luigi Russolo*, 19–24.
32 Quoted in ibid, 20. Russolo, of course, cites the onomatopoetic art of Words-in-Freedom, particularly Marinetti's poem "Zang Tumb Tumb," as an example of the noises of language, thus underscoring the vibratory potential of noise.
33 Marinetti, "La Radia," in *Futurism: An Anthology*, 294.
34 Ibid. Punctuation unaltered.
35 Quoted in Chessa, *Luigi Russolo*, 21
36 Ibid.
37 Carlo Carrà, "The Painting of Sounds, Noises, and Smell," in *Futurism: An Anthology*, 156.
38 Ibid.
39 In many cases, such as the 1896 experiments of Hippolyte Barduc, such plates were simply held to one's forehead, thus receiving the imprint of one's emanating brainwaves. This experiment began with the French neurologist Hippolyte Baraduc. See Anthony Enns, "Vibratory Photography," in *Vibratory Modernism*, 182.
40 Quoted in Enns, "Vibratory Photography," 185.
41 Russolo, *Art of Noises*, 39.
42 Ibid., 39.
43 Chessa, *Luigi Russolo*, 80.
44 Quoted in ibid., 94.
45 Giovanni Lista, *Futurisme: Manifestes, Proclamations, Documents"* (Lausanne: L'age d'homme, 1973), 60. See Chessa, *Luigi Russolo*, 103.
46 Francesco Balilla Pratella, "Futurist Music: Technical Manifesto," in *Futurism: An Anthology*, 81.
47 Russolo, *Art of Noises*, 62.
48 Ibid., 62.
49 Carlo Carrà, "Painting of Sounds" (emphasis mine).
50 To be sure, the piano is the well-tempered system's main representative in the world of instruments. Russolo and his fellow Futurists preferred instruments with the capacity for free intonation such as the violin. That said, insofar as

the piano's keys in *La Musica* are endless, one may take the keyboard as invoking his enharmonic ideals.
51 Russolo, *Art of Noises*, 62
52 Ibid., 64.
53 Ibid., 76.
54 Ibid., 69.
55 Ibid.
56 Ibid., 68.
57 Quoted in Chessa, *Luigi Russolo*, 134.
58 Barclay Brown, "Introduction," in *Art of Noises*, 19.
59 Russolo, *Art of Noises*, 68.
60 See Bijsterveld, *Mechanical Sound*, 144–51.
61 Chessa, *Luigi Russolo*, 138.
62 Quoted in ibid., 162.
63 Quoted in ibid., 157.
64 See ibid., 216.
65 Quoted in ibid., 212. Translations are Chessa's.
66 Quoted in ibid., 151.
67 Marinetti, "La Radia," in *Futurism: An Anthology*, 294.

Chapter Two

1 I have chosen to italicize *Symphony of Sirens*, though other scholars place the title in quotation marks. This is to avoid confusion between the *Symphony of Sirens* and articles that Avraamov wrote on the *Symphony of Sirens*, which all bear the title "Symphony of Sirens."
2 Russolo, "Art of Noises," in *Futurism: An Anthology*, ed. Lawrence S. Rainey, Christine Poggi, and Laura Wittman (New Haven, CT: Yale University Press, 2009), 138.
3 Of these, only the Baku Worker score remains. See Arseny Avraamov, "Nakaz po 'Gudkovoi simfonii," *Bakinskii rabochii* 250 (November 1922): 3. For a discussion of the discrepancies between the *Gorn* and *Baku Worker* instructions, see pt. 2 below.
4 Here, with some modifications, I've relied on Mel Gordon's translation of the *Symphony of Sirens*. Arseny Avraamov, "The Symphony of Sirens," in *Wireless Imagination: Sound, Radio, and the Avante-Garde*, trans. Mel Gordon, ed. Douglas Kahn and Gregory Whitehead (Cambridge, MA: MIT Press, 1994), 252. For the original Russian see, Arseny Avraamov, "Simfoniia Gudkov," *Gorn* 9 (November 1923): 116. Modifications to Gordon's translation will be noted in the footnotes.
5 Gordon's *Wireless Imagination* translation presents this region as two separate districts, "Bibi" and "Abot" (250).

6 Here, Gordon's *Wireless Imagination* translation misreads "sound thunderously from the road" as "head off to the road roaring" (250). This has given scholars the impression that a chorus of automobiles driving from one part of the city to the other was part of the Symphony.
7 A typo in Gordon's translation reads "Mrs. Avraamov" instead of Ars. Avraamov.
8 On "Black Town," see Delia Duong Ba Wendel, "The 1922 'Symphony of Sirens' in Baku, Azerbaijan," in *Journal of Urban Design* 17, no. 4 (2012): 554.
9 Rene Fuelop-Miller, *The Mind and Face of Bolshevism* (New York: Harper and Row, 1962), 184.
10 See, e.g., Claire Bishop, *Artificial Hells: Participatory Art and the Politics of Spectatorship* (London: Verso, 2012), 41–75.
11 See Michel Chion, *Sound: An Acoulogical Treatise*, trans. James A. Steintrager (Durham, NC: Duke University Press, 2016), 69.
12 See Amy Nelson, *Music for the Revolution: Musicians and Power in Early Soviet Russia* (University Park: Penn State University Press, 2004), 27–9; Wendel, "1922 'Symphony of Sirens'" Andrei Smirnov, *Sound in Z: Experiments in Sound and Electronic Music in Early 20th Century Russia* (London: Koenig Books, 2013), 147–50; Adrian Curtin, *Avant-garde Theatre Sound* (New York: Palgrave Macmillan, 2014), 186–98; Marina Frolova-Walker and Jonathan Walker, *Music and Soviet Power* (Rochester, NY: Boydell Press, 2012), 81.
13 Sergei Rumiantsev, *Ars Novyi, ili Dela i prikliucheniia bezustal'nogo kazaka Arseniia Avrramova* (Moscow: Deka-vs, 2007), 38–9. According to Rumiantsev, Krasnokutsky is in fact Avraamov's original name – the rest are pseudonyms. The source of most biographical information about the composer, Rumiantsev's monograph includes a number of Avraamov's letters and articles in abridged and unabridged form. These include Avraamov's 1943 letter to the Communist Party; his correspondence with his lover, Revecca Zhiv; and multiple articles on music theory that Avraamov published before and after the October Revolution (reproduced in their entirety). The letters and correspondences come from the private archives of Avraamov's friends and relatives – especially his son, German Avraamov, and Revecca Zhiv. I have not been able to see these correspondences first-hand. Throughout this article, I will be relying on materials from Rumiantsev's book. If a passage is quoted as part of a discussion in Rumiantsev's book, I will write "Quoted in Rumiantsev ..."; if it is reproduced in its entirety or near entirety, I will write "Reproduced in Rumiantsev ... " All translations of these materials are my own.
14 Nikolai Izvolov, "From the History of Graphic Sound in the Soviet Union; or, Media without a Medium," trans. Sergei Levchin, in *Sound, Speech, Music in Soviet and Post-Soviet Cinema*, ed. Lilya Kaganovsky and Masha Salazkina (Bloomington: Indiana University Press, 2014), 34.
15 Ibid.
16 Ibid., 35.

17 Quoted in ibid., 32.
18 Quoted in ibid., 31.
19 Avraamov, "Symphony of Sirens," 245 / "Simfoniia Gudkov," 109 (translation modified).
20 Quoted in Arseny Avraamov, "Symphony of Sirens," in *Baku: Symphony of Sirens: Sound Experiments in the Russian Avant-garde: Original Documents and Reconstructions of 72 Key Works of Music, Poetry and Agitprop from the Russian Avantgardes (1908–1942)*, ed. Miguel Molina Alarcón, trans. Deidre MacCloskey (London: ReR Megacorp, 2008), 70. This article bears the same title as Avraamov's 1923 article for *Gorn*. Alarcón's document is a translation from Spanish of the Russian original, first published in 1924 in the journal *Khudozhnik i zrtiel'* (*Artist and Viewer*). I have verified the translation against Mayakovsky's original: Vladimir Mayakovsky, "Prikaz po armii iskusstv," *Dlia Golosa* (Berlin: R.S.F.S.R. gos. izd., 1923), 33. For Avraamov's original article, see Arseny Avraamov, "Simfoniia Gudkov," *Khudozhnik i zritel'* 1 (January 1924): 50. Modifications to Alarcón's translation will be noted in the footnotes.
21 On Soviet festivals, see Richard Stites, *Revolutionary Dreams: Utopian Visions and Experimental Life in the Russian Revolution* (Oxford: Oxford University Press, 1989), 79–101; James von Geldern, *Bolshevik Festival, 1917–1920* (Berkeley: University of California Press, 1993); Katerina Clark, *Petersburg: Crucible of Cultural Revolution* (Cambridge, MA: Harvard University Press, 1995), 100–43; Malte Rolf, *Soviet Mass Festivals, 1917–1991* (Pittsburgh: University of Pittsburgh Press, 2013); Kristin Romberg, "Festival," in *Revoliutsiia! Demonstartsiia! Soviet Art Put to the Test*, ed. Mathew S. Vitovsky and Devin Fore (Chicago: Art Institute of Chicago, 2017), 250–80.
22 Quoted in Lionel Trilling, *Sincerity and Authenticity* (Cambridge, MA: Harvard University Press, 1971), 65.
23 Clark, *Petersburg*, 139.
24 Ibid., 138.
25 Avraamov, *Symphony of Sirens, Artist and Viewer*, 70 / "Simfoniia Gudkov," *Khudozhnik i zritel'*, 50. Rumiantsev notes, however, that there is no independent verification of the performance of the *Symphony of Sirens* in Nizhny Novgorod outside of Avraamov's own account. Rumiantsev, *Ars Novyi*, 88.
26 On the proceedings of the Baku Congress, see *To See the Dawn: Baku, 1920–First Congress of the Peoples of the East*, ed. John Riddell (New York: Pathfinder, 1993).
27 Quoted in Stephen White, "Communism and the East: The Baku Congress, 1920," in *Slavic Review* 33, no. 3 (September 1974): 492. For Wendel's account, see Wendel, "1922 'Symphony of Sirens,'" 556.
28 See Hélène Carrère d'Encausse, *The Great Challenge: Nationalities and the Bolshevik State* (New York: Holmes and Meier, 1992); Yuri Slezkine, "The USSR as a Communal Apartment, or How a Socialist State Promoted Ethnic Particularism," *Slavic Review* 53 (Summer 1994): 414–52; Jeremy Smith, *The*

Bolsheviks and the National Question, 1917–1923 (Basingstoke, UK: St Martin's Press, 1999); Terry Martin, "Affirmative Action Empire," in *A State of Nations: Empire and Nation-Making in the Age of Lenin and Stalin*, ed. Ronald Grigor Suny and Terry Martin (Oxford: Oxford University Press, 2001), 67–90; Benjamin Loring, "Colonizers with Party Cards: Soviet Internal Colonialism in Central Asia, 1917–39," *Kritika* 15, no. 1 (Winter 2014): 77–102.

29 Martin, "Affirmative Action Empire," 77–8.
30 Vladimir I. Lenin, "Critical Remarks on the National Question," in *V.I. Lenin Collected Works*, vol. 20 (Moscow, 1977 [1913]), 17–45; Lenin, "The Rights of Nations to Self-Determination," in *Collected Works*, vol. 20, 393–455; Lenin, "The Question of Nationalities or Autonomisation" (1922), accessed 5 September 2023, www.marxists.org/archive/lenin/works/1922/dec/testamnt/autonomy.htm.

Of course, Lenin was particularly concerned with appearances. In Azerbaijan, many of the Bolshevik's policies with respect to nationalities covered the pursuit of natural resources. See Audrey L. Altstadt, *The Politics of Culture in Soviet Azerbaijan, 1920–40* (London: Routledge, 2016), 34–7.

31 The letter is reproduced in Rumiantsev, *Ars Novyi*, 10–37.
32 Reproduced in ibid., 23–4.
33 Ibid., 24.
34 Ibid., 25.
35 Ibid., 25.
36 Frolova-Walker and Walker, *Music and Soviet Power*, 44–5.
37 The following argument is indebted to Wendel's "1922 'Symphony of Sirens.'"
38 Altstadt, *Politics of Culture*, 4.
39 1901 was the peak year for Baku's oil production. Audrey L. Altstadt, *The Azerbaijani Turks: Power and Identity under Russian Rule* (Stanford, CA: Stanford University Press, 1992), 22.
40 Altstadt, *Azerbaijani Turks*, 21.
41 Ibid., 27.
42 Ibid., 32.
43 Ibid., 44.
44 Ibid., 44–5.
45 See Ronald Grigor Suny, *The Baku Commune 1917–1918: Class and Nationality in the Russian Revolution* (Princeton, NJ: Princeton University Press, 1972), 214–34. On ethnic conflict in Baku and Azerbaijan, see also Tadeusz Swietochowski, *Russia and Azerbaijan: A Borderland in Transition* (New York: Columbia University Press, 1995).
46 Wendel, "1922 'Symphony of Sirens,'" 550.
47 For studies on noise that may have inspired scholars such as Wendel and Curtin, see Jacques Attali, *Noise: The Political Economy of Music*, trans. Brian Massumi (Minneapolis: University of Minnesota Press, 1985); Douglas Kahn,

Noise, Water, Meat: A History of Sound in the Arts (Cambridge, MA: MIT Press, 1999); Craig Dworkin, "The Politics of Noise," in *Reading the Illegible* (Evanston, IL: Northwestern University Press, 2003); Paul Hegarty, *Noise/Music: A History* (New York: Continuum, 2007); Karin Bijsterveld, *Mechanical Sound: Technology, Culture, and Public Problems in the Twentieth Century* (Cambridge, MA: MIT Press, 2008); Salomé Voegelin, *Listening to Noise and Silence: Toward a Philosophy of Sound Art* (London: Continuum, 2010); Hillel Schwartz, *Making Noise: From Babel to the Big Bang and Beyond* (New York: Zone Books, 2011); Greg Hainge, *Noise Matters: Towards an Ontology of Noise* (New York: Bloomsbury Academic, 2013).

48 Frolova-Walker and Walker, *Music and Soviet Power*, 81. Frolova-Walker and Walker also mention that a "subsequent attempt to mount the event in Petrograd failed." This is an error. Avraamov's subsequent and final attempt to mount the *Symphony of Sirens* occurred in Moscow in 1923. Frolova-Walker and Walker may be thinking here of an initial attempt to stage the performance in Petrograd in 1918. Avraamov briefly mentions this performance in a 1924 article for the journal *Artist and Viewer*.

49 Wendel, "1922 'Symphony of Sirens,'" 551–6.

50 One of the reasons for the recent popularity of the *Symphony of Sirens* is the publication of Miguel Molina Alarcón's *Baku: Symphony of Sirens: Sound Experiments and the Radio Avant-garde* (2003) and Andrei Smirnov's *Sound in Z* (2013). These two publications have brought Avraamov's mass spectacle into the mainstream, at least as far as *musique concrete* and noise art are concerned. Indeed, Alarcón's reconstruction of the symphony using live recording and audio samples masquerades on YouTube as a recording of the actual performance. Meanwhile, Smirnov's book, as well as his article for the Red Bull Music Academy website, has inspired noise lovers and musicians to take an interest in Avraamov's work and ideas on subjects ranging from the mass spectacle to microtonal composition and sound synthesis. To be sure, this interest is very much welcome. One of its drawbacks, however, is that it tends to magnify the scale of the symphony beyond what can be reasonably inferred from Avraamov's text and limited biography. See "Arseny Avraamov – Symphony of Factory Sirens (Public Event, Baku 1922)," YouTube video, 28:12, uploaded by Miguel Negrón Oyarzo, 27 May 2011, www.youtube.com/watch?v=Kq_7w9RHvpQ&t=1s; Andrey Smirnov and Sasha Kloptsov, "Revolutionary Arseny Avraamov," Red Bull Music Academy Daily, 28 July 2017, http://daily.redbullmusicacademy.com/2017/07/revolutionary-arseny-avraamov.

51 Wendel, "1922 'Symphony of Sirens,'" 550. Relying on Wendel's analysis, the sound-studies scholar Adrian Curtin has speculated as to how the symphony's overpowering noises may have affected the ears and bodies of Baku's listeners and performers. In his estimation, the symphony is a manifestation of soundscape design avant la lettre. Curtin, *Avant-garde Theatre Sound*, 191–5.

52 In his monograph, Rumiantsev provides facing reproductions of both instructions for comparison. These are too long to reproduce here (Rumiantsev, *Ars Novyi*, 81–4). For the original *Baku Worker* instruction, see "Nakaz po 'Gudkovoi simfonii," *Bakinskii rabochii* 250 (November 1922): 3. Like those printed in *Gorn*, the *Baku Worker* instructions provide limited information. It is doubtful that the instructions were enough to mobilize and inform a massive crowd of listener-performers, particularly since they were published the day before the performance. Rather, it is more likely the case that, in Baku, the instructions served to inform residents and crowds of the day's events. Indeed, such "instructions" as "the noon cannon is cancelled" read like elements of a concert program.

53 Not being able to read Azerbaijani, I cannot say whether there are any mentions of the event in the Azerbaijani-language press. That said, none of the English-language historical literature on Azerbaijan during this period that I've consulted mentions the existence of such articles. Given that, as I show below, most Russian-language articles connect back to Avraamov himself, it seems reasonable to suspect a similar state of affairs in the Azerbaijani-language press. It is also possible that the event did not garner any attention in these publications, perhaps because it did not take place as described. Nevertheless, I cannot prove this conclusively.

54 Reproduced in Rumiantsev, *Ars Novyi*, 123.

55 The mandate was most likely secured with the help of Pyotr Ivanovich Chagin, then secretary of the Azerbaijan Communist Party and editor of the *Baku Worker*. Chagin is mentioned in the reproduction of the *Baku Worker* instruction in *Gorn*. Avraamov, "Symphony of Sirens," *Wireless Imagination*, 252 / "Simfoniya Gudkov," *Gorn*, 116.

56 Rumiantsev, *Ars Novyi*, 123. Rumiantsev also mentions two articles about the Baku Symphony that had been published in the *Baku Worker*, though both were written in November 1923, after the performance of the Moscow Symphony (Rumiantsev, *Ars Novyi*, 86–7). Neither suggest events occurring at anywhere near the scale of the Symphony, though they do mention the wailing of sirens.

57 Lydia Ivanova, *Vospominaniia. Kniga ob ottse* (Moscow: n.p., 1992), 113–14, accessed 5 September 2023, www.v-ivanov.it/lv_ivanova/01text/02.htm#h2_5, quoted in Sergei Khismatov, "Simfoniia Gudkov," *Opera Musicologia* 6, no. 4 (2010): 109–10 (translation mine).

58 Avraamov, "Symphony of Sirens," *Wireless Imagination*, 246 / "Simfoniia Gudkov," *Gorn*, 110.

59 "Я таки не ошибся в моем пророчестве (начало 'Симфонии гудков') – Мировой Октябрь вот он уж у порога … и знаешь, есть слухи, что сигналом к восстанию будет во всех городах Германии – Гудковая симфония"; reproduced in Rumiantsev, *Ars Novyi*, 100. "I was thus not mistaken in my prophecy (the beginning of the *Symphony of Sirens*) – the world October Revolution is on

the threshold ... and you know, there are rumors that the signal for the uprising will be in all German cities – the *Symphony of Sirens*" (translation mine).
60 Quoted in Pheng Cheah, "Nondialectical Materialism," *Diacritics* 38, nos 1–2 (Spring–Summer 2008): 143.
61 Cheah, "Nondialectical Materialism," 143.
62 Ibid., 144.
63 Theodor Adorno, *Philosophy of New Music*, trans. Robert Hullot-Kentor (Minneapolis: University of Minnesota Press, 2006), 52–3.
64 This is not to say that staging such a city symphony is impossible, but only that it requires a great deal more reflection on the artifice of the composition and the heterogeneity of the space.
65 Franco Moretti, *Modern Epic: The World System from Goethe to García Márquez* (London: Verso, 1996), 5.
66 Vivian Sobchack, "Cities on the Edge of Time: The Urban Science Fiction Film," in *Liquid Metal: The Science Fiction Film Reader*, ed. Sean Redmond (New York: Columbia University Press, 2005), 78.
67 Morretti, *Modern Epic*, 5.
68 Marjoire Perloff, "Epic Ecologies (Review: Modern Epic by Franco Moretti)," *electronic book review* 4 (13 December 1998): https://electronicbookreview.com/essay/epic-ecologies/.
69 Ibid.
70 Pheng Cheah, "Nondialectical Materialism," 144.
71 "Symphony of Sirens," *Pravda* (14 November 1923): 5, quoted in Khismatov, "Simfoniia Gudkov," 107 (translation mine). At the same time, the reporter suggests, Gnesin cautiously encouraged the mass spectacle's experimental project: "With regard to harmony, Gnesin found the results very interesting. He recommends the continuation of work in this area: the music of factory sirens may replace the sound of church bells as a means of collective organization" (ibid). This speaks to the religious quality of mass spectacles, what Katerina Clark calls their "thirst for the sacred"; Clark, *Petersburg*, 2. For more critical responses see "Simfoniia Gudkov, *Izvestiia VTsIK* (9 November 1923): 6; A. Uglov, "Zvuki Moskvy v Oktiabr'skuiu godovshchinu," *Izvestiia VTsIKa* (11 November 1923): 5; "Simfoniia Gudkov," *Rabochaia gazeta* (9 November 1923): 4.
72 Uglov, "Zvuki Moskvy," 5, quoted in Khismatov, "Sinfonia Gudkov," 108 (ellipses Khismatov's, translation mine). As Khismatov points out, Uglov appears unaware of the existence of the Baku Symphony.
73 Avraamov, "Symphony of Sirens," *Artist and Viewer*, 71 / "Simfoniia Gudkov," *Khudozhnik i zritel'*, 51.
74 Reproduced in Rumiantsev, *Ars Novyi*, 133.
75 "Obrashchenie Moskovskogo Proletkul'ta k fabrichno-zavodskim komitetam Moskvy o simfonii gudkov vo vremia prasdnovaniia VI godovshchiny Oktiabria"; reproduced in Rumiantsev, *Ars Novyi*, 126. As Rumiantsev points

out, this appeal was most likely written by Avraamov himself. In it, Avraamov refers readers to his article in *Gorn*. The *Gorn* article, however, did not appear until after the Moscow performance. This supports the idea that Avraamov understood the *Gorn* article as helping to facilitate the Moscow performance. The appeal also shows that the scale of the Moscow performance was quite a bit smaller than that of the Baku Symphony.

76 Rumiantsev, *Ars Novyi*, 128–9.
77 Reproduced in Rumiantsev, *Ars Novyi*, 131. There was no repeat performance. Avraamov writes "ReveccA" in Latin script with the last letter capitalized on purpose as if to echo the resonance of her name (ellipses Rumiantsev's).
78 Reproduced in Rumiantsev, *Ars Novyi*, 137–9. Avraamov does not give Eva's family name.
79 Vladimir Solovyov, *The Meaning of Love*, trans. Thomas R. Beyer Jr (Edinburgh: Lindisfarne Press, 1985).
80 The letter was in fact written on 19 August 1923; reproduced in Rumianstev, *Ars Novyi*, 58–62.
81 Ibid., 60.
82 Clark, *Petersburg*, 140.
83 Reproduced in Rumiantsev, *Ars Novyi*, 61.
84 Ibid.
85 See Smirnov, *Sound in Z*, 28.
86 Ibid., 31–2.
87 Quoted in Izvolov, "From the History of Graphic Sound," 36.
88 For a comparison of Avraamov's work on sound synthesis with that of other sound-synthesis pioneers like Rudolph Pfenninger and Oskar Fischinger, see Thomas Y. Levin, "Tones from Out of Nowhere: Rudolf Pfenninger and the Archaeology of Synthetic Sound," *Grey Room* 12 (2003): 32–79.
89 Although he never realized a synthetic *Symphony of Sirens* on such a grand scale, Avraamov and his contemporaries were able to create a number of synthetic musical pieces that are both acoustically and visually pleasing.
90 Quoted in Smirnov, *Sound in Z*, 152.
91 I have placed "live" and "synthetic" in scare quotess since it is of course possible in a musical composition for synthesizers to be performed "live" in front of an audience. The distinction I'm driving at here, however, is between a performance performed for and by an audience of listener-participants (the *Symphony of Sirens* in Baku and Moscow) and a composition based on synthesized sound that can be listened to in any context and any time whatsoever.
92 Reproduced in Rumiantsev, *Ars Novyi*, 196.
93 Ibid., 195–6.
94 Ibid.
95 Reproduced in Rumiantsev, *Ars Novyi*, 195. I would like to thank one of the anonymous reviewers at *Slavic Review* for this translation.

96 Avraamov, "Symphony of Sirens," *Artist and Viewer*, 70 / Avraamov, *Khudozhnik i zritel'*, 50.

97 As such, the symphony anticipates Soviet radio practices of the late 1920s, especially public broadcasts via wired loudspeakers. See Stephen Lovell, "How Russia Learned to Listen: Radio and the Making of Soviet Culture," *Kritika: Explorations in Russian and Eurasian History* 12, no. 3 (November 2011): 591–615.

98 "У нас еще так недавно был Танеев и Скрябин ... У кого? Где это 'у нас'? В Москве? В Петрограде? Ведь даже первопрестольный Киев знает Скрябина лишь по нескольким гастролям, а крупнейшие произведения Танеева там – даже в Киеве – никогда не исполнялись"; reproduced in Rumiantsev, *Ars Novyi*, 194.

99 Ibid., 196.

100 Quoted in E. Kan-Novikova, *Sobiratel'nitsa Russkikh Narodnykh Pesen, Evgeniia Lineva* (Moscow: n.p., 1952), 46 (translation mine). For more on Lineva and her collection of folk music, see James Bailey, "A Collection of Translations of Russian Folk Songs: E. E. Lineva's Visit to America (1892–1896)," *Slavic and East European Folklore Association* 4, no. 1 (1999): 24–34.

101 Eugenie Linieff, *Folk Songs of the Ukraine: An Experiment in Recording Ukrainian Folksongs by Phonograph during a Musical Ethnological Excursion to Poltova in 1903*, trans. Maria Safonoff (Illinois, n.d.). This songbook would in turn inspire the great works of Russian composers such as Igor Stravinsky, as well as go on to inform performances and revivals of Russian and Ukrainian folk music around the world. For Lineva's influence on Stravinsky, see Richard Taruskin, *Stravinsky and the Russian Traditions* (Berkeley: University of California Press, 1996), 727–35.

102 Walter Benjamin, "The Work of Art in the Age of Its Technological Reproducibility," in *The Work of Art in the Age of Its Technological Reproducibility, and Other Writings on Media*, ed. Michael W. Jennings, Brigid Doherty, and Thomas Y. Levin (Cambridge, MA: Belknap Press, 2008), 23.

103 Jonathan Sterne, *The Audible Past: Cultural Origins of Sound Reproduction* (Durham, NC: Duke University Press, 2003), 219.

104 Vsevolod Pudovkin, "The Problem of Rhythm in My First Sound Film," in *Vsevolod Pudovkin: Selected Essays*, ed. Richard Taylor (London: Seagull Books, 2006), 213.

Chapter Three

1 See, e.g., John Grierson, "First Principles of Documentary," in *Grierson on Documentary*, ed. Forsyth Hardy (Berkeley: University of California Press, 1966), 19–30; Siegfried Kracauer, *From Caligari to Hitler: A Psychological History of German Film*, ed. and intro. Leonardo Quaresima, rev. and exp. ed. (1947; Princeton, NJ: Princeton University Press. 2004); Jire Kolaja and Arnold W.

Foster, "'Berlin, Symphony of a City' as a Theme of Visual Rhythm," *Journal of Aesthetics and Art Criticism* 23, no. 3 (1965): 353–8; James Donald, *Imagining the Modern City* (London: Routledge, 1999); Alexander Graff, "Paris – Berlin – Moscow: On the Montage Aesthetic in the City Symphony Films of the 1920s," in, *Avant-garde Critical Studies: Avant-garde Film*, ed. Graf and Dietrich Scheunemann (Amsterdam: Brill/Rodopi, 2007): 77–93; Nora M. Alter, *"Berlin, Symphony of a Great City* (1927): City, Image, Sound," in *Weimar Cinema: An Essential Guide to Classic Films of the Era*, ed. Noah Isenberg (New York: Columbia University Press, 2009), 193–217; Kim Knowles, "Travels with a Camera: Speed and Embodiment in Early French Avant-garde Film," *Studies in French Cinema* 13, no.1 (2012): 17–31; Margaret Werth, "Heterogeneity, the City, and Cinema in Alberto Cavalcanti's *Rien que les heures*," *Art History* 36, no. 5 (2013): 1018–41; Bollerey and Grafe, "Introduction" to *Eselsohren: Journal of History of Art, Architecture and Urbanism* 2, nos 1–2 (2014): 5–8; Jon Gartenberg, "NY, NY: A Century of City Symphony Films," *Framework* 55, no. 2 (2014): 248–76; Ling Zhang, "Rhythmic Movement, the City Symphony and Transcultural Transmediality: Liu Na'ou and *The Man Who Has a Camera* (1933)," *Journal of Chinese Cinemas* 9, no. 1 (2015): 42–61; Steven Jacobs, Anthony Kinik, and Eva Hielscher, "Introduction: The City Symphony Phenomenon 1920–40," in *The City Symphony Phenomenon: Cinema, Art, and Urban Modernity between the Wars*, ed. Steven Jacobs, Anthony Kinik, and Eva Hielscher (New York: Routledge, 2019), 3–44. Grierson, Kracauer, Kolaja and Foster, Sitney, Graf, Alter, and Zhang all address the symphonic analogy directly in their analysis of film rhythm and composition. The others take the musical analogy as a point of departure for investigations into topics such as heterogeneity (Werth, "Heterogeneity, the City") and architecture (Gartenberg, "NY, NY"). Many more articles that take the musical analogy of the city symphony as their starting point are collected in Jacobs, Kinik, and Hielscher's edited volume, *City Symphony Phenomenon*.
2 Carolyn Birdsall is a notable exception. Birdsall, "Resounding City Films: Vertov, Ruttmann and Early Experiments with Documentary Sound Aesthetics," in *Music and Sound in Documentary Film*, ed. Holly Rogers (New York: Routledge, 2015), 20–38.
3 Eva Hielscher, "Symphonic Rotterdam or the Flowing City: Von Barsy's and Von Maydell's 'The City that Never Rests,'" *Eselsohren: Journal of History of Art, Architecture and Urbanism* 2, nos 1–2 (2014): 161.
4 David Bordwell, "The Musical Analogy," *Yale French Studies* 60 (1980): 142. Quoted in the introduction.
5 See William Moritz *Optical Poetry: The Life and Work of Oskar Fischinger* (Bloomington: Indiana University Press, 2004); Simon Shaw-Miller, *Eye hEar the Visual in Music* (London: Routledge, 2016); Aimee Mollaghan, *The Visual Music Film* (London: Palgrave MacMillan, 2015); and Danijela Kulezic-Wilson, *The Musicality of Narrative Film* (London: Palgrave Macmillan, 2015).

6 The borders between these techniques are, of course, fluid. A technique from the first category may have a corollary in the second or third. To a certain extent, it depends on what aspect of the technique one chooses to focus on.
7 Quoted in Andrei Smirnov, *Sound in Z: Experiments in Sound and Electronic Music in Early 20th Century Russia* (London: Koenig Books, 2013), 26.
8 Ibid., 26.
9 John Cage, *Silence* (London: Marion Boyars, 1999), 3.
10 Dziga Vertov, "We. Variant of a Manifesto," in *Kino-Eye: The Writings of Dziga Vertov*, ed. Annette Michelson, trans. Kevin O'Brien (Berkeley: University of California Press, 1984), 8.
11 See, e.g., Andy Birtwistle, "Photographic Sound Art and the Silent Modernity of Walter Ruttmann's *Weekend* (1930)," *The New Sound Track* 6, no. 2 (2016): 123. Birtwistle's article is very informative, but it unfortunately concludes with a caricature of Vertov's cinematic practice as an example of the type of medium specificity that supposedly eclipsed more intermedial experiments such as Ruttmann's *Weekend* (see chap. 4). By contrast, I think that Vertov's films actually support Birtwistle's overarching argument for intermediality.
12 Quoted in Sabine Hake "Ruttmann's *Berlin, Symphony of the Big City*," in *Dancing on the Volcano: Essays on the Culture of the Weimar Republic*, ed. Thomas W. Kniesche, Stephen Brockmann, and Brian Keith (Columbia, SC: Camden House, 1994): 131.
13 On implied sound in Ruttmann's film, see Birdsall, "Resounding City Films." According to Carolyn Birdsall, *Berlin* also made heavy use of Edmund Meisel's musical score to amplify these elements (32–3). That said, the same techniques are successful in connoting sound regardless of the score and are regularly used in films such as *Man with a Movie Camera* for which there are no written scores, only verbal notes.
14 Michel Chion, *Film: A Sound Art*, trans. Claudia Gorbman (New York: Columbia University Press, 2003), 3.
15 Ruttmann performs a similar trick in his first sound film, *Melody of the World* (1930).
16 Birdsall, "Resounding City Films," 32–3. Such was the fate of Russolo's noisemakers, especially the noise harmonium. Instead of becoming the basis for independent concerts, this instrument generated the most interest as accompaniment for silent films, particularly at Fox's Studio 28 in Paris. See Barclay Brown, "Introduction" to Luigi Russolo, *The Art of Noises* (New York: Pendragon Press, 1987), 9.
17 Jonathan Berger, "How Noise Makes Music," *Nautilus* (2016), https://nautil.us/how-noise-makes-music-236017/.
18 See Berlin-Brandenburgische Akademie der Wissenschaften, *Deutsches Wörterbuch von Jakob Grimm und Wilhelm Grimm* (Trier Center for Digital Humanities, 1998–2017): http://woerterbuchnetz.de/.

19 "Den Rausch der Bewegung erleben, nicht wissen, woher ihr Rausch kommt" (translation mine); Walter Ruttmann, "Wie ich meine BERLIN-Film drehte," in *Walter Ruttmann. Eine Dokumetation*, ed. J. Goergen (Berlin: Freunde der Deutschen Kinemathek, 1989), 80.
20 John MacKay, "Introduction: *Man with a Movie Camera* (Dziga Vertov, 1929)," 10–11 (unpublished article, courtesy of the author).
21 Lynn Mally, *Culture of the Future: The Proletkult Movement in Revolutionary Russia* (Berkeley: University of California Press, 1990).
22 John MacKay, "Disorganized Noise: *Enthusiasm* and the Ear of the Collective," *KinoKultura* 7 (January 2005), pt. 4, p. 12, www.kinokultura.com/articles/jano5-mackay.html. For more on this idea, see chap. 5.
23 Mikhail Bakhtin, "Forms of Time and of the Chronotope in the Novel," in *The Dialogic Imagination*, trans. Caryl Emerson and Michael Holquist (Austin: University of Texas Press. 1981), 170.
24 Michael Temple, *Jean Vigo* (London: Faber and Faber, 1998), 26–7.
25 Douglas Kahn, *Noise, Water, Meat: A History of Sound in the Arts* (Cambridge, MA: MIT Press, 1999), 72.
26 Friederich A. Kittler, *Gramophone, Film, Typewriter*, trans. Geoffrey Winthrop-Young and Michael Wutz (Stanford, CA: Stanford University Press, 1986), 24–5.
27 Dziga Vertov, "We. A Version of a Manifesto," in *The Film Factory: Russian and Soviet Cinema in Documents 1896–1939*, ed. Richard Taylor and Ian Christie (London: Routledge, 1988): 71.
28 The Russian word is the same as the English.
29 Quoted in Graf, "Paris – Berlin – Moscow," 83.
30 Ibid.
31 Vertov, "We," 72.
32 Smirnov, *Sound in Z*, 175–237.
33 On drawn sound, see Smirnov, *Sound in Z*, 175–239; and Nikolai Izvolov, "Designed Sound in the USSR," *KinoKultura* 24 (2009), www.kinokultura.com/2009/24-izvolov.shtml.
34 Kahn, *Noise, Water, Meat*, 8–10.
35 Christa Blümlinger, "Minor Paris City Symphonies," in *City Symphony Phenomenon*, 70.
36 This account follows Hake, "Ruttmann's *Berlin*," 137.
37 Thomas Y. Levin, "'Tones from Out of Nowhere': Rudolf Pfenninger and the Archaeology of Synthetic Sound," *Grey Room* 12 (2003): 52–3.
38 Quoted in ibid., 53.
39 Quoted in ibid., 57.
40 Ibid., 58. Levin quotes Max Lenz, "Der Gezeichnete Tonfilm," *Die Umschau* 36, no. 49 (1932): 971–3.
41 Levin, "'Tones from Out of Nowhere,'" 59.
42 Ibid., 59.

43 Alter, "Berlin," 211.
44 Hake, "Ruttmann's *Berlin*," 137.
45 Sabine Mainberger, "In the Vortex of the Spiral Tendency: Questions of Aesthetics, Literature and Natural Sciences in the Work of Goethe," *Estudos Avançandos* 24, no. 69 (2010): 205.
46 Chion, *Film*, 6.
47 See, e.g., Jonathan Crary, *Techniques of the Observer: On Vision and Modernity in the Nineteenth Century* (Cambridge, MA: MIT Press, 1990); Brian Price, "Frank and Lilian Gilbreth and the Motion Study Controversy, 1907–30," in *A Mental Revolution: Scientific Management since Taylor*, ed. Daniel Nelson (Columbus: Ohio State University Press, 1992), 58.
48 Michael Cowan, *Technology's Pulse: Essays on Rhythm in German Modernism* (London: Institute of Germanic and Romance Studies, 2011), 30.
49 Ibid., 32.
50 Ibid.
51 Émile Benveniste, *Problems in General Linguistics*, trans. Mary Elizabeth Meek (Miami: University of Miami Press, 1971), 287.
52 Ibid., 285–6.
53 Ibid., 287.
54 John MacKay, *Dziga Vertov: Life and Work*, vol. 1, *1896–1921* (Boston: Academic Studies Press, 2018), 115. As Cowan points out, Bücher based his findings on ethnomusicological studies of traditional work songs, as well as "so-called 'zoo-humains' or 'Völkershauen'" at the Paris World's fair. Like Klages, he believed that rhythm was an expression of human vitality and collectivity, but he did not interpret this to mean that human rhythm was irrational or unsystematic. Rather, evincing an understanding of the body as, in the words of Anson Rabinbach, a "human motor," Bücher argued that rhythm "regulates all the natural movements of the animal body to generate the most efficient use of energy. Trotting horses and loaded camels" – those famous subjects of chronophotography – "move rhythmically no less than oarsmen in a ship or blacksmiths wielding the hammer." Quoted in Cowan, *Technology's Pulse*, 24.
55 Quoted in MacKay, *Dziga Vertov*, 117.
56 Ibid., 118.
57 Vertov, "We," 5.
58 MacKay, "Man with a Movie Camera," 10–11.
59 Michael Cowan, *Walter Ruttmann and the Cinema of Multiplicity: Avant-garde – Advertising – Modernity* (Amsterdam: Amsterdam University Press, 2014), 19.
60 Ibid., 24.
61 Ibid., 31.
62 For more on psychophysics, see Anson Rabinbach, *The Human Motor: Energy, Fatigue, and the Origins of Modernity* (Berkeley: University of California Press, 1992).

63 For more on Gastev and his influence on the Soviet avant-garde, see Julia Vaingurt, *Wonderlands of the Avant-garde: Technology and the Arts in Russia of the 1920s* (Evanston, IL: Northwestern University Press, 2013).
64 Vertov, "We," 71.
65 Ibid.
66 For a detailed account of the pace of this planning in terms of a single project, see Stephen Kotkin, *Magnetic Mountain: Stalinism as a Civilization* (Berkeley: University of California Press, 1995).
67 Devin Fore, "Metabiotic State: Dziga Vertov's *The Eleventh Year*," *October* 145 (2013): 6.
68 Stuart Elden, "Rhythmanalysis: An Introduction," in Henri Lefebvre, *Rhythmanalysis: Space, Time, and Everyday Life*, trans. Stuart Elden and Gerald Moore (London: Bloomsbury Academic, 2013), 5.
69 Lefebvre, *Rhythmanalysis*, 45.
70 Elden, "Rhythmanalysis," 4.
71 Ibid.
72 Quoted in ibid., 8.
73 Vertov, "We," 8.

Chapter Four

1 For a closer analysis of Stone's cover design, see Kurt W. Foster, "The City That Cannot Stay Silent: Döblin's *Berlin Alexanderplatz*," *Log* 33 (Winter 2015): 48–50.
2 Stephen Lovell, "How Russia Learned to Listen: Radio and the Making of Soviet Culture," *Kritika: Explorations in Russian and Eurasian History* 12, no. 3 (2011): 593.
3 Jonathan Sterne, *The Audible Past: Cultural Origins of Sound Reproduction* (Durham, NC: Duke University Press, 2003), 89.
4 Foster, "City," 50.
5 Peter Jelavich, *Berlin Alexanderplatz: Radio, Film, and the Death of Weimar Culture* (Berkeley: University of California Press), 93–125.
6 As Jelavich points out, at a dinner in his honour, Eisenstein suggested that Döblin and his contemporaries did not understand the essence of his films; Jelavich, *Berlin Alexanderplatz*, 15.
7 Jelavich, *Berlin Alexanderplatz*, 13–16. Tom Gunning, "The Cinema of Attraction[s]: Early Film, Its Spectator and the Avant-garde," in *The Cinema of Attractions Reloaded*, ed. Wanda Strauven (Amsterdam: Amsterdam University Press, 2006), 381–9.
8 Quoted in Jelavich, *Berlin Alexanderplatz*, 14.
9 See, e.g., Alfred Döblin, "Theater of the Little People," in *German Essays on Film*, ed. Richard W. McCormick and Alison Guenther-Pal (New York: Continuum, 2004), 1–3.

10 Georg Simmel, "Metropolis and Mental Life," in *Simmel on Culture*, ed. David Frisby and Mike Featherbone (London: Sage Publications, 2000).
11 Alfred Döblin, *Berlin, Alexanderplatz*, trans Michael Hofmann (New York: New York Review of Books, 2018), 8. For the German original, see Alfred Döblin, *Berlin, Alexanderplatz* (Frankfurt am Main: Fischer Verlag, 2013), 16. Subsequent citations will provide the English page number followed by the German – e.g., Döblin, *Berlin Alexanderplatz*, 8/16.
12 Döblin, *Berlin, Alexanderplatz*, 8/16.
13 Foster, "City," 44.
14 Döblin, *Berlin, Alexanderplatz*, 183. Here it is necessary to quote from the German original to get a sense Döblin's onomatopoeia.
15 Döblin, *Berlin, Alexanderplatz*, 163.
16 Ibid., 183.
17 Ibid., 178.
18 Döblin, *Berlin, Alexanderplatz*, 329. For a detailed list, see Toni Bernhart, "Stadt hören: Auditive Wahrnehmung in *Berlin, Alexanderplatz* von Alfred Döblin," *Zeitschrift für Litteraturwissenschaft und Linguistik* 149 (2008): 52–4.
19 Quoted in Foster, "City," 43. Hofmann's translation reads: "The words, sound waves, sonorities filled with meaning." Foster's, however, is closer to the original: "Die Worte, tönende Wellen, Geräuschwellen, mit Inhalt gefüllt." See Döblin, *Berlin, Alexanderplatz*, 76/94.
20 Quoted in Foster, "City," 39–40.
21 Quoted in ibid.," 43.
22 Döblin, *Berlin, Alexanderplatz*, 51.
23 Jelavich, *Berlin Alexanderplatz*, 93.
24 Ibid.
25 Quoted in ibid., 94.
26 Ibid., 95.
27 Ibid., 100.
28 Heinrich Heine, *The North Sea*, trans. Howard Mumford Jones (Chicago: Open Court, 1916; repr. New York: New Directions Books, 1951), 71–6. Page numbers include the German original and facing translation.
29 Daniel Gilfilan, *Pieces of Sound: German Experimental Radio* (Minneapolis: University of Minnesota Press, 2009), 22.
30 Ibid., 23.
31 Heine, *North Sea*, 72. The German original is on page 73 of this bilingual volume. In the above translation, I replaced the word "vessel" with "ship" to translate the German "Schiff."
32 Ibid., 74/75.
33 Ibid., 76/77.
34 Jelavich, *Berlin Alexanderplatz*, 63.

35 Ibid.
36 Ibid., 87.
37 Ibid., 74.
38 Bertolt Brecht, "The Radio as a Communications Apparatus," in *Bertolt Brecht on Film and Radio*, ed. and trans. Marc Silberman (Methuen Drama, 2016), 42/"Der Rundfunk als Kommunikationsapparat," in *Werke* 21 (Berlin: Suhrkamp, 1988), 552.
39 Friedrich Kittler, "Wellenartillerie," *Kunstradio*, 27 October 1988 (radio broadcast).
40 Brecht, "Radio," 41.
41 Quoted in Gilfillan, *German Experimental Radio*, 39.
42 Ibid., 29.
43 Ibid., 29–30.
44 Ibid., 31.
45 Quoted in ibid., 40.
46 The bureaucrat was Erich Scholz, the undersecretary of the Reich Interior Ministry; quoted in Jelavich, *Berlin Alexanderplatz*, 39.
47 Ibid., 39.
48 Ibid., 46.
49 Ibid., 73.
50 Ibid., 81.
51 Walter Ruttmann, "Weekend: Hörspiel," in *Walter Ruttmann: Eine Dokumentation*, ed. Jeanpaul Goergen (Berlin: Freunde der Deutschen Kinemathek), 130.
52 Jelavich, *Berlin Alexanderplatz*, 81.
53 Helmut Heißenbüttel, "Die Geschichte vom Franz Biberkopf und Weekend; gehört von Helmut Heißenbüttel," Deutsches Rundfunkarchiv, A23/16. Translation mine. "Ich erkenne Klänge und Geräusche der eigenen Kindheit. Das ist Stadt für mich. Der Charakter der Metropole Berlin charakterisiert sich am ehesten durch die Dialektfärbung der Sprachteile. Zugleich höre ich hier" – that is, in *Weekend* – "zum erstenmal Elemente einer akustischen Collage. Vieles, das uns heute formal geläufig ist, wird hier als Entdeckung hörbar, als etwas, das zugleich naiv und kühn erscheint."
54 Ibid.
55 Rudolf Arnheim, *Radio*, trans. Margaret Ludwig and Herbert Read (London: Faber and Faber, 1937), 32.
56 Ibid., 30–1.
57 Ibid., 29–30.
58 Ibid., 123–4.
59 Quoted in ibid., 123–4.
60 Ibid., 60.
61 Ibid., 95.

62 Ibid., 52.
63 Ibid., 96.
64 Ibid., 98.
65 Vsevolod Pudovkin, *Film Technique and Film Acting*, ed. and trans. Ivor Montagu (New York: Grove), 1970), 68–71. For an excellent summation and evaluation of Pudovkin's ideas, see Vance Kepley Jr., "Pudovkin and the Continuity Style: Problems of Space and Narration," *Discourses* 17, no. 3 (Spring 1995): 85–100.
66 Arnheim, *Radio*, 122.
67 Lotte Eisner, "Walter Ruttmann schneidet ein Film-Hörspiel," in *Walter Ruttmann* (ed. Jeanpaul Goergen), 131. Translation mine.
68 Andy Birtwistle, "Photographic Sound Art and the Silent Modernity of Walter Ruttmann's *Weekend* (1930)," *New Soundtrack* 6, no. 2 (September 2016): 119.
69 This notion is perhaps most famously articulated in Clement Greenberg, "Avant-garde and Kitsch," in *Art and Culture: Critical Essays* (1961; Boston: Beacon Press, 1989), 3–21.
70 Birtwistle, "Photographic Sound Art," 119.
71 Quoted in ibid.
72 That is, in Greenberg's essay, cited above.
73 Birtwistle, "Photographic Sound Art," 116.
74 Eisner, "Walter Ruttmann," 131 (translation mine).
75 Michel Chion, *Audio-Vision*, trans. Claudia Gorbman (New York: Columbia University Press, 1994), 29.
76 Christian Beyer, "Edmund Husserl," in *The Stanford Encyclopedia of Philosophy*, sec. 6, 28 February 2003, substantive revision 17 October 2022, https://plato.stanford.edu/entries/husserl/.
77 Chion, *Audio-Vision*, 29.
78 Ibid., 30.
79 Ibid., 30.
80 Ibid., 29.
81 Friedrich Kittler, "Wellenartillerie" (transcript from radio broadcast; no page numbers given). "Der Schützengraben ist tatsächlich der Vater des Massenradios" (translation mine).
82 Ibid. "Das Hörspiel [ist] Feedback eines Weltkrieges."
83 Quoted in Gilflan, *Pieces of Sound*, 36.
84 See, e.g., Steven Levy, *Hackers: Heroes of the Computer Revolution* (New York: Penguin, 1994).
85 Bruno Latour, "On Actor-Network Theory: A Few Clarifications," *Soziale Welt* 47, no. 4 (1996): 370.
86 Ibid., 372.
87 Ibid., 375.

Chapter Five

1 Yuri Lotman, *Universe of the Mind: A Semiotic Theory of Culture*, trans. Ann Shukman (London: I.B. Tauris, 1990), 191.
2 Ibid., 192.
3 Counterpoint was one of the main topics discussed at what was arguably the world's first film festival – a meeting of avant-garde filmmakers, including many of those mentioned in this paragraph, in La Sarraz, Switzerland. See Thomas Elsaesser and Malte Hagener, "Walter Ruttmann: 1929," in *1929 Beiträge zur Archäologie der Medien*, ed. Stefan Andriopoulos and Bernhard J. Dotzler (Berlin: Suhrkamp, 2002), 316–44.
4 Sergei Eisenstein, Vsevolod Pudovkin, and Grigori Alexandrov, "Statement on Sound," in *The Film Factory: Russian and Soviet Cinema in Documents 1896–1939*, ed. Richard Taylor and Ian Christie (London: Routledge, 1988), 234.
5 Examples of this technique can be found, to varying degrees, in the films of Grigori Kosintsev and Leonid Trauberg (*Alone*, 1931), Dziga Vertov (*Enthusiasm: Symphony of the Donbass*, 1931), Esfir Shub (*KShE*, 1931), Joris Ivens (*Komsomol: Youth Speaks*, 1931), Bertolt Brecht (*Kuhle Wampe*, 1931), Vsevolod Pudovkin (*Deserter*, 1933), Erwin Piscator (*Revolt of the Fishermen*, 1934), and many others.
6 Kristin Thompson, "Early Sound Counterpoint," *Yale French Studies* 60 (1980): 120.
7 Ibid.
8 Ibid.
9 Ian Christie, "Soviet Cinema: Making Sense of Sound, a Revised Historiography," *Screen* 23, no. 2 (July–August 1982): 39.
10 J. Peter Burkholder, Donald Jay Grout, and Claude V. Palisca, *A History of Western Music* (New York: Norton, 2014), 112.
11 E.g., Kazimir Malevich's "Black Square," as an "irreducible, extraspatial, extratemporal, and extrahistorical" form, attempted to outstrip progress in painting through a "reduction of all possible concrete content." Boris Groys, *On the New*, trans. G.M. Goshgarian (London: Verso, 2014), 25.
12 Lilya Kaganovsky, *The Voice of Technology: Soviet Cinema's Transition to Sound, 1928–35* (Bloomington: Indiana University Press, 2018), 74.
13 Dziga Vertov, "The Radio-Eye's March," in *Film Factory*, 300.
14 Michel Chion, *Audio-Vision*, trans. Claudia Gorbman (New York: Columbia University Press, 1994), 38.
15 Ibid., 40.
16 Elsaesser and Hagener, "Walter Ruttmann."
17 Walter Ruttmann, "Principles of the Sound Film," trans. Alex H. Bush, in *The Promise of Cinema: German Film Theory, 1907–33*, ed. Anton Kaes, Nicholas Baer, and Michael Cowan (Oakland: University of California Press, 2016), 556.

18 Lev Manovich, *The Language of New Media* (Cambridge, MA: The MIT Press), xv–xxxvi. Using Vertov's *Man with the Movie Camera*, Manovich presents the symphony film as a kind of data set.
19 Translation mine. The original reads: "Dem Geiste der Gemeinsamkeit unter den Völkern hat die Hamburg-Amerika-Linie ihr Schiffartsnetz zur Vergnügung gestelltund eine Filmexpedition um die Erde gesandt, um das Verständnis für die mannigfachen Formen menschlichen Lebens zu vermehren und das Verbindende unter den Menschen zur Darstellung zu bringen. Sie wurde bei ihrer Arbeit unterstützt durch die Regierungen von Deutschland, Groß-Britannien, Frankreich, Italien, der Vereinigten Staaten von Nordamerika, von Holland, Griechenland, Indien, Siam, China, Japan, Panama und Cuba, deren Gebiete die Expedition auf ihrer Reise durchforschte. Die Hamburg-Amerika-Linie dankt den Vertretern dieser Regierungen und allen, die sich für diese Arbeit eingesetzt haben, für ihre Mithilfe an diesem Werk menschlicher Lebens- und Arbeits-Gemeinschaft."
20 Walter Benjamin, "The Work of Art in the Age of Its Technological Reproducibility," in *The Work of Art in the Age of Its Technological Reproducibility and Other Writings on Media*, ed. Michael W. Jennings, Brigid Doherty, and Thomas Y. Levin (Cambridge, MA: Harvard University Press, 2008), 37.
21 Siegfried Kracauer, *From Caligari to Hitler: A Psychological History of the German Film*, ed. and intro. Leonardo Quaresima, rev. and exp. ed. (1947; Princeton, NJ: Princeton University Press, 2004), 184.
22 Ibid.
23 See Corey Anton, Robert K. Logan, and Lance Strate, eds, *Taking Up McLuhan's Cause: Perspective on Media and Formal Causality* (Bristol, UK: Intellect, 2017).
24 Aristotle, *Physics*, bk. 2, chap. 3, in *The Basic Works of Aristotle*, ed. Richard McKeon (New York: Modern Library, 2001), 240–1.
25 Eric McLuhan, "Forward," in *Taking Up McLuhan's Cause*, vii–xiii.
26 See, e.g., Tom Gunning, "Tracing the Individual Body: Photography, Detectives, and Early Cinema," in *Cinema and the Invention of Modern Life*, ed. Leo Charney and Vanessa R. Schwartz (Berkeley: University of California Press, 1995), 15–45.
27 On the disruptive powers of the "ethical scream," see Avital Ronell, "Trauma TV: Twelve Steps beyond the Pleasure Principle," in *Finitude's Score: Essays for the End of the Millenium* (Lincoln: University of Nebraska Press, 1998), 311–12.
28 Chion, *Audio-Vision*, 46.
29 Dziga Vertov, "Speech to the First All-Union Conference on Soviet Sound," in *Film Factory*, 304.
30 Vertov took extensive notes during these trips that included the reactions of the audience. Adeleheid Heftberger, "Propaganda in Motion: Dziga Vertov's and Aleksandr Medvedkin's Film Trains and Agit Steamers of the 1920s and 1930s," in *Apparatus: Film, Media and Digital Cultures in Central and*

Eastern Europe 1 (2015): doi: http://dx.doi.org/10.17892/app.2015.0001.2. See also John MacKay, *Dziga Vertov: Life and Work*, vol. 1 *1896–1921* (Boston: Academic Studies Press, 2018), 234–41; Vladimir Tolstoi, ed., *Agitmassovoe Iskusstvo Sovetskoj Rossii. Materialy i dokumenty. Agitpoezda i agitparokhody. Peredvizhnoi teatr. Politicheskii plakat. 1918–1932* (Moscow: Iskusstvo, 2002). For images of agit-trains, see David King, *Red Star over Russia. A Visual History of the Soviet Union from the Revolution to the Death of Stalin* (New York: Tate, 2009), 78–86.

31 King, *Red Star*, 68, quoted in Heftberger, "Propaganda in Motion," 12.
32 Political leaders were often part of the spectacle offered by agit-trains. As John MacKay notes, figures such as Nadezhda Krupskaia, Viacheslav Molotov, Lunacharsky, and Mikhail Kalinin all travelled aboard agit-trains to mass meetings across the country; MacKay, *Dziga Vertov*, 238.
33 Ibid.
34 Ibid.
35 Vertov worked with a sound-recording system designed by Alexander Shorin (1890–1941). For more on Shorin's system, see Andrei Smirnov's *Sound in Z: Experiments in Sound and Electronic Music in Early 20th Century Russia* (London: Koenig Books, 2013), 155–7.
36 Vertov, "Speech to the First All-Union Conference," 305.
37 Ibid.
38 Ibid.
39 Vertov, "We," 71.
40 Gilles Deleuze, *Cinema*, 2 vols (Minneapolis: University of Minnesota Press, 1986), 1:82, quoted in John MacKay, "Disorganized Noise: *Enthusiasm* and the Ear of the Collective," *KinoKultura* 7 (January 2005), pt. 1, pp. 5–6, www.kinokultura.com/articles/jano5-mackay.html.
41 As well as the editor. She (Elizaveta Svilova) is also featured in Vertov's film in one of its most important sections, the frozen-motion sequence. Nevertheless, the film's emphasis remains the mobile acrobatics of the cameraman while acknowledging that, without the editor, these acrobatics would never amount to a full-fledged film.
42 Oksana Bulgakowa, "The Ear against the Eye: Vertov's Symphony," *Monatsheft* 98, no. 2 (2006): 227.
43 Ibid., 228.
44 MacKay, "Disorganized Noise," intro, p. 4.
45 Devin Fore makes a similar point when he writes that "*Enthusiasm* presents a variety of machine discourse and syntax, from the radiotelegraph and the intervallic Morse signals to the factory whistle that is manipulated by Vertov to sound distinct musical notes. The human voice is but one instrument of communication in the contemporary industrial landscape"; Devin Fore, "Dziga Vertov, The First Shoemaker of Russian Cinema," *Configurations* 18 (2011): 372–3.

46 Dziga Vertov, "O Radio-Glaze," in *Iz naslediia*, ed. A.S. Deriabin and D.V. Kruzhkova, 2 vols (Moscow: Eizenshtein tsentr, 2008), 1:163. Original is in all capital letters.
47 Slava Gerovitch, "Love-Hate for Man-Machine Metaphors in Soviet Physiology: From Pavlov to 'Physiological Cybernetics,'" in *Science in Context* 15, no. 2 (2002): 343.
48 MacKay, *Dziga Vertov*, 70–84.
49 T.J. Clark, *Painting of Modern Life: Paris in the Art of Manet and His Followers* (New York: Knopf, 1985), 49, quoted in McKenzie Wark, *The Spectacle of Disintegration: Situationist Passages out of the 20th Century* (London: Verso, 2013), 33.
50 MacKay, "Disorganized Noise," pt. 3.

Coda

1 Karen Tei Yamashita, *Tropic of Orange* (Minneapolis: Coffee House Press, 1997), 34.
2 Ibid., 32.
3 Ibid., 33.
4 Ibid., 32.
5 Ibid., 33.
6 Ibid., 34.
7 Ibid., 33.
8 Ibid., 32.
9 Jean-Luc Nancy, *Listening*, trans. Charlotte Mandell (New York: Fordham University Press, 2007), 66.
10 Ibid., 67.
11 Ibid.
12 Ibid., 10. Nancy notes that these two tendencies – the mimetic and the methexic – intermingle in sonorous activity; indeed, they cannot be separated.
13 Ibid., 41.
14 Ibid., 49–59.

Index

Adorno, Theodor, 79, 164, 180
all sound, 115–6
Aristotle, 172
Arnheim, Rudolf, 21, 151–5, 164
ars nova, 151, 165–6
Attali, Jacques, 29, 53, 57, 79, 125
auscultation, of the city, 132–41
avant-garde: modernism, 156; mythopoesis, 13; sound art, 21; Soviet, 89, 100; theories of, 13
Avraamov, Arseny: Baku, 18, 59–64, 73–80, 89, 94, 182; "The Coming Musical Science and the New Era in Music History" (1916), 89; global Petrograd, 65–73; mass spectacle, 91–3; mechanical reproduction, 87–93; Moscow, 65, 80–8; *Symphony of Sirens*, 23, 27–9, 59–95, 170–1
Azerbaijani-Armenian conflict, 72–3

Bakhtin, Mikhail, 108, 111
Baku, First Congress of the Peoples of the East (1920), 68. See also Avraamov, Arseny: Baku; Avraamov, Arseny: *Symphony of Sirens*,
Balázs, Béla, 164
Bekhterev, Vladimir, 124
Benjamin, Walter, 12, 87–92, 131, 171
Benveniste, Émile, 122–3, 128
Bergson, Henri, 121, 128
Besant, Annie, and C.W. Leadbeater, 41, 45
Bijsterveld, Karin, 29
Boccioni, Umberto, 41–3, 54–5; *Città che sale* (1910–11), 42–3

Bolshevik propaganda, 14, 63–5, 69–73, 132
Bolshoi Theatre, 127
Brecht, Bertolt, 21, 159, 165; *The Flight of the Lindberghs* (1929), 140, 144–8, 159. See also radio: bi-directional
Bücher, Karl, 123
Busoni, Ferruccio, 53–4
Buzzi, Paolo, 55–6

carnival, 46, 101, 106, 111–12. See also Bakhtin, Mikhail
Carrà, Carlo, 40–3, 48
Cavalcanti, Alberto, 164
Chion, Michel, 28, 101, 121, 167; reduced listening, 158–9
Chladni, Ernst, 38, 113
Chomette, Henri: *Jeux des reflets et de la vitesse* (1925), 116
city space, 78, 81
constructivism, 106
contrapuntal sound, 24, 164–8, 173–5, 180

Delius, Frederick, 26
Döblin, Alfred, 81, 131–40, 149–50; *Alfred Döblin: In the Book, at Home, on the Street* (1928), 131–2; *Berlin, Alexanderplatz* (1927; novel), 131–8, 149; *Kinostil*, 134; *The Story of Franz Biberkopf* (unaired radio adaptation), 134, 138–41, 148, 150, 161; use of onomatopoeia, 135–7. See also Hörspiel

Eisenstein, Sergei, 101, 168
Eisler, Hans, 164
Eisner, Lotte, 155–7
Elgar, Edward, 56
enharmony, 46–58. See also Russolo, Luigi; microtonality

Fischinger, Oskar, 8, 119
Flesch, Hans, 21, 132, 149, 151; *Zauberei auf dem Sender* (1924), 140
Futurism, 27, 38–9, 48–9, 56, 71, 138

Gastev, Alexei, 65–7, 126
globalization, 163–4, 169, 185
Goethe, Johann Wolfgang von, 120
Groys, Boris, 166

Heißenbüttel, Helmut, 150–1
Heine, Heinrich: *Sea Apparition* radio recital, 141–3, 149–50
Helmholtz, Hermann von, 38
Hörbild, 140, 148–50, 158–60. See also Ruttmann, Walter: *Weekend*
Hörspiel, 134, 141–4, 148–51, 158. See also Döblin, Alfred: *Berlin, Alexanderplatz*; Döblin, Alfred: *Story of Franz Biberkopf*
Husserl, Edmund, 158

intermediality, 10–13, 156–7
internationalism, 72, 170
intonarumori, 21, 30, 50, 56–7. See also Russolo, Luigi
Ivanov, Aleksandr, 117
Ivanova, Lydia, 75
Ivens, Joris: *Komsomol: Youth Speaks* (1931), 163
Ives, Charles, 26

Jacques-Dalcroze, Émile, 123
Jules-Marey, Étienne, 114–21

Kaufman, Mikhail, 106–7, 124
Kiel mutiny (3 November 1918), 145
Kittler, Friedrich, 38, 113, 159–60; "The City as Medium," 13–17
Klages, Ludwig, 121–3
Kracauer, Siegfried, 12, 164, 172

Latour, Bruno, 161–2
Lefebvre, Henri, 128–30
Lenin, Vladimir, 66, 69–71, 107, 179; "The Rights of Nations to Self-Determination" (1913), 176
Levin, Thomas Y., 7, 116–18
Lichtspiele, 101
Lotman, Yuri, 162
Lukàcs, György, 123

Marinetti, Filippo Tommaso, 40, 50, 56, 138
"Marseillaise" (anthem), 59, 62–3, 110
mass spectacle, 18, 23, 59, 68, 88–96, 188. See also Avraamov, Arseny: *Symphony of Sirens*
materialism, 79
Mayakovsky, Vladimir: "Orders for the Army of Art" (1918), 68
McLuhan, Marshall, 172–3
mechanical reproduction, 6, 23–5, 65, 87–94, 97–100
medium, city as, 8, 13–17, 32–46, 93, 132–3
medium specificity, 99, 100, 156–7. See also Vertov, Dziga
Meyerhold, Vsevolod, 106, 114
microtonality, 27, 50, 66–7, 87, 114. See also enharmony
modernism, 13, 112, 125, 156
Moholy-Nagy, László: "Dynamic of the Metropolis," 3–8; *Impressions of the Old Marseille Port* (1929–32), 5
montage, 96, 102, 134, 149, 155–6, 169–71, 185; cross-sectional, 134, 169, 171–3; sound, 99, 155–6

Mosolov, Alexander, 27, 100
musical analogy, 11–12, 19, 96
Muybridge, Edweard, 114, 121

Nancy, Jean-Luc, 189–90
network, of noises (Russolo), 33–9, 56–8; German radio, 132–3, 138, 140–5, 157–62, 169–70; *Symphony of Sirens*, 93;. See also Kittler, Friedrich; medium; radio
New Economic Policy, 71, 109
Nietzsche, Friedrich, 13, 40, 68, 129
noise, 9, 21, 27–9, 94, 98, 100–5, 129, 136; dialectic of, 29–30, 112; instruments, 32, 51; urban, 32, 190. See also Russolo, Luigi; *intonarumori*; enharmony

occult, 19, 27–8, 33–50, 54–7, 64–5
October Revolution, 23, 18, 59, 89–90, 176–7
onomatopoeia, 98, 135, 138

Pfenninger, Rudolf, 23, 88, 97, 116–9, 124–5
phonograph, 7, 10, 92–3, 99, 116
Plekhanov, Georgi, 79
Proletarian Cultural Organization, 71, 107
propaganda, 20–1, 78, 132, 176, 177–8
Pudovkin, Vsevolod, 94, 154
Pythagoras: logic of intervals, 113

radio: bi-directional, 147–8, 159; broadcast genres, 136–9, 141–4; the city as a radio network, 159–60; German, 24, 143–50, 160; sound and city space, 150–9; Soviet, 132; Swedish Mast, 24, 60, 90; technology, 24, 143–5, 159; use of headphones, 144; Wolff'sche Telegraphenbüro, "Funkerspuk," 145–7. See also Brecht, Bertolt; *Hörbild*; *Hörspiel*; network
reduced listening; 158–9. See also Chion, Michel
re-mediation, 17, 132, 141–57
rhythm, 121–30
Rousseau, Jean-Jacques, 68
Russolo, Luigi, 33–58, 60, 100, 136; *Al di là materia*, 44, 55; *The Art of Noises* (1913), 21, 33, 36–7, 46–54, 57–8; *Awakening of a City*, 22, 53–5, 64, 163; *La Musica* (1912), 46; *Lineeforza della folgore* (1912), 44–6; *Luncheon on the Terrace of the Kursaal Hotel*, 33; *Maschere* (1907–8), 46; *Meeting of Automobiles and Aeroplanes*, 33; noise instruments, 37, 50, 54–6, 151; *The Revolt*, 43; synesthetic experiments, 40–2, 44–6, 57–8. See also enharmony
Ruttmann, Walter, 24, 100–2, 149–75; *Berlin, Symphony of a Great City* (1927), 97, 100–2, 169–74; cross-sectional approach, 172; inaudible sound technique, 102; intermediality, 156; *Lichtspiel: Opus I–V* (1921–25), 101; linearity and circularity, 127; *Melody of the World* (1930), 24, 163, 169–75, 184; optical-acoustic counterpoint ,168; *Weekend* (1930), 24, 134, 140, 149–61. See also *Hörbild*

Schlegel, Friedrich, 11–13
Schwitters, Kurt, 5, 138
Shklovsky, Viktor: *Ostranenie* (defamiliarization), 165
Sholpo, Evgeny, 8, 66–7, 114
Shub, Esfir, 163
Simmel, Georg, 6, 12, 123, 135, 185
Siodmak, Robert, 101
socialism, 68, 71–2, 183–4

socialist realism, 20, 166
Solovyov, Vladimir, 85
sound, 17–19; synthesis, 67, 88, 119, 190; recording and transmission, 100; visual representation, 114
Soviet-Taylorism, 65–8, 84, 126. *See also* Gastev, Alexei
Stalin, Joseph, 109, 127, 183
stethoscopes, 131–2. *See also* auscultation, of the city
Stone, Sasha, 131
Symbolism, French, 39–40
synesthesia, 13, 40–2, 44

Tatlin, Vladimir, 85–6
Tonbild-Syndikat, 169

Ulmer, Edgar G., 101

Vertov, Dziga, 99–113, 156, 162–8, 175–86; cine-ambulance, 176–8; cine-scales, 114; *Enthusiasm: Symphony of the Donbass* (1931), 24, 165, 177, 179–85; inaudible sound, 130; Kino-Eye, 111, 183; *Kinochestvo*, 99, 129, 156; "Laboratory of Hearing," 98, 110; *Man with a Movie Camera* (1929), 24, 97–9, 106, 124–7, 178; movement interval, 113–15, 126, 129, 178; Radio-Eye, 183; *A Sixth Part of the World* (1926), 163–7, 185–6; sympathetic, 37, 40, 42, 56–7; vibration 19, 36–46
Vigo, Jean: *À propos de Nice*, 20, 23, 101–2, 106–7, 110–15
Voinov, Nikolai, 66, 114, 117

Wagner, Richard, 13, 27, 68
Wolf, Werner, 11–12

Yamashita, Karen Tei: *Tropic of Orange* (1997), 187–90
Yankovsky, Boris, 114